*Teaching
Arguments*

Teaching Arguments

Rhetorical Comprehension, Critique, and Response

Jennifer Fletcher
Foreword by Carol Jago

STENHOUSE PUBLISHERS
PORTLAND, MAINE

Stenhouse Publishers
www.stenhouse.com

Credits
Page 18: "How Old Is Grand Canyon? New Study Puts Age at 70 Million Years" by Alicia Chang. Used with permission of the Associated Press Copyright © 2012. All rights reserved.

Page 214: "The Olympic Contradiction" by David Brooks. Article from the *New York Times*, July 26. © 2012 the *New York Times*. All rights reserved. Used by permission and protected by the Copyright Laws of the United States. The printing, copying, redistribution, or retransmission of this Content without express written permission is prohibited.

Page 63: "South Korean president Park Geun-hye (L) shakes hands with Microsoft founder Bill Gates before their meeting at the presidential Blue House in Seoul on April 22, 2013." AFP PHOTO / Lee Jin-man / Getty Images. Reproduced with permission.

Page 55: CALVIN AND HOBBES © 1989 Watterson. Reprinted with permission of UNIVERSAL UCLICK. All rights reserved.

Page 230: "A Lifetime of Learning," keynote address given by Diana Garcia at the AVID (Advancement Via Individual Determination) Writers Conference, on March 22, 2011, at California State University, Monterey Bay. Reprinted with permission of Diana Garcia.

Library of Congress Cataloging-in-Publication Data
Fletcher, Jennifer, 1972–
  Teaching arguments : rhetorical comprehension, critique, and response / Jennifer Fletcher ; Foreword by Carol Jago.
    pages cm
  Includes index.
  ISBN 978-1-57110-999-6 (pbk. : alk. paper) -- ISBN 978-1-62531-043-9 (ebook) 1. Persuasion (Rhetoric)--Study and teaching. 2. English language--Rhetoric--Study and teaching. 3. Report writing--Study and teaching. I. Title.
  P301.5.P47F54 2015
  808--dc23
                              2014032440

Cover and interior design by Blue Design

Manufactured in the United States of America

PRINTED ON 30% PCW
RECYCLED PAPER

21 20 19 18 17 16   9 8 7 6 5 4 3

To the students and teachers of Buena Park High School
And in memory of Jeanne Tillman, with love and gratitude

CONTENTS

Prompts for Argument Essays

List of Nonfiction Readings

Foreword

On March 11, 1924, British Prime Minister Stanley Baldwin spoke against a Cambridge Union motion "That this House has the highest regard for rhetoric." Baldwin's claim? "To tell the truth needs no art at all." He went on to defend his argument with the assertion, "Let us remember this: when we come to big things we do not need rhetoric. Truth, we have always been told, is naked. She requires very little clothing." Those in attendance were more than a little puzzled that the prime minister should challenge the Cambridge Union's very raison d'être. Assembled company being unimpressed by Baldwin's "rhetoric," the motion passed.

Jennifer Fletcher's book might have helped Stanley Baldwin understand why he lost the argument. Truth is rarely naked. All discourse is clothed with purpose, occasion, audience, ethos, logos, and pathos. It shouldn't have been a surprise to Baldwin that a Cambridge debating club would not be a receptive audience for the claim that rhetoric is extraneous ornamentation. Even his status as prime minister, his ethos, wasn't enough to win over a room full of undergraduates in love with the sound of their own voices.

In *Teaching Arguments: Rhetorical Comprehension, Critique, and Response,* Fletcher makes a powerful case for the teaching of rhetoric as an essential thread in the fabric of every child's education. It isn't something to be reserved for the most able students. Understanding the warp and woof of argumentation is critical not only for academic success but also, and even more important, to read the world around us. Anyone naïve to the uses of language is vulnerable to its abuse. Every one of us is surrounded by able rhetorical manipulators, from ad men to politicians, from preachers to tweeters.

Fletcher demonstrates how to parse instruction in argumentation throughout a course of study, offering students repeated and various entry points for entering the world of academic discourse both as readers and as writers. She also tells stories from her own classroom experiences—successes and shortcomings—that will resonate for every English teacher. Reading about her attempts at teaching the argument essay by having students develop a question, conduct research, and write papers reminded me of my own early fumblings. Why didn't I see the folly of asking students to write their thesis before having any idea what they were talking about? Like Fletcher, "I had put the cart before the horse; it's hard to ask a question about an ongoing conversation if you don't listen to the conversation first." If only this book had been published twenty years ago I would owe far fewer students a refund.

Most important, Fletcher captures the vital nature of our work in the classroom. Teaching isn't just about helping students pass exams and get into good colleges. We need to arm young people with the rhetorical tools they need to survive in a world full of conflicting and sometimes dangerous messages. I don't want my students to be innocents abroad.

—Carol Jago

Acknowledgments

My guiding hope for this book has been that it would be honest and helpful. If I've achieved this goal, the credit goes to the many people who have helped me throughout the writing process and who have taught me about rhetoric and college readiness over the past ten years. First, thanks go to the members of the California State University Expository Reading and Writing Course (ERWC) Advisory Committee for transforming my understanding of academic preparation. You helped me to see that the rigorous analysis and relentless attention to text that I had previously thought appropriate only for Advanced Placement courses could, in fact, help all students be better prepared for life after high school. You also showed this literature junkie that high-interest, superbly written nonfiction could be just as exciting to read and teach as my beloved Charles Dickens. An extra special thank-you to John Edlund for deepening my regard for and understanding of Aristotelian rhetoric, and to Nancy Brynelson for her extraordinary service and leadership. How reassuring it's been to know that these smart, good people are working tirelessly on behalf of our students!

I wish to express my appreciation, too, to those teachers who so generously took the time to pilot these materials in their classrooms: Nolina Beauchamp, Jackie Linstead, Emma Thompson, Silva Shamassian, Tammy Rodriguez-Kam, and Michelle Muncy-Silva.

To the students who have graciously shared their work for this project, including the superb Cat Cardenas: Thank you for helping me learn how to be a better teacher!

Many thanks, as well, to my colleagues, friends, and family who kindly gave me feedback on chapter drafts and extended my thinking about rhetoric and learning: Robby Ching, Glen McClish (who also gave the gift of one of the best sentences in the book), Nelson Graff, John Edlund, Ernest Stromberg, Coreen Cardenas, and Dorothy Kimble. And thanks to Dan Kimble for special "technical assistance." I love when brilliant minds help me do my work.

I am deeply grateful to the Stenhouse editors and reviewers whose astute and helpful comments made this a better book, especially Jill Cooley, Erin Trainer, Glenda Funk, and Joseph

Wiederhold. Sometimes I cringe when I think of the things I'd have missed if there hadn't been so many sharp eyes and excellent brains on this project. You all have brought the book much closer to what I wanted it to be from the start.

Additional thanks are due to the following outstanding folks:

Diana Garcia and Ernest Stromberg, my Cal State Monterey Bay colleagues, for sharing their writing, assignments, and encouragement.

Jill Cooley and the editorial board at Stenhouse, for taking a chance on a new writer and an ancient approach.

Carol Jago, for feedback on an early proposal for this project and for permission to use previously published material from *California English,* the journal of the California Association of Teachers of English. I'm also indebted to Carol for consistently making me feel good about being an English teacher.

The California Reading and Literature Project (CRLP), for permission to use lesson exemplars created for CRLP's Secondary Academic Language Tools.

Linda Clinard, for ongoing mentoring and inspiration.

Robbye Kimble and Rose Fletcher, for their love and encouragement.

California State University, Monterey Bay, for a much needed and appreciated CSU Faculty Research, Scholarship and Creative Activity Fellowship.

Jennifer Benge for her fabulous artwork.

And my family: Ken, Dryden, and Ellerie. Thank you for all your patient support and healthy perspectives. I love you!

Introduction: Crossing the Threshold

Argumentative writing is writing that reasons its way to a conclusion. It addresses ideas that the writer takes seriously enough to want to explore and support with good reasons.

—JOHN T. GAGE

For my birthday this year, I finally got something I've wanted for most of my adult life: a real camera. On the advice of a friend who's an amateur photographer, I asked my husband to get me a Canon EOS Rebel T3 as a good starter camera for someone who wants to learn how to do more than point and shoot. That was six months ago. So far, I've read the manual a few times, watched tutorial videos, and taken loads of pictures, but I still just point and shoot.

As I was taking pictures at my niece's birthday party with no more skill than I'd used with my cell phone camera, it occurred to me that I might be bumping up against what researchers call a "threshold concept" in learning. All learning involves some kind of movement from surface to depth; that's just the normal developmental trajectory, the struggle toward mastery we experience in our "zone of proximal development" (Vygotsky 1978, 84). But sometimes that trajectory hits an obstacle that's hard to get past, even with support. When the struggle for a deeper understanding involves more than garden-variety confusion, chances are you're on the doorstep of a threshold concept.

In "Threshold Concepts and Troublesome Knowledge," Jan H. F. Meyer and Ray Land describe a threshold concept "as akin to a portal, opening up a new and previously inaccessible way of thinking about something" (2003, 1). Once learned, threshold concepts are difficult to unlearn because they transform the way we think about our subject matter—and sometimes our world. For instance, Darwin's theory of evolution by natural selection is a threshold concept that changes how we view the life sciences. Or, to give a nonexample, a concept like "storytelling" in English language arts is not a threshold concept because most students have an intuitive grasp of this idea. Personal narrative comes naturally to students. In contrast, threshold concepts mark both a major stumbling block and point of no return in learning since successfully passing through the portal depends on learning to think differently, even counterintuitively.

Curious to know if I might be headed for new territory in picture-taking, I did a quick Internet search on "threshold concepts" and "photography." Hits came from around the globe identifying "visualization" as a threshold concept that forever changes the way we use cameras. I thought photography was just about recognizing and capturing beauty. I didn't realize that I could be visualizing the work of art I wanted to create before determining the conditions to create it. Training myself to see the finished image instead of what's before my eyes? That's transformative learning indeed. I find I can hold this new idea in my head just so long before I slip back to my old dependence on my viewfinder. This is the oscillation between superficial and deep learning Meyers and Land (2003) describe as endemic to the process of threshold crossing.

Threshold Concepts in Argumentation

I think this transitional place is where most of our high school students are when it comes to argumentation. They certainly have plenty of practical experience with arguing and responding to arguments. And whether the term is new to them or not, our students know a lot about rhetoric. They have experience trying to persuade different audiences for different purposes, adjusting their persona to suit different occasions, and using logic and emotion to get what they want. Think of the many times students have tried to talk you into giving them a higher grade. What teenagers typically don't have a lot of experience with is how to do more than the basics. Like me with my camera, our students are in possession of tools they haven't mastered yet because they don't have a deep sense of their transformative capacities.

We can work with that.

If we want our students to do more than just point and shoot when it comes to argumentation, we need to teach them what rhetoric is and does. Rhetorical reading and writing are the gateway practices behind effective argumentation. Within rhetoric itself, we find several threshold concepts that change how students approach texts: occasion, audience, purpose, ethos, pathos, and logos. All are integrative and transformative.

This book is about opening doors to deeper learning for all our students through a rhetorical approach to arguments—an approach based on situational awareness and responsiveness instead of rules and formulas. Throughout the chapters, you'll find detailed examples of activities, such as the rhetorical précis, descriptive outlining, and the doubting and believing game, that show students how to move beyond a superficial response to texts. Many students who aspire to higher education are not in Advanced Placement classes—and many more students with the ability to succeed in college and career don't initially see their own potential. They (and sometimes their teachers) might think they're just not "college material." Rhetorical knowledge helps all of us see more than what's before our eyes.

Why Rhetoric Matters

Rhetoric—in addition to being versatile—has always been both eminently rigorous and practical. Throughout the centuries, rhetoric has been a remarkably adaptive means to prepare critical thinkers and effective communicators for real-world decisions. Rhetoric develops what literacy researchers Richard Beach, Amanda Haertling Thein, and Daryl Parks identify as an equalizing competency for working-class teens: the ability to "negotiate the competing demands of diverse social worlds" (2008, viii).

I've spent my twenty years in education working with students who face significant obstacles on the path to high school graduation and college completion. I always knew which classes I was teaching by how much stuff my kids brought with them to class. I could barely walk the aisles in my AP class, so crowded was it with overloaded backpacks, badminton rackets, and violin cases. Students in my "regular" classes, on the other hand, often strolled in with rolled-up spiral notebooks in their back pockets. Then there were those souls who traveled so lightly that they didn't even bring a pen to class. On many days, my primary "student engagement technique" was brokering deals between the students without school supplies and their more provident peers so we could all just get on with our work.

For the many low-income, underrepresented, and multilingual students for whom higher education is an alien world, the study and practice of rhetoric offers essential training in the imaginative and empathic capacities that enable writers to write for diverse audiences, purposes, and occasions. Rhetoric helps us inhabit other social worlds and identities. In the final chapter of this book, "Aristotle's Guide to Becoming a 'Good' Student," you'll find activities specifically designed to give students a boost of support as they build rhetorical knowledge and academic confidence. If your students could use some extra help *preparing* to be academically prepared, you might want to read Chapter 7 first.

What's Rhetoric?

Rhetoric targets the conventions and processes of high academic literacy, including the sophisticated responsiveness to context that characterizes college and workplace writing. Writing rhetorically means writing with the attention to argument, purpose, audience, authority, and style demanded by academic texts. It means discovering, as Aristotle explains, the best available means of persuasion—such as the skillful use of evidence and appeals. In the rhetorical tradition, argument and persuasion go hand in hand. We make arguments to persuade people. When the Common Core State Standards (CCSS) call for students to "determine an author's point of view or purpose in a text in which the rhetoric is particularly effective," it's asking students to analyze the way a writer's persuasive choices contribute to a text's meaning and power (NGA/CCSSO 2010, CCSS.ELA-Literacy.RI.11-12.6).

To use a technology metaphor, rhetoric isn't just an app that enhances instruction in argumentation; rhetoric is the operating system. As a matter of fact, the study of how to read and write arguments comes to us from the rhetorical tradition. In classical rhetoric, argument was an advanced "assignment" type that students mastered in a sequence of increasingly complex tasks (Corbett and Connors 1999). Rhetoric is larger than argument. If you prefer a nontech metaphor, you might think of rhetoric as the Swiss Army knife of critical communication, of which argument comprises several blades.

In the many centuries following the classical period, argumentation continued to be the bread and butter of rhetoric courses, and rhetoric continued to be a central discipline in schools. Rhetoric has a history older than the idea of public education itself—older, in fact, than Christianity, Euclidian geometry, or the Great Wall of China. Since the fourth century BCE, rhetoric has been standard fare for students. Rhetoricians Sharon Crowley and Debra Hawhee describe the central importance of rhetoric to civic life in the classical age: "In ancient times, people used rhetoric to make decisions, resolve disputes, and to mediate public discussion of important issues" (2009, 1). While the enduring importance of rhetoric is clear, the meaning of the term can be a little fuzzy.

One of the challenges in trying to fix a definition to rhetoric is that it is both process and product, activity and artifact. As Erika Lindemann (2001) points out in *A Rhetoric for Writing Teachers,* the term *rhetoric* itself can refer alternately to a practice, theory, discipline, or even a type of book (instructors assign a "rhetoric" as the textbook in many college classes).

And then, of course, there are those definitions of rhetoric as "empty words" or "manipulation." Crowley and Hawhee are quick to rectify misunderstandings of the term:

> What often passes for rhetoric in our own time—repeatedly stating
> (or shouting) one's beliefs at an "opponent" in order to browbeat him
> into submission—is not rhetoric. Participation in rhetoric entails that
> every party to the discussion be aware that beliefs may change during
> the exchange and discussion of points of view. All parties to a rhetorical
> transaction *must be willing to be persuaded by good arguments.* (2009, 6;
> emphasis added)

Composition scholar Andrea Lunsford's broad and helpful definition of rhetoric suggests its capacity to contain multitudes. She calls rhetoric "the art, practice, and study of human communication" (quoted in Eidenmuller 2014).

Seeing Past the Surface: Teaching Arguments Rhetorically

What you'll find throughout this book are ways to help students see past their first impressions. When we teach students to think about arguments rhetorically, we build up their powers of observation. We want students to pay closer attention to the acts of meaning around them, to notice rhetorical, and yes, persuasive, strategies that might not be apparent at first glance.

Like this, for example. During a visit to the world-famous Monterey Bay Aquarium a few years ago, I noticed an interesting sign in the restroom: "paper towels = trees." It's a simple but powerful message. And it makes a clear argument: If we use paper towels, we are consuming trees. Most people who saw this sign likely accepted it as an important conservation reminder without considering the persuasive strategies behind the message. The logical equation of paper to trees seems so reasonable and irrefutable that it's easy to accept at face value. But if we look at the sign as an argument—a claim requiring support—rather than a statement of fact, we can uncover several choices the writer of this message has made to convince us of its probable truth:

- The equals sign (=) makes the claim seem like a mathematical certainty (logos).
- The word *trees* (instead of *wood pulp, tree plantation,* or *tree farm*) suggests unspoiled forests (pathos).
- The message comes from the Monterey Bay Aquarium—a leader in ocean conservation (ethos).
- Placing the sign on paper towel dispensers takes advantage of an opportune moment (*kairos*).

This little argument uses logical, emotional, and character appeals to achieve its purpose: reducing the waste of natural resources. If we dig deeper, we might notice a lack of evidence, qualifiers, or counterarguments. We might also start to question the extent to which we agree or disagree with the message. Does using paper towels really equate to cutting down trees? What are the effects of logging? What about recycled paper or alternative materials? Why doesn't the aquarium just use electric hand dryers?

When I returned to the Monterey Bay Aquarium this spring, I noticed that the signs in the restrooms had changed to "Even recycled towels started as trees, so please use as few as possible." (See Figure 1.)

FIGURE 1
Monterey Bay Aquarium's second, modified sign

I can only guess that the new message and persuasive strategies were in concession to questions and counterarguments like those I raised about the original notice. You can easily imagine the ongoing conversation that led to the modified towel sign.

Our world is full of arguments like these. Andrea A. Lunsford and John J. Ruszkiewicz even suggest that "everything's an argument" (2010, vii), meaning all the messages we encounter, whether through words or images, have a particular purpose and point of view. Arguments ask for some kind of response. Being college and career ready—or "life ready" as one teacher friend puts it—requires an ability to respond to these messages critically.

The CCSS recognize the connection between proficiency in argumentation and postsecondary success. For instance, many of the CCSS's Writing Standards for Grades 11–12 affirm the importance of understanding, creating, and supporting arguments. Consider the following:

> 1. Write arguments to support claims in an analysis of substantive topics or texts, using valid reasoning and relevant and sufficient evidence.
>
> a. Introduce precise, knowledgeable claim(s), establish the significance of the claim(s), distinguish the claim(s) from alternate or opposing claims, and create an organization that logically sequences claim(s), counterclaims, reasons, and evidence.
>
> b. Develop claim(s) and counterclaims fairly and thoroughly, supplying the most relevant evidence for each while pointing out the strengths and limitations of both in a manner that anticipates the audience's knowledge level, concerns, values, and possible biases.
>
> c. Use words, phrases, and clauses as well as varied syntax to link the major sections of the text, create cohesion, and clarify the relationships between claim(s) and reasons, between reasons and evidence, and between claim(s) and counterclaims. (NGA/CCSSO 2010, CCSS. ELA-Literacy.W.11-12.1)

When we analyze and develop arguments, we have to consider more than just the printed words on the page. We have to consider the full social world in which the argument does its work. Arguments try to accomplish something; they seek a specific outcome, a change in people's actions or beliefs—such as not recklessly wasting paper towels. And to change people, we have to understand them. We have to anticipate their concerns and objections and know the opportune moments and best means to make our pitch. Rhetoric teaches us how to do these things. "When we practice rhetoric," writes Erika Lindemann in *A Rhetoric for Writing Teachers,* "we make decisions about our subject, audience, point of view, purpose, and message. We select our best evidence, the best order in which to present our ideas, and the best resources of language to express them" (2001, 40–41).

The Shift Toward Argumentation and Rhetoric

The CCSS is just one of several converging academic preparation efforts now shifting K–12 instruction toward a greater focus on argument literacy and rhetorical knowledge. For instance, the Reading Framework for the 2009 National Assessment of Educational Progress (National Assessment Governing Board 2008) and 2011 *Framework for Success in Postsecondary Writing* (the latter a document collaboratively prepared by the Council of Writing Program Administrators [CWPA], the National Council of Teachers of English [NCTE], and the National Writing Project [NWP]) also see the ability to analyze and evaluate arguments rhetorically as essential to college and career readiness. This shift has important implications for how we teach reading and writing in high school English classes. CWPA, NCTE, and NWP's *Framework* recommends that today's teachers help students develop "rhetorical knowledge" by providing opportunities to do the following:

> learn and practice key rhetorical concepts such as audience, purpose, context, and genre through writing and analysis of a variety of types of texts . . .
>
> write for real audiences and purposes, and analyze a writer's choices in light of those audiences and purposes . . .
>
> contribute, through writing, their own ideas and opinions about a topic to an ongoing conversation. (2011, 6)

New resources have been published in response to our changing educational climate. The 2011 *Teaching Argument Writing, Grades 6–12* by influential composition scholar George Hillocks, for example, offers step-by-step methods for teaching how to evaluate and write arguments. Hillocks identifies proficiency in argumentation as a key factor in postsecondary success: "For college and career one needs to know how to make an effective case, to make a good argument" (xvii). As we move toward this focus on argument literacy, we're being challenged to teach in new ways.

One challenge we face arises from the nature of academic and workplace arguments—which can be pretty different from the personal or political arguments students are often most familiar with. For one, arguments between scholars or coworkers do not usually have clear winners and losers. Scientists are not going to take a vote on the age of the Grand Canyon or the ability of coral to adapt to climate change, nor will most businesses consider only two options for expanding their markets. For another, since the participants in academic and workplace arguments are in the same disciplinary or professional community, they tend (mostly) to respect each other; they're not starting with the assumption that people who disagree with them are crazy. This is not always the case in the arenas of politics and public opinion. Thus, debating the pros and cons of issues like gun control or abortion, or trying to persuade parents to extend their curfew, doesn't necessarily prepare students for reading and writing the kinds of complex, situated, and open-ended arguments they will encounter in college or their careers.

We're expecting a lot from our high school students. Teenagers may be great at expressing their views, but argumentation—as the Common Core and academia see it—is not simply about encouraging students to voice their opinions on controversial topics; it's about, in John T. Gage's phrase, "an intellectual journey into the realm of ideas" (2000, xvi). Making that journey successfully depends upon advanced literacy skills. Past Modern Language Association (MLA) President Gerald Graff emphasizes this point in his identification of key competencies of "argument literacy":

listening to viewpoints different from one's own

summarizing them in ways others can recognize

comparing and contrasting positions

spotting contradictions and non sequiturs

coming to conclusions that contribute to a continuing conversation of ideas (2003, 23)

"This argument literacy," Graff asserts, "is rightly viewed as central to being educated" (2003, 3). The intellectual leap from topic-based opinion writing to text-based argument literacy is what makes argumentation of this kind a "threshold concept"—and what makes a rhetorical approach to teaching arguments so important.

> While it's probably fair to say we're not just teaching persuasive writing anymore, we can't separate argumentation from the intent to persuade.

Bringing the Conversation to Life

The idea that academic texts represent real acts of communication and a real community of diverse, quirky, and often contentious individuals can take a little getting used to for many high school students. It can be a pretty big imaginative leap to see beyond a battered, school-issued anthology to a real writer, struggling away at her computer or typewriter or manuscript (especially a manuscript!), and the real readers in their homes or on trains or at cafés or wherever. And it takes excellent listening skills to be able to "hear" the other voices in a written conversation. Our students need help understanding that, as Charles Bazerman puts it, "the social context of voices that surround us frames each particular writing situation" (1995, 4).

Helping students to read and write rhetorically is thus largely about bringing the conversations they're joining to life. We want students to transform the two-dimensional surface of a written text into a three-dimensional social world. There's a thrill of discovery in finding that writers read other writers, share ideas and audiences, talk back to their critics, and comment on each other's work. Here's Charlotte Brontë, for instance, on William Makepeace Thackeray: "Not that by any means I always agree with Mr. Thackeray's opinions, but his force, his penetration, his pithy simplicity, his eloquence . . . command entire admiration" (Gaskell 1857/2005, 432). My students often react to these kinds of writer-to-writer connections with surprise: "Wait . . . these people knew each other?!"

I bring in as many pictures as I can get of writers' and publishers' work spaces to give my students a better sense of the messy, labor-intensive, and collaborative business that produces the writing they read. Some of my favorites include photos of Karl Marx's and Virginia Woolf's tables in the British Library's Reading Room, Charles Dickens's study at Gad's Hill Place, and T. S. Eliot's office at Faber and Faber in London's Bloomsbury Square. Poet Robinson Jeffers's lovely Tor House (see Figure 2) in Carmel, California, is particularly good because you can see the marks in the ceiling right under his second-floor writing desk where his wife, Una, would whack the planks with a broomstick to keep her husband on task; he apparently paced when distracted. Bazerman sums up this social complexity nicely: "Writing involves other people" (1995, 2).

Until students can see this bigger picture, it's hard to explain to them what we mean by *rhetorical situation.* We can define the terms *audience, purpose,* and *occasion,* but these can too easily seem like new vocabulary words to be added to the weekly eight-to-ten. We want students to be able to visualize a scene and construct a backstory for each of these terms when applied to a specific text. How can students understand the occasion for the Gettysburg Address unless they see Lincoln's train steaming through the war-torn countryside on its way to the newly created cemetery? How can they understand the audience for a Bob Herbert op-ed piece in the *New York Times* if they've never seen the advertisements in this newspaper or read the reader comments on the web page? This shift to a full understanding of a text's rhetorical context is one of the most important developmental milestones on the road to academic preparation.

FIGURE 2
Tor House, home of poet Robinson Jeffers
Photo by Jennifer Fletcher

Seeing writing as communication—instead of just a school requirement—additionally transforms students' understanding of the conditional effectiveness of a writer's rhetorical choices. What works depends on the situation. Compare the following two sentences from the same adult writer, an attorney from Monterey, California. The sentences are the opening lines of two different texts written on different occasions for different purposes and audiences:

1. I am writing to you as a volunteer member of the Legal Committee of the American Civil Liberties Union, Monterey County Chapter, to express the concern of ACLU with the prior restraints and limitations on freedom of speech contained in the draft Facilities Use Policy.

2. Monterey County should put the brakes on further expanding its jail.

Which sentence begins a formal business letter? Which one begins an op-ed piece in a newspaper? How do you know? What does it mean that the same person could write in two such different styles? How are these different stylistic choices suited to the texts' genres? When our students can understand and perform these same kinds of rhetorical style makeovers, we know they're well prepared to join a variety of written conversations.

Chapter Overview: Integrating and Applying Threshold Concepts

The chapters in this book offer explicit strategies for moving students from a superficial to a deep understanding of argumentation's threshold concepts. In many ways, reading and writing arguments rhetorically is about, in Peter Elbow's phrase, "embracing contraries" (1986). Those contraries come from many sources:

The diverse views we encounter in our reading (see Chapter 1)

The tension between our belief and doubt (see Chapter 2)

The dynamics of occasion, audience, and purpose (see Chapters 3 through 5)

The interplay of reason, emotion, and character (see Chapter 6)

Our own identities and experiences as readers and writers (see Chapter 7)

For students who have crossed the threshold into deep learning, creating order from contraries doesn't come at the cost of complexity. Instead, these writers are able to produce cohesive arguments that nevertheless show a tolerance for ambiguity. They resist oversimplification, integrating and applying rhetorical concepts without narrowly defining them.

This book, for instance, meets multiple rhetorical purposes: It informs, analyzes, evaluates, and proposes a solution. And it answers multiple questions about rhetoric and teaching argumentation rhetorically:

What is rhetoric? *(A question of definition.)*

What impact does the ability to read and write arguments rhetorically have on students' college and career readiness? *(A question of fact.)*

What are the benefits of teaching rhetoric to high school students? *(A question of quality.)*

Why should teachers use a rhetorical approach to argumentation? *(A question of policy.)*

You'll find the classical strategy I used to generate these questions in the discussion of stasis theory in Chapter 1.

A Few Final Notes on Reading This Book

Before you pass under the lintel into the rest of these pages, I'd like to offer a quick cook's tour of what you'll find. First, each chapter offers a doorway into a critical concept in rhetorical theory and practice. Because the doubting and believing game, the rhetorical situation (occasion, audience, and purpose), and the rhetorical appeals (ethos, pathos, and logos) are all interrelated, most chapters can either be read in order or with a kind of "Choose Your Own Adventure" approach. For instance, teachers who first want to deepen their students' knowledge of ethos, pathos, and logos could skip straight to Chapter 6 (although I hope you'll come back and check out the other chapters another time). If at any point in the reading you think, "This'll never work with my students," you can take a quick detour to Chapter 7. While Chapters 1 and 2 are a package deal, the rest can pretty much stand on their own. The point is that argumentation's threshold concepts are simultaneously present in acts of communication and that we don't need to teach our students these concepts in the sequence they're presented here.

Second, you'll find extensive modeling of rhetorical analysis in all chapters. If we want students to develop and internalize advanced literacy practices, then we all need to increase the amount of time we spend inside a text. Let me just say at the beginning, it's hard work to analyze a text. It's also hard work to help students analyze a text.

At some point in my career as an English teacher I came to the unhappy realization that if I was going to be well prepared to teach rhetorical analysis to my students, I was going to have to do the analyses myself. In my more rebellious moods, I'd sometimes like to be exempt from doing the work I've asked my students to do. But this reluctance doesn't help me show my students what I mean when I ask them to read and write rhetorically. Although I still think I start every heavy analytical task with a sigh, I've learned that my job requires more than giving definitions and directions.

That doesn't mean, however, that the hard work isn't fun. One of my operating assumptions is that anything that takes the joy out of teaching and learning is probably not a good idea. Pulitzer Prize–winning novelist Junot Diaz says we are our best selves when we respond deeply to art; a slow, careful study of great writing can fill readers with joyful, self-forgetting admiration and interest—and can engage reluctant students in exciting textual discoveries despite their best defenses. That's why I've been so picky about the "informational texts" I've included in this book. I'm a literature junkie myself, but I've learned that a brilliantly written piece of nonfiction can lift the spirit of a classroom as delightfully as a Billy Collins poem.

And third, some of the activities in this book are what rhetoricians might call *heuristic strategies*—tools or shortcuts to speed up learning. These include graphic organizers and mini-lessons on context, audience, purpose, and the rhetorical appeals that are not meant as ends in themselves but rather as experiments or exercises that can help students grasp troublesome knowledge. The point is to find creative ways to help students see what they might be missing about a concept—for instance, the mistaken notion of a text being written for "everyone"—so that they can apply this concept with greater depth and precision later on. Once students have crossed this threshold, we want them working with authentic academic texts, tasks, and contexts. We don't put the training wheels back on after our kids have learned to ride a bike.

At the end of each chapter, you'll find two lists: "Points to Remember" for teachers and "Prompts for Quick-Writes or Pairs Conversations" for students. The student prompts offer a quick formative assessment of the rhetorical skills, strategies, and concepts targeted by that chapter. These can be used before, during, or after a lesson to help students make connections and reflect on their learning.

Now, a brief word about Aristotle. While this book relies heavily on principles of Aristotelian rhetoric, there are moments, I admit, when I find it hard to take Aristotle seriously myself. For instance, in explaining that the use of persuasive speech is to lead to decisions, he adds stiffly, "When we know a thing, and have decided about it, there is no further use in speaking about it" (1984; Book II, Chapter xviii). (You'll see that I cite Aristotle by book and chapter number to make it easier for you to find these references in your own copies of his works.) My husband might be glad if I followed this precept, but I find compliance impossible. Poet Thomas Gray famously said that reading Aristotle's lecture notes is a bit like eating dried hay. I wouldn't go quite this far, but the reading I did for this project certainly necessitated that I up my caffeine intake. Yet despite Aristotle's stiffness and antiquated social views, his *Rhetoric* remains an enduring intellectual model that continues to significantly inform the theory and practice of critical communication. He's still a great teacher.

Lastly, this book recognizes that high school students have different emotional and intel-lectual needs from college students. College and career readiness, moreover, is a different goal from advanced placement. Many students who are not ready for accelerated high school classes will thrive on college campuses. Our students need appropriately rigorous instruc-tion in inclusive classrooms—instruction that invites and prepares them to critically engage arguments in a variety of postsecondary contexts. Adolescent literacy researcher Wayne H. Slater reminds us of the stakes: "If we expect all students to attain high literacy, so that they can flourish in higher education, the competitive world of work, and our free society, many more need to be achieving at the *advanced* level" (2004, 43; original emphasis). By teaching arguments rhetorically, we can help make that happen.

CHAPTER 1

Starting with Open-Minded Inquiry

The beginning of all discourse is a topic, a question, a problem, an issue.
—EDWARD P. J . CORBETT AND ROBERT J. CONNORS

Most of the things about which we make decisions, and into which therefore we inquire, present us with alternative possibilities.
—ARISTOTLE

Like many teachers, I sometimes wish I could find all those students I taught my first few years in the classroom and apologize for my rookie mistakes. For instance, here's how I used to teach the argument essay: I would ask students to choose an issue, develop a research question on their issue, and *then* read lots of articles and books to find their answer.

While this approach produced writing that generally matched the form of academic arguments, the substance was off. Claims were not well aligned with support, the reasoning felt forced, and there was often little sense of an authentic issue or context. Instead of reading-based writing, I had shoehorning and cherry-picking. As I learned more about rhetoric, I came to see that I had put the cart before the horse; it's hard to ask a question about an ongoing conversation if you don't listen to the conversation first.

A rhetorical approach to texts acknowledges that writing begins with reading. As a California report on college readiness notes, "College students and faculty do not think in isolation. They think with, around, and against other thinkers in a culture of academic literacy" (ICAS 2002, 12). How do students know which topics are current in their field of inquiry unless they begin by reading published works? How do they know their own position on an issue unless they can articulate the extent to which they agree or disagree with other writers? And what kind of credibility or ethos can writers have if they ignore the viewpoints of those who are most deeply impacted by an issue?

Starting with open-minded inquiry means starting by finding the questions other writers are asking. It's ultimately our students' job to figure out the hot topics, bones of contention, and sticking points of the day through careful reading and analysis of different texts. This chapter offers teachers several ways we can help.

Getting Ready to Enter the Conversation

When I teach argument essays today, my students and I begin by listening to the conversations we wish to join. Listening is hard work. It involves, as William H. Armstrong, Newbery Award–winning author of *Sounder,* explains, "subjecting the mind of the listener to the speaker" (1995, 8). When we listen, we have "to coordinate [our] mental powers with an outside force" (Armstrong 1995, 8). That means making an effort to understand a writer's argument on its own terms and not jumping to conclusions or pouncing on one or two juicy statements.

Why are we listening so carefully? We listen because we're trying to get ourselves situated. Have you ever had the experience of showing up to a meeting not knowing what to expect and being concerned about making a wrong move? Perhaps you were a new member of an English department, school site team, PTA, or leadership council. What did you do? If you're like me, you probably sat quietly and listened to everyone else until you could gauge the pulse of the room.

Writers do the same kind of reconnaissance listening when they prepare to enter a written conversation. This is a new and transformative idea for most of my students: in other words, a threshold concept. In the preface to *Threshold Concepts and Transformational Learning*, editors Jan H. F. Meyer, Ray Land, and Caroline Baillie write that "all journeys begin with leaving that familiar [interior] space and crossing over into the riskier space beyond the threshold" (2010, ix). Threshold concepts, you might recall from the introduction, allow "things formerly not perceived to come into view" (ix). They are "gateway concepts" (ix) that require us to let go of our usual way of viewing things and that empower us to see what we couldn't see before. We want high school students to see writing as dialogue—and to understand that attentive listening helps us communicate in informed and responsible ways.

Kenneth Burke, a giant in the field of twentieth-century rhetoric, offers a good reason for why listening should precede speaking: We can't just barge into a discussion without knowing what it's about. What's more, the people who are already involved in a conversation aren't going to stop talking and fill us in on everything we missed. We have to catch up on our own.

In his famous parlor conversation metaphor, Burke characterizes academic argumentation as an ongoing discussion that requires participants to pay careful attention to what has already been said (and yes, students will ask, "What's a parlor?"):

Imagine that you enter a parlor. You come late. When you arrive, others have long preceded you, and they are engaged in a heated discussion, a discussion too heated for them to pause and tell you exactly what it is about. In fact, the discussion had already begun long before any of them got there, so that no one present is qualified to retrace for you all the steps that had gone before. You listen for a while, until you decide that you have caught the tenor of the argument; then you put in your oar. Someone answers; you answer him; another comes to your defense; another aligns himself against you, to either the embarrassment or gratification of your opponent, depending upon the quality of your ally's assistance. However, the discussion is interminable. The hour grows late, you must depart. And you do depart, with the discussion still vigorously in progress. (1941, 110–111)

We have to listen long enough ("for a while") until we understand the substance of the argument; we can't just react based on a flimsy first impression if we want other people to listen to us.

Learning to Pay Attention

"Hear and attend and listen!" Thus Rudyard Kipling repeatedly commands his "Best Beloved" in *Just So Stories* (1902), as if he suspects his audience is a little inclined toward distraction. Paying attention to something means we give it the gift of our full consciousness. This is not a payment that can be made with a quick swipe of a debit card. This is an old-school transaction that requires time and an undivided focus.

Try this: Tell students that you're going to look closely at a painting together for a full

ten minutes. Their task will be to notice every little detail they can see in the painting during the allotted time, and you're going to record how long it takes them to notice different details. I use John Singleton Copley's *Boy with a Flying Squirrel* (1765)—you'll see why soon—but any sufficiently complex image will do. (See Figure 1.1.) It helps to use a ready-made time sheet (Figure 1.2) so that you can just take notes on what students say minute by minute. Now, reveal the painting and start the timer.

FIGURE 1.1

John Singleton Copley's *Boy with a Flying Squirrel* (1765)

FIGURE 1.2

Observation Time Sheet

MINUTES	OBSERVATIONS
1	
2	
3	
4	
5	
6	
7	
8	
9	
10	

Record what the class notices throughout your shared examination of the artwork, noting the time of each observation. Guide your class through the activity, repeatedly asking, "What do you notice?" and "Anything else?" When students say, "That's it. We've seen everything," tell them, "Look again" and "Look harder." If students need more help, ask them to think about the colors, shapes, patterns, curves, and lines of the painting. Can they find any hidden clues to the painting's meaning? After the ten-minute timer goes off, debrief the activity with questions like these:

- What did students notice first?
- What details took longer for students to see? Why?
- What details would they have missed if they had looked at the painting for only one minute?

You can let the debriefing continue through a pairs conversation and quick-write:

- Pairs Conversation: With a partner, discuss the time differences of the class's observations. Why are these differences significant?
- Quick-Write: "What does it take to see past the surface of something?"

Lastly, bring the whole class back together for a quick discussion of other kinds of first impressions that can be deepened by a closer look. Do students remember their first impression of their best friend? Their middle school or high school? Their favorite teacher? How has extended experience and more intimate knowledge helped them to see past the surface appearance in these examples? Can they think of a time when their first impression of something was wrong?

There's a secret to this activity that I save until the end. When we've finished our discussion, I reveal to students that this activity is based on an assignment designed by Harvard University art historian Jennifer L. Roberts—and that she requires her students to contemplate the same painting *for three hours!* Gasps and looks of horror. At least one student usually says, "I'd die." But I push students to entertain this idea. What do they think *they'd* see after an hour? After three hours? What might this Harvard lesson teach high school students about the role of patience in close reading?

In "The Power of Patience: Teaching Students the Value of Deceleration and Immersive Attention," Roberts discusses the importance of learning patiently. She says of the values of "critical attention, patient investigation, and skepticism about immediate surface appearances" that "few skills . . . are more important in academic or civic life in the twenty-first century" (2013). Roberts has put this principle into practice. Not only does she ask her students to spend what she admits is a "painfully long time" observing an image, but she's undertaken this task herself.

And what did Roberts, who has a PhD from Yale, notice after contemplating *Boy with a Flying Squirrel* for three straight hours? What she says about her own experience reveals the way that even expert brains might need extensive nudging past first impressions:

> It took me nine minutes to notice that the shape of the boy's ear precisely echoes that of the ruff along the squirrel's belly—and that Copley was making some kind of connection between the animal and the human body and the sensory capacities of each. It was 21 minutes before I registered the fact that the fingers holding the chain exactly span the diameter of the water glass beneath them. It took a good 45 minutes before I realized that the seemingly random folds and wrinkles in the background curtain are actually perfect copies of the shapes of the boy's ear and eye, as if Copley had imagined those sensory organs distributing or imprinting themselves on the surface behind him. And so on. (2013)

> If you try this activity with *Boy with a Flying Squirrel*, be sure to have your students look again at the painting to see if they can see what Roberts saw. The similarity between the squirrel's belly and the inside of the boy's ear usually draws the biggest "Oh, wow!"

Roberts's reflections on patient learning make an elegant point: "Just because something is available instantly to vision does not mean that it is available instantly to consciousness" (2013). Patience, she tells us, is power.

Listening with an Open Mind

We want students to practice this same art of patience when they listen to written texts. Patience is essential so that we don't prematurely foreclose any interpretive possibilities or force our own perspectives on the situation too soon. We attempt to suspend all judgment and personal reactions as we work to understand a writer's meaning.

In *Embracing Contraries,* Peter Elbow calls this noncritical approach to reading playing "the believing game," because we willingly give the writer the benefit of the doubt, at least for a time (1986, 261). I tell my students that this kind of intentional belief (Elbow calls it "methodological belief" [1986, 255]) is a threshold concept because it can be difficult and disorienting—and hard to unlearn once we've experienced its benefits. The CCSS clearly value this ability; the introduction to the English Language Arts standards describes college-ready students as "engaged and open-minded—but discerning—readers and listeners" who "work diligently to understand precisely what an author or speaker is saying" (NGA/CCSSO 2010, 7). This practice has also been described as "reading with the grain" (Batholomae and Petrosky 2002, 11) or "listening to the text" (Bean, Chappell, and Gillam 2014, 47), and *listening* is a great word for the supportive attention we give a writer during this initial part of the reading process.

My students will be the first to tell you that this isn't easy to do. Ana Lorena, for instance, says that this approach "is difficult because once you begin to read, you must set your initial emotions aside." Her classmate Stephanie describes this act as turning off our one-way vision. Another student, Brandon, says he can't help but take an early stance on an issue although "this makes it hard to hear the other side if it isn't yelling at me loud enough."

Listening to a text and postponing judgment, in fact, might require even more brain muscle (and good manners) than the critical analyses we'll conduct later. We're not just waiting for our turn to respond; we're engaging in reading as discovery or "invention," searching for the questions other writers are asking. We try to comprehend a text before we critique it. As one of my students put it, "If you contradict what you are reading, you won't really get the point of the passage."

MODELING THE BELIEVING GAME

We can help kids develop their capacity to listen with an open mind by modeling the believing game with a full text. For the following example, I've used David Brooks's (2012) opinion piece "The Olympic Contradiction" from the *New York Times,* but any well-crafted written argument will work. You might substitute an article from your local paper or a nonfiction piece from your anthology that appeals to your students' interests and experiences.

We read "The Olympic Contradiction" as part of a series of arguments on the place and value of sports in our culture. In this piece, Brooks celebrates the paradoxical tension between competition and cooperation at the heart of the Olympic experience. While students have loads to say about overly competitive coaches and parents, they are less ready to slow down and really engage Brooks's written argument—which, it turns out, is not actually about the Olympics or sports at all. Because most of my students find it much easier to respond to a topic than to listen to a text, I try to disrupt their usual approach through a teacher-led think-aloud.

First, I frontload my students with the definitions of a few key terms from the article: *monomaniac, virtue, opposable, pinnacle,* and *contradiction* (you might choose different words based on your students' needs). I also ask students to skim the article briefly on their own just to get the gist of Brooks's argument. Then, to make clear how much effort and attention are required to listen to a text, I lead my class through a detailed think-aloud of this article in which I model how to play the believing game. I tell students that at this point our belief is only provisional or hypothetical; in other words, we're temporarily trying on the writer's ideas for size. Modeling this process lets me show my students why learning to play the believing game can change the way they read.

This activity also works well as an "interrupted reading," in which I display one paragraph from the text at a time using a data projector (many thanks to Marilyn Elkins, rhetoric queen, for this terrific strategy). Letting students see only one section of text at a time helps defamiliarize the reading process for students and makes visible the difference between superficial and deep reading. As you show each section, ask, "What do you notice?" Students can also take charge of an interrupted reading using lines from the text on PowerPoint slides. I like slides that contain only a couple of sentences each so that students really have to look closely at the writer's language.

While I model the believing game as a think-aloud, my students complete the following "Checklist for Listening to a Think-Aloud" (Appendix 1), an activity I adapted from a unit designed by Mira-Lisa Katz and Meline Akashian for the CSU Expository Reading and Writing Course (ERWC Task Force 2013, 11). Students use this same checklist when I later demonstrate how to play the doubting game. Since the doubting game happens on another day, I remind students to bring their checklist back to class. They then compare the differences between what readers do when reading supportively versus what they do when reading critically (see Chapter 2).

Checklist for Listening to a Think-Aloud: Playing the Believing Game and the Doubting Game

Directions to Students: As your teacher models how to do a think-aloud, keep track of what he or she does while playing the believing game and the doubting game. You'll be using this same checklist for both games. First, place a plus sign (+) by everything you hear your teacher do during the believing game. Then, place a minus sign (–) by everything your teacher does when demonstrating the doubting game later on. Be sure to hang on to your checklist since you'll probably be playing the believing game and doubting game on different days. Some reading strategies may get both a plus and a minus sign.

___ Identify the main idea

___ Postpone judgment

___ Identify underlying assumptions

___ Question the writer's authority

___ Identify the context

___ Notice text structure and organization

___ Evaluate the effectiveness of the writer's rhetorical choices

___ Identify important examples

___ Paraphrase key claims

___ Summarize the writer's argument

___ Question the relevance of the evidence

___ Challenge the writer's claims

___ Notice what paragraphs say and do

___ Identify the writer's purpose

___ Notice key transitions

___ Offer a personal response

___ See the issue from the writer's point of view

___ Suggest potential counterarguments

___ Question the writer's reasoning

___ Give the writer the benefit of the doubt

___ Clarify key terms

___ Disagree with the writer

> When playing the believing game, it helps to reassure students that they will eventually get the chance to disagree with the writer, but that they're going to have to wait until it's time to play the doubting game (see Chapter 2).

"The Olympic Contradiction" by David Brooks: Believing Game Think-Aloud

My comments to my students are in italics. For the complete text without commentary, please see Appendix 2.

"The Olympic Contradiction" by David Brooks
New York Times, July 26, 2012

Abraham Lincoln said that a house divided against itself cannot stand. He was right about slavery, but the maxim doesn't apply to much else. In general, the best people are contradictory, and the most enduring institutions are, too.

OK, Brooks says the longest-lasting institutions and best people are divided and contradictory; that sounds like one of his main claims. It also looks like he's challenging a long-held belief that internal divisions are a problem.

The Olympics are a good example. The Olympics are a peaceful celebration of our warlike nature.

Now Brooks has moved from a principle to an example. I think I see where he's going.

FIGURE 1.3
Men's marathon, 2012 Summer Olympics in London
Photo by Jennifer Fletcher

The opening ceremony represents one side of the Olympic movement. They are a lavish celebration of the cooperative virtues: unity, friendship, equality, compassion and care. In Friday's ceremony, there'll be musical tributes to the global community and the Olympic spirit. There will be Pepsi commercial-type images of the people from different backgrounds joyfully coming together. There will be pious speeches about our common humanity and universal ideals.

And there will be a lot of dancing. Because we're social, semi-herdlike creatures, we take a primordial pleasure in the sight of a large number of people moving in unison. Dance is physical, like sports, but, in many ways, it is the opposite of sports. In dance, the purpose is to blend with and mirror each other; in sport, the purpose is to come out ahead. Dancers perform for the audience and offer a gift of emotion; athletes respond to one another and the spectators are just there to witness and cheer.

This paragraph is all about the spirit of cooperation at the Olympics as represented in the opening ceremony. Brooks mentions dance as a specific example of an emotional, community-based activity that is noncompetitive.

Dancers, especially at the opening ceremony, smile in warmth and friendship. No true sport is ever done smiling (this is the problem with figure skating and competitive cheerleading).

After the opening ceremony is over, the Olympics turn into a celebration of the competitive virtues: tenacity, courage, excellence, supremacy, discipline and conflict.

Brooks sees a real difference between the "warmth and friendship" of dance and the competitive virtues of a "true sport." This paragraph seems to be a turning point in his argument; he's shifting from cooperation to competition. I'm not sure how serious he is here.

The smiling goes away and the grim-faced games begin. The marathoner struggling against exhaustion, the boxer trying to pummel his foe, the diver resolutely focused on her task. The purpose is to be tougher and better than the people who are seeking the same pinnacle.

If the opening ceremony is win-win, most of the rest of the games are win-lose. If the opening ceremony mimics peace, the competitions mimic warfare. It's not about the brotherhood of humankind. It's about making sure our country beats the Chinese in the medal chart.

Through fierce competition, sport separates the elite from the mediocre. It identifies the heroes and standards of excellence that everybody else can emulate (a noble loser can serve as well as a talented winner). The idea is not to win friendship; it's to win glory. We get to see people experiencing the thrill of victory from the agony of defeat and judge how well they respond.

In sum, the Olympic Games appeal both to our desire for fellowship and our desire for status, to the dreams of community and also supremacy. And, of course, these desires are in tension. But the world is, too. The world isn't a jigsaw puzzle that fits neatly and logically together. It's a system of clashing waves that can never be fully reconciled.

There's a lot going on here. Brooks gives several examples of athletic scenes that show why "the grim-faced games" are not about friendship. He then describes a list of opposites. Let's see, there's win-win and win-lose, peace and warfare, victory and defeat, community and supremacy. Anything else? I'm not sure if he intends friendship and glory to be opposites, too. The last sentences of this paragraph bring all the opposites together in the image of clashing waves and suggest we can't really sort out these differences.

The enduring popularity of the Olympics teach the lesson that if you find yourself caught between two competing impulses, you don't always need to choose between them. You can go for both simultaneously. A single institution can celebrate charitable compassion and military toughness. A three-week festival can be crassly commercial, but also strangely moving.

F. Scott Fitzgerald famously said that the mark of a first-rate intelligence is the ability to hold two contradictory thoughts in your mind at the same time. But it's not really the mark of genius, just the mark of anybody who functions well in the world. It's the mark of any institution that lasts.

A few years ago, Roger Martin, the dean of the University of Toronto's management school, wrote a book called "The Opposable Mind," about business leaders who can embrace the tension between contradictory ideas. One of his examples was A. G. Lafley of Procter & Gamble.

Some Procter & Gamble executives thought the company needed to cut costs and lower prices to compete with the supermarket store brands. Another group thought the company should invest in innovation to keep their products clearly superior. Lafley embraced both visions, pushing hard in both directions.

Now we're coming back to Brooks's thesis—the idea that it's actually good to be contradictory. Brooks gives several examples of why choosing "both" instead of "either/or" helps us "to function well in the world." This is the lesson we should learn from the Olympics.

The world, unfortunately, has too many monomaniacs—people who pick one side of any creative tension and wish the other would just go away. Some parents and teachers like the cooperative virtues and distrust the competitive ones, so, laughably, they tell their kids that they are going to play sports but nobody is going to keep score.

Brooks now says that choosing one opposite over another can actually cause problems. To him, a monomaniac is a person who can see only one side.

Politics has become a contest of monomaniacs. One faction champions austerity while another champions growth. One party becomes the party of economic security and the other becomes the party of creative destruction.

Here's a scaled-up example of groups who can't support contradictory ideas. Brooks moved from the personal to the political.

The right course is usually to push hard in both directions, to be a house creatively divided against itself, to thrive amid the contradictions. The Olympics are great, but they are not coherent.

This is the final restatement of Brooks's thesis. Does that make three times he has stated his argument? "Right course" makes it sound like embracing contradictions is not just an effective way to live or work but is actually a better moral or intellectual choice. He seems to be evaluating the ability to accept opposites simultaneously.

> After we complete the think-aloud, I ask my students to compare their checklist with a partner's and then tell me what they noticed. This open-ended question invites them to share their initial thoughts about the text or the believing game. Most students really enjoy "The Olympic Contradiction." I knew I'd scored a hit in terms of student interest when I heard one student athlete whisper to her friend, "I kind of love this article."

Debriefing the Activity

Much of what I'm doing in the think-aloud, of course, is just paraphrasing or mirroring Brooks's words as a way of checking my comprehension. The question I'm trying to answer is "What is Brooks saying?"; *how* and *why* he says what he says will come later. I'm also searching for the implicit question behind Brooks's thesis. While Brooks can't tell me if I'm on the right track, the act of articulating another writer's argument aloud can give us a good sense of our understanding—and my students are welcome to correct me if they think I've gotten it wrong. After we've done this in class a few times, I ask student volunteers to lead the think-aloud with sections of other texts. Students can also try this in small groups. The goal is for this kind of supportive paraphrasing to eventually become an internalized, independent practice.

Now for a confession—Do I really forgo any analysis until after I've worked hard to understand the writer's position? Well, no. Some meanings—for example, in many poems—can be impossible to discover without analysis. Often, we have to work from part to whole. And with a writer like David Brooks, ignoring things like tone and humor at the outset can actually lead to serious misreadings down the road. But, in general, when my students and I work with expository texts, we try to focus on comprehension as a precondition for critique—even as we recognize that some insights happen simultaneously.

Bringing the Conversation to Life

Another threshold concept that can be difficult to grasp is this: Texts bear traces of other voices in the conversation the writer is joining. We can often figure out who else is in the "parlor" (to use Burke's metaphor) by noting the names in a writer's sources, references, allusions, and footnotes. When my students are first learning this idea, I ask them to draw a sketch representing all the different voices they hear in a text. Stick figures are fine. The point is for students to be able to see these references or sources as real people. (See the student directions just before Figures 1.4 and 1.5.)

When we read David Brooks's article "The Olympic Contradiction," we thus have to imagine the other voices who are a part of the conversation he's entering. His reference to Lincoln's aphorism about "a house divided" is a clue that Brooks is engaging a long-standing cultural discussion (Emerson and Whitman certainly had lots to say about contradictions). We can infer that some of Brooks's contemporaries have probably expressed concern about the mixed messages sent by the Olympic Games. Other voices in this conversation appear as supporting sources in the article itself: F. Scott Fitzgerald, Roger Martin, and the executives at Procter & Gamble. A conversation—and the issue it addresses—can be limited to a specific historical moment or can span the centuries. In this case, the participants share a common interest in the question of whether it's good or bad to entertain two opposing ideas at the same time.

Directions to Students: Draw a sketch representing all the different voices you hear in David Brooks's "The Olympic Contradiction." You may want to conduct a quick Internet search for images of the people Brooks mentions in his article to see what they look like. These are the

people who have contributed something to the conversation he's joining. Be sure to include Brooks himself in your sketch. Stick figures are fine—the point is for you to be able to see these references or sources as real people!

Ana Lorena's sketch (Figure 1.4) captures the diversity of voices in Brooks's article.

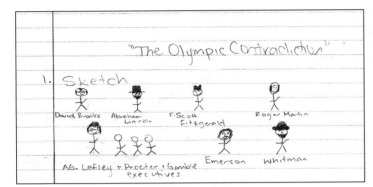

FIGURE 1.4
Student Ana Lorena's sketch of the voices in Brooks's "Olympic Contradiction"

And I loved the humor of Karen's drawing! (See Figure 1.5.)

You can imagine the pictures ninth graders would draw if you asked them to sketch the different voices in, for example, Martin Luther King Jr.'s "Letter from Birmingham Jail": clergymen, merchants, Socrates, Reinhold Niebuhr, a five-year-old child, and St. Thomas Aquinas, among others.

It's also helpful to know who and what are *not* a part of a conversation. Brooks's article is not about the best format for the opening ceremony or about why dancers or cheerleaders should not be considered athletes (although many students may want to attack Brooks on this front). These conversations exist, too, but they're not the ones Brooks is engaging in. In my work helping to develop the criteria for placement in college writing courses in California, I repeatedly encounter this kind of misreading of rhetorical context as a mark of a student who is not yet college ready. The scoring guide used for the California State University English Placement Test, for instance, notes that below-adequate papers may demonstrate

FIGURE 1.5
Student Karen's sketch of the voices in Brooks's "Olympic Contradiction"

"an inaccurate understanding of the [reading] passage" or "may wander off topic or discuss irrelevant aspects of the topic" (CSU 2009, 15).

Discovering the Question at Issue

Reading with the grain like this is a great way to help kids find the key question a writer responds to in an argument-based text. Because we've already identified three places where Brooks states his position on the importance of accepting contradictions, we know that this article is not just about the Olympics or competition versus cooperation. We've tracked Brooks's examples through the think-aloud activity, noting the way he offers specific instances in support of larger claims, so we know the issue here is about the principles behind the illustrations. If we didn't do this careful work first, we might fall for the trap of reacting to Brooks's provocative statements about dance or figure skating or boxing without engaging the question at issue Brooks himself is answering.

I can now check students' reading comprehension by asking them to identify the implicit question behind Brooks's thesis and to give a brief justification of their choice:

Sample Formative Assessment

Directions to Students: Identify the central question Brooks responds to in "The Olympic Contradiction." Then explain why you chose the answer you selected.

A.   Can competitive virtues coexist with cooperative virtues?

B.   What is the reason for the enduring popularity of the Olympics?

C.   Is dance a true sport?

D.   Is an acceptance of opposites a characteristic of intelligence?

E.   Is it good to embrace the tension between contradictions?

F.   Is competition better than cooperation?

G.   Should the Olympic Games be less competitive?

Justification for your selection:

I'm hoping that my students will choose "E"—a question that calls for an evaluation, rather than a definition, explanation, or policy recommendation. "D" might be a good distractor because it implies a positive judgment about the acceptance of opposites, but "intelligence" doesn't figure as a main idea in the article. Some students might also be drawn to "A," but the question of the existence of these dualities is not at issue. Brooks assumes their coexistence and argues that these opposing tensions are not a problem. His thesis is that these kinds of contradictions are productive and beneficial, not an instance of hypocrisy or destructive incoherence. "E" is the real question at issue.

Think your students would have a hard time choosing "E"? Hang tight. There's a way to make this easier.

WHAT'S A QUESTION AT ISSUE?

John T. Gage, author of *The Shape of Reason: Argumentative Writing in College,* offers a helpful explanation of a question at issue: "A question is at issue when members of a community agree that it is important to answer and there is uncertainty or disagreement as to the best answer" (2000, 42). Both the importance of the question and the uncertainty of the answer are key. Without shared concerns and differing viewpoints, there's no reason to engage in argumentation. Although my fourth-grade son has loads of opinions about the graphics, options, music, and characters in Minecraft, my own lack of experience with the computer game makes it unlikely that a question at issue regarding the game's content will arise between us. Now, *how much time he should spend playing the game*—that's an issue I can argue about.

HOW DO I MAKE THIS EASIER? (HINT: TRY STASIS THEORY)

The ability to identify different question types makes it easier for students to respond to the arguments of other writers appropriately. Enter stasis theory. Stasis theory is my secret weapon for dispelling confusion over the central question a text asks.

Believed to have been first developed by Hermagoras of Temnos, a Greek rhetorician who taught in Rome during the first century BCE, stasis theory offers a means by which participants in a conversation can identify the question at issue (Edlund 2006). Stasis is the fixed point upon which an argument hinges. Gage explains, "The stasis of any argument is the specific point on which the controversy rests, that one point on which one person says 'yes' but another says 'no' or 'I'm not sure'" (2000, 40).

If we can't settle on the point of disagreement, we can't engage in argumentation because we'll either be talking at cross-purposes or just to ourselves. For instance, a group that wants to talk about why capital punishment is morally wrong hasn't reached stasis with a group that wants to evaluate the financial costs of capital punishment. They're not part of the same conversation. To engage an audience, we need to achieve stasis.

While rhetoricians sometimes list up to six different kinds of stasis questions, I find the following four (modified from *Everything's an Argument* [Lunsford 2010] and the CSU Expository Reading and Writing Course [ERWC Task Force 2013]) work well for my purposes:

Question of Fact:	Did something happen? Is it real? What is its origin or cause?
Question of Definition:	What is its nature? What are its parts? How is it classified?
Question of Quality:	What is its quality? Is it good or bad? Harmful or helpful?
Question of Policy:	What actions should be taken? How can we make things better?

We can generate similar questions under these general categories (e.g., Is something better or worse than something else? How are the parts related to the whole? What are its character-istics?), but these four basic types of questions work well for most of the kinds of arguments that high school students encounter in academic reading.

Consider how stasis theory can help students identify the question at issue in "The Olympic Contradiction."

A: Question of Fact: Can competitive virtues coexist with cooperative virtues?

B: Question of Fact: What is the reason for the enduring popularity of the Olympics?

C: Question of Definition: Is dance a true sport?

D: Question of Definition: Is an acceptance of opposites a characteristic of intelligence?

E: Question of Quality: Is it good to embrace the tension between contradictions?

F: Question of Quality: Is competition better than cooperation?

G: Question of Policy: Should the Olympic Games be less competitive?

Viewed through the lens of stasis theory, it's easier to see the very different kinds of conversa-tions these questions frame. Brooks makes extensive comparisons and evaluations throughout his article, a circumstance that should point students pretty quickly toward a question of quality. From there, it's not too hard to pinpoint what he's actually judging—and it's not the value of competition.

When I give the preceding quiz to students without identifying the stasis theory question behind each answer choice, I find students are more easily fooled by distractors. For instance, Eddie (who took the quiz *sans* the stasis theory enhancement) offered a justification for why he chose "D" that showed he understood the passage but had trouble articulating its thesis:

> I believe the central question that Brooks responds to is "Is an acceptance of opposites a characteristic of intelligence?" Brooks talks about the idea of monomaniacs, people who pick one side of any tension and wish the other would go away. But Brooks also mentions that there are too many monomaniacs. He demonstrates this through F. Scott Fitzgerald that "the mark of a first-rate intelligence is the ability to hold two contradictory thoughts in your mind at the same time." This is the question that is most prominently answered.

Eddie mistakes a key supporting claim for the central thesis. The example he cites is certainly important to the meaning of the passage as a whole, but Brooks's overarching question is not about whether something is or is not a characteristic of intelligence, a question of definition.

In contrast, Lucas's stasis-informed justification for choosing "E" shows he was able to keep the big picture and the big question in mind: "Since the beginning of the article . . . David Brooks gave examples to prove that it is good to embrace tension between contradictions."

FINDING QUESTIONS

A trick to finding the stasis question behind an argument is what Gage calls the "yes, but" question (2000, 40). As readers, we have this reaction when we encounter a generally plausible statement that nevertheless gives us pause; we feel a strong urge to doubt and qualify. Reading-based writing prompts built on these kinds of statements can be great fun to create. I like to offer my students a seemingly reasonable prompt with a little bit of crazy tacked on. I find it helps them identify that point on a slippery slope when they want to slam on the brakes. A generally defensible assertion rounded off with a sweeping generalization or improbable solution works nicely: for instance, a passage that claims that sugary sodas contribute to childhood obesity and tooth decay . . . and we should therefore establish a minimum age of eighteen for drinking soda (this kind of thesis responds both to a question of fact, "What's causing childhood obesity?" and a question of policy, "What should we do about it?"). I'm looking for a response that shows the students are willing to follow the writer's logic up to a certain point but not ready to take that extra leap into an untenable position. The reaction I'm after is "Uh huh, uh huh, uh huh—wait a minute!"

Where do we look for these questions? Riffling through another writer's introduction or conclusion is a good place to start. We're looking for a strong thesis we can trace back to an engaging question at issue, a solid proposition, or "a complete sentence that asserts or denies something about the subject" (Corbett and Connors 1999, 27). Brooks offers his thesis in the beginning, middle, and end of his article, making his main argument relatively easy to find.

Running with a thesis question that is already in play, so to speak, avoids one of the pitfalls of generic research assignments: It can be really hard to take a randomly selected topic from a teacher-generated list (e.g., cell phones, global warming, health care, cheating, etc.), spin out an array of potential research questions that could be asked about that subject, and *then* find relevant readings. Again, we're putting the cart before the horse. Say, for instance, you have a student who's interested in the history of ska bands in Southern California. Now, you could have this student brainstorm a series of questions on this topic using stasis theory:

Question of Fact:	What are the origins of this genre of music?
Question of Definition:	What are the key characteristics of ska? To what other forms of music is ska related?
Question of Quality:	Is ska more entertaining than reggae or rock?
Question of Policy:	Should ska be included in music appreciation courses?

This is an interesting intellectual exercise and not a bad way to illustrate the way different questions influence the structure and purpose of our responses, but what happens if no one else is asking and answering any of these questions? What happens if all the readings we find, for example, are actually about the social tensions within the ska fan base? Choosing a question that nobody else is talking about is akin to abruptly changing the subject in a conversation; people might still listen to you if your new topic is truly worth engaging, but they'll probably find your behavior a bit rude or irritating. I think of the story a colleague tells about a student who asked, "What do you do if you can't find any support for your thesis?" Find a new thesis, of course. For this reason, I like stasis theory best as an analytical reading strategy, not as a decontextualized prewriting strategy.

To be sure, there are certainly many real-world instances when questions come before research because of a genuine need to know a specific answer. For instance, an insurance company might need to know how past case law will impact its policies in the coming year—or a library might need to know the best-selling books in order to have enough copies available to loan. But these are not questions at issue. Finding an answer to a closed-ended question doesn't require engaging multiple perspectives or an ongoing conversation and is not a typical academic task.

Beyond the Pros and Cons Essay

As stasis theory makes clear, academic arguments can address more than just a question of policy. Yet often, instruction in argumentation gets limited to pro and con views of a social issue—the perennial proposition and support essay that asserts what we should do about a particular problem:

> Should high schools have dress codes?
>
> Should abortion be illegal?
>
> Should sex education be taught in public schools?
>
> Should we repeal the death penalty?
>
> Should we legalize marijuana?

The problem with teaching academic argumentation exclusively through these types of questions is that scholars are interested in more than just questions of policy. The following article by Associated Press science writer Alicia Chang, for instance, describes a debate among researchers over a question of fact about the Grand Canyon (Figure 1.6):

"How Old Is Grand Canyon? New Study Puts Age at 70 Million Years"

LOS ANGELES—The awe-inspiring Grand Canyon was probably carved about 70 million years ago, much earlier than thought, a provocative

FIGURE 1.6

The Grand Canyon, south rim, spring 2012

Photo by Coreen Cardenas

new study suggests—so early that dinosaurs might have roamed near this natural wonder.

Using a new dating tool, a team of scientists came up with a different age for the gorge's western section, challenging conventional wisdom that much of the canyon was scoured by the mighty Colorado River in the last 5 million to 6 million years.

Not everyone is convinced with the latest viewpoint published online Thursday in the journal *Science.*

Critics contend the study ignores a mountain of evidence pointing to a geologically young landscape and they have doubts about the technique used to date it.

The notion that the Grand Canyon existed during the dinosaur era is "ludicrous," said geologist Karl Karlstrom of the University of New Mexico in Albuquerque.

How the Grand Canyon became grand—with its vertical cliffs and flat plateaus—has been debated since John Wesley Powell navigated the whitewater rapids and scouted the sheer walls during his famous 1869 expedition.

Some 5 million tourists flock to Arizona each year to marvel at the 277-mile-long chasm, which plunges a mile deep in some places. It's a geologic layer cake with the most recent rock formations near the rim stacked on top of older rocks that date back 2 billion years.

Though the exposed rocks are ancient, most scientists believe the Grand Canyon itself was forged in the recent geologic past, created when tectonic forces uplifted the land that the Colorado River later carved through.

The new work by researchers at the University of Colorado Boulder and California Institute of Technology argued that canyon-cutting occurred long before that. They focused on the western end of the Grand Canyon occupied today by the Hualapai Reservation, which owns the Skywalk attraction, a horseshoe-shaped glass bridge that extends from the canyon's edge.

To come up with the age, the team crushed rocks collected from the bottom of the canyon to analyze a rare type of mineral called apatite. The mineral contains traces of radioactive elements that release helium during decay, allowing researchers to calculate the passage of time since the canyon eroded.

Their interpretation: The western Grand Canyon is 70 million years old and was likely shaped by an ancient river that coursed in the opposite direction of the west-flowing Colorado.

Lead researcher Rebecca Flowers of the University of Colorado Boulder realizes not everyone will accept this alternative view, which minimizes the role of the Colorado River.

"Arguments will continue over the age of Grand Canyon, and I hope our study will stimulate more work to decipher the mysteries," Flowers said in an email.

It's not the first time that Flowers has dug up evidence for an older Grand Canyon. In 2008, she authored a study that suggested part of the eastern Grand Canyon, where most tourists go, formed 55 million years ago. Another study published that same year by a different group of researchers put the age of the western section at 17 million years old.

If the Grand Canyon truly existed before dinosaurs became extinct, it would have looked vastly different because the climate back then was more tropical. Dinosaurs that patrolled the American West then included smaller tyrannosaurs, horned and dome-headed dinosaurs and duckbills.

If they peered over the rim, it would not look like "the starkly beautiful desert of today, but an environment with more lush vegetation," said University of Maryland paleontologist Thomas Holtz.

Many scientists find it hard to imagine an ancient Grand Canyon since the oldest gravel and sediment that washed downstream date to about 6 million years ago and there are no signs of older deposits. And while they welcome advanced dating methods to decipher the canyon's age, Karlstrom of the University of New Mexico does not think the latest effort is very accurate.

Karlstrom said it also defies logic that a fully formed canyon would sit unchanged for tens of millions of years without undergoing further erosion.

Geologist Richard Young of the State University of New York at Geneseo said his own work suggests there was a cliff in the place of the ancient Grand Canyon.

Flowers "wants to have a canyon there. I want to have a cliff there. Obviously, one of us can't be right," he said.

Whatever the age, there may be a middle ground, said Utah State University geologist Joel Pederson.

> Researchers have long known about older canyons in the region cut
> by rivers that flow in a different direction than the Colorado River. It's
> possible that a good portion of the Grand Canyon was chiseled long ago
> by these smaller rivers and then the Colorado came along and finished
> the job, he said. (Chang 2012)

Chang's prose is rich with the language of academic argumentation. Because the team of scientists "challeng[es] conventional wisdom," not everyone "is convinced" or "will accept this alternative view." Chang's verbs also characterize this scholarly conversation as an argument; researchers "contend," "believe," and "argued." The question at issue is "how the Grand Canyon became grand"—a question of fact.

This is exactly how Gerald Graff and Cathy Birkenstein characterize argumentation in *"They Say/I Say": The Moves That Matter in Academic Writing* (2010). Graff and Birkenstein's popular resource for student writers "demystifies academic argumentation" (xv) through the use of sentence templates that help students frame the multiple perspectives they must engage when they summarize and respond to ongoing debates. The models Graff and Birkenstein offer look very much like Chang's sentences:

> Conventional wisdom has it that _____.
> X argues that _____.
> X claims that _____.
> X denies/does not deny that _____. (163–165)

Students who begin by reading authentic arguments from other writers (instead of choosing a topic from a list) can see that questions of fact can be just as contentious and exciting as questions of policy.

Analyzing the Stasis Question

If students are able to score a good stasis question from their reading, they can take their understanding of the subject and its rhetorical context further by asking questions about the stasis question itself. The following helpful list comes from *Reading Rhetorically*:

Prompts for Question Analysis

1. What question do you plan to investigate—and hope to answer—in this paper?

2. What makes this question worth pursuing—to you and others?

3. What kind of expert would be able to provide good answers or the current best thinking about possible answers?

4. Where do you expect to find particularly good information about the matter?

5.   How recent must materials be to be relevant? What factors might make information outdated?

6.   What individuals or interest groups have a major stake in answering your question in a particular way?

7.   What kinds of bias do you need to be especially alert for on this particular question?

8.   What words or phrases might be useful for some initial searching? (Bean, Chappell, and Gillam 2011, 108)

These questions provide a road map to the conversation a student would be joining in answering a particular stasis question. As students think about the scope and membership of this conversation, its participants' qualifications and interests, and the language used in this discourse community, they get a better sense of what other sources they should read. They also learn more about their audience and occasion.

Something for rhetoric fans to note—stasis theory is close kin to another classical tool for developing arguments: the common topics. These include definition (How can you classify the subject?), comparison (What are the similarities and differences?), relationship (What are the causes and effects?), and circumstance (What is possible and impossible?), among others (Corbett and Connors 1999, 87). Both stasis theory and the common topic are invention strategies—ways of developing and supporting arguments. The point is not to have students memorize or choose between systems for finding questions—after all, both are just schema—but to help students activate their radar to the different kinds of questions writers ask. I'm happy if my students recognize that "What is it?" is a very different sort of question from "Did it happen?" or "Is it good?"; I don't need them to remember the terms *stasis theory* or *common topics*.

Writing as Inquiry

Writing-to-learn activities are another excellent form of inquiry. To be sure, writing is itself a questioning strategy; Gage talks about "writing as reasoned inquiry" (2000, xiii). Taking up a pen or pencil or sitting down at a computer is always an act of discovery. When we write, we're exploring what we think and know. Although we may have a particular idea we want to express when we first begin writing, we often find that the process of writing itself leads to surprising insights that make us question our original assumptions. Providing students with multiple writing-to-learn experiences is a good way to help them investigate their subject before taking their own position on a question at issue.

In addition to quick-writes, reading journals, and reflections, I like to use a modified version of Peter Elbow's "loop writing" (1998a, 59) to nudge my students beyond a superficial understanding of a question at issue. I learned this strategy from Sharon Hunter, one of my master teachers, and find it most effective after students have already done some reading and writing on the issue they're studying. Here's how it works:

I share the following four prompts with my students on a document camera or LCD projector, uncovering one prompt at a time. Each time I show a new prompt, students have five minutes to freewrite their response. The entire looped sequence takes a little over twenty minutes and allows students to investigate *one* issue in depth. This part is important: While students might be tempted to stray from their subject after so much writing, I keep pulling them back to their chosen issue. The purpose of "loop writing" is to dig past knee-jerk or surface-level understandings to a new perspective on the subject.

Prompts (Show one at a time, keeping the others hidden until their turn.)

> When I first think of my issue, I think of . . .
>
> Next I think of . . .
>
> Then it occurs to me . . .
>
> Now I wonder . . .

After students finish responding to all four prompts (and shaking out their cramped hands), they often find that what they've written looks very much like an essay. The transitions in the prompts—*first, next, then, now*—and the switches between the verbs *think, occurs,* and *wonder* move students through a reevaluation of their understanding. They frequently find that what they thought they knew was either inaccurate or insufficient and that there's a lot more to their topic than they had first assumed. Very often the last two prompts encourage students to question things they'd taken for granted—like the universality of a key principle or the values of their intended audience. The loops help the writers to spiral up into alternative points of view.

Cherllyn's loop writing on her research question shows the way this activity can encourage exploration and reflection:

> When I first think of my research topic . . . I think of a stadium. More like an Olympic stadium. There are so many ideas in my head, but I cannot break them up to see where I want to go. Do I want to stick to one sport? Or think more broadly? I know I want to delve into sports and can use a million anecdote[s], but finding good sources makes me nervous. I'm not sure if I'm going to be able to find enough to get all my thoughts into words. I know I need to research before I really throw myself into a topic, but I'm afraid there will not be enough time.
>
> Next, I think of . . . where do I want to go? What do I want to accomplish researching the meaning of sports? Is there anything in particular that I need to include? I really want to use 1 or 2 personal anecdotes about swimming and water polo, but I'm not sure I understand what I want to know yet. I need to think of how I could focus on 1 or

2 less popular ones all the while continuing the broad questions for all
sports.

Then it occurs to me . . . that I can add gender trouble, college readiness,
and childhood to this. By talking about if sports can help children be ready
for college or if athletics can help children with sour pasts move on. I
could also research how playing sports/spreading oneself so thin could be
a bad thing in high school.

Now I wonder . . . why did I start playing water polo? What makes us
want to play those more violent sports? Uh oh, here comes more ideas:
What is it about being competitive [that] makes some human beings feel
whole? Why do we need sports? Where did we get this idea that exercise
was a good thing? All it does is kill your knees, arms, muscles, and joints.

Cherylln's last two "loops" show how her brainstorming progressed from practical con-
siderations of the assignment to an intellectual engagement of the subject.

Conclusion

In the rhetorical tradition, argumentation begins with asking questions. The special name classical rhetoric gives to the exploratory stage when we find the issues, positions, and evidence
we want to engage—*invention*—captures this sense of discovery. Invention doesn't mean
fabrication; it means generating content through inquiry. Revered rhetoricians Edward P. J.
Corbett and Robert J. Connors explain that invention is particularly important in expository
and argumentative writing because in description and narration writers have more opportunities to create their own material (1999). In exposition and argumentation, writers have to find
it. In *A New History of Classical Rhetoric,* George A. Kennedy describes invention as being
focused on "thinking out the subject matter" (1994, 4).

This early stage of reading is also about scoping out the rhetorical situation. Rhetorician
Charles Bazerman tells student writers, "You have to read well enough to see what people
are really discussing, what the real issues are. You need to understand what has already been
written to decide intelligently what you can contribute" (1995, 4–5). We might need to do a
little reconnaissance listening before we're ready to join the conversation.

Asking questions is about reading a variety of sources with an open mind. It's about postponing judgment and tolerating ambiguity, reading with the grain, and playing the believing
game. When academic writing begins with open-ended inquiry, students have an authentic
opportunity to understand and respond to real-world arguments.

Points to Remember

As you plan your lessons and teach the concepts described in this chapter, you might want to refer to the following list of points to remember:

1. Academic writing begins with academic reading.

2. When we read and write for academic purposes, we join a conversation already in progress.

3. Reading "with the grain" enhances our ability to understand the arguments of other writers.

4. Argumentation involves asking and answering questions.

5. The question at issue is the point of disagreement—or pivot point—on which an argument hinges.

6. Knowing the kinds of questions writers can ask helps us to identify arguments more easily.

7. Stasis theory questions include questions of fact, definition, quality, and policy.

8. Achieving stasis means the speaker/writer and audience agree on the question at issue. In other words, they're engaged in the same conversation, not addressing separate topics.

9. Open-minded reading and listening are essential preparation for academic writing.

10. A well-developed questioning habit is a key trait of college-ready students.

Prompts for Quick-Writes or Pairs Conversations

The following prompts can be used before, during, or after a lesson to help students make personal connections, deepen their understanding, and reflect on their learning:

1. How do you know if something is true or only an opinion?

2. How do you decide if something is better or worse than something else?

3. Describe a time you had to classify or sort something. What kind of categories did you use? How did you decide where things belonged? What did you do if something didn't fit the categories?

4. Describe a time when you decided something was more important than something else. How did you reach this decision?

5. Describe a policy at your school (e.g., dress code, tardy policy, lunch passes, detention, homework) that you would like to see changed. What future policy would you recommend? How will the new policy make things better?

6. Describe a time when you found it hard to play "the believing game" while reading a text. What did you do, if anything, to overcome your doubt?

7. When is it difficult for you to listen to the words of another writer? Why? What can you do about this?

8. What kinds of conversations do you like to join? What do you enjoy talking about?

9. Describe a time when you were able to see something from a different point of view. What helped you to understand a new perspective?

10. Describe a time when you read something that caused you to strongly agree with the writer's viewpoint. What would you say to this writer?

11. Respond to the following question of fact: Can we change the impact that our family relationships have on us?

12. Respond to the following question of definition: What do college ready and career ready mean to you?

13. Respond to the following question of quality: Is it better to have loved and lost or never to have loved at all?

14. Respond to the following question of policy: What should teachers do to prevent cheating?

CHAPTER 2

From Comprehension to Critique

Ender noticed that without exception they had lined up with their heads still in the direction that had been up in the corridor. So Ender deliberately took hold of what they were treating as a floor and dangled from it upside down. "Why are you upside down, soldier?" he demanded. . . .

"From now on, you forget about gravity before you go through that door. The old gravity is gone, erased. Understand me? Whatever your gravity is when you get to the door, remember—the enemy's gate is down."

—ORSON SCOTT CARD, FROM *ENDER'S GAME*

In Orson Scott Card's sci-fi novel *Ender's Game,* the title character makes a transformative discovery: We can strategically change our perceptions. Ender Wiggin teaches his soldiers that orientation is a matter of tactical choice in the zero-gravity battle room. The whole book, in fact, is about the power of perspective, about the new understandings we gain when we look with different eyes.

When we shift from reading a text supportively to reading it critically, we are strategically choosing to reorient ourselves. We intentionally change our vantage point so that we can take a full survey of a text's complexities before we determine the extent to which we agree or disagree with its claims.

This turn from comprehending a text to critiquing it can feel unsettling, which is part of what makes "methodological doubt" a threshold concept (Elbow 1986, 264). If we've deliberately postponed our judgment during our initial reading of a text, it can be a challenge to turn around and give our critical doubt free rein. Whereas before we imagined what it felt like to agree with a writer, now we imagine what it feels like to disagree. In both cases, we're trying on a perspective that might not come naturally to us—and that might ultimately be different from our own view. We do this so we can, as the Common Core introduction puts it, "evaluate other points of view critically and constructively" as we prepare to join the conversation ourselves (NGA/CCSSO 2010, 7).

Playing the Doubting Game

Peter Elbow calls doubting and believing "among the most powerful root acts we can perform with our minds" (1986, 268). In my experience, doubting often comes easier than believing, which is why we have to work so hard to understand a text before we critique it. But skepticism certainly requires brain power, too—especially if we are the choir the writer's preaching to. Sometimes it's our belief we have to suspend.

When we switch from playing the believing game to playing the doubting game, I give my students the heads-up that this transition in thinking can be difficult. One of my students, Alex, described this challenge in a quick-write: "The doubting game is very difficult for me once I have already gone through a text believing everything about it. I feel like I trust the author and their words are law. I have a lot of trouble finding flaws in the argument." Another student said that she found it really hard to play the doubting game unless she knew a lot about the topic.

Elbow describes doubt as associated with "resisting authority," "holding back," and "tentativeness" (1986, 264–265). When we doubt a writer's claims, we create a critical distance between ourselves and the text, reserving our conviction (or "trust," as Alex put it) until we've analyzed all the evidence. We're no longer trying to see the issue exclusively through the writer's eyes. Here's where the word *discerning* in the Common Core's description of a college-ready student comes into play (NGA/CCSSO 2010, 7). While the CCSS encourages open-minded reading and listening, it also calls for students to "question an author's or speaker's assumptions and premises and assess the veracity of claims and the soundness of reasoning" (NGA/CCSSO 2010, 7). At this stage of the reading process, students move from listening to a text to interrogating it.

We deliberately create this critical distance in preparation for taking our own stance on an issue. The authors of *Reading Rhetorically* explain that the goal of reading against the grain is to "apply your own critical thinking so that you can 'speak back' to texts with authority and insight in both oral and written conversations" (Bean, Chappell, and Gillam 2011, 41). Guiding kids through what Kelly Gallagher calls "second-draft reading" (2004, 80) gets them ready to have their say. It also develops a key rhetorical competency: the ability to understand and integrate multiple perspectives.

> No surprise, many students don't like having to read something more than once. By showing students that there are different ways of reading, we give them a reason to return to a text. We can say, "You may have already read this, but you haven't read it *this* way yet."

PLAYING THE DOUBTING GAME WITH "THE OLYMPIC CONTRADICTION" BY DAVID BROOKS

To see how we can help high school students learn to play the doubting game, let's take a second look at David Brooks's "The Olympic Contradiction." Remember, Brooks responds to the question of whether internal contradictions are good or bad (a question of quality) by saying, in a nutshell, that contradictions are good. Once students understand what Brooks is saying, they can evaluate the effectiveness of his argument. Do they find his reasons and examples compelling? His ethos credible? His logic convincing? His humor apt? A critical rereading of the text—this time *against the grain*—can help students find their answers.

Those reluctant skeptics who find the believing game easier than the doubting game can keep a sticky note on their desk or text to remind them to read against the grain during this activity. Remember: The object of the game is *disbelief*! On their sticky note, students can write some cues to prompt their mistrust of the text:

> While there are lots of times when fluent readers unconsciously slip between reading with the grain and reading against it, the ability to *choose* to do one or the other despite our natural inclinations takes intentional effort and extended practice.

- Does the writer say anything that bothers me?
- Are any of the writer's claims unsupported?
- Does the writer draw any dubious conclusions?
- Does the writer contradict himself or herself?
- Do I disagree with any of the writer's claims or assumptions?
- Are there any reasons not to trust this writer?
- Does the writer leave anything out?

I also share my own critical questions and responses in a continuation of the think-aloud activity we did for the first reading. And I warn students that they're going to have to ramp up their effort during this activity. As I annotate, they annotate. Students keep track of what we're doing when we play the doubting game by using the same Checklist for Listening to a Think-Aloud I introduced for the believing game (see Chapter 1, page 7), only now students mark the strategies with minus signs (–) instead of plus signs (+). They should notice some key differences from the reading strategies they marked on their checklist during the believing game.

> On the days when we teach threshold concepts like the doubting game, we need to let our students know that it's not going to be business as usual; we're going to ask them to do something with their brains that they probably haven't done before and that will take extra time and practice to master. Threshold concepts can't be taught in stand-alone lessons. I might be able to teach a literary term like *personification* in a single class, but I can't teach reading against the grain in just one day.

Annotation Cue Cards

When students are new to annotation, I like to use a document camera or projector to model how I underline key words and write marginal comments on the pages of something I'm reading. I also use

Annotation Cue Cards to help students learn the kinds of comments and questions fluent readers write during a rhetorical analysis of a text. (I got the idea for this activity from the "Conversation Cue Cards" used by teachers at Buena Park High School to encourage class discussion.) The cards serve as a support structure for our whole-class critique of a text. The idea is to be flexible and organic with the discussion by using the cue cards as an optional support structure to build upon. Appendix 3 and the list that follows show the cue cards I created for our analysis of "The Olympic Contradiction." I used the thoughts and questions from my own annotations but put them into more student-friendly language. So, you'll see similarities between my original annotations (right margin) and some of the cue card text (listed before the article that follows and in Appendix 3).

Directions to the Teacher: **To make the Annotation Cue Cards for an analysis of Brooks's article, type and print the comments and questions, cut them into strips, and glue the strips onto individual index cards for durability. It's best if the cards aren't in order when you give them to the students. You may not have enough cue cards for each student to have one, but you should have enough "plants" around the room so that you get lots of responses when you ask your students to help you annotate an article. A few students will receive "wild cards" on which they can write their own comments or questions—you can add more wild cards as students become more proficient in annotation. Let students know that they should always feel welcome to contribute their own original ideas and questions as well.**

Read the article aloud, calling for those students with cue cards to add their comments or questions at the relevant moments. Encourage students to put their cue card's comment or question in their own words. Add your own critical think-aloud comments as appropriate. (You'll see a transcript of my think-aloud in italics between paragraphs of the article that follows.) Be sure to pause frequently to ask if anyone has anything to contribute, and remind students to annotate their own copies of the article during this process. Let students know it's OK if they don't see a spot to share their cue card; they can make up their own comments or questions instead. If students are reluctant to share their comments or questions, try increasing your wait time.

Annotation Cue Card Comments and Questions for "The Olympic Contradiction" by David Brooks

Comment: That's a pretty strong claim.

Question: What does Brooks mean by "best"? Most successful? Most admirable?

Question: Is this an oxymoron or paradox?

Question: Do they represent only one side?

Comment: This is a strong image—Brooks sounds pretty sarcastic.

Comment: I find this sentence annoying.

Question: Is Brooks a cynic?

Question: Why is Brooks so negative here?

Question: Does Brooks mean too much dancing?

Question: Aren't these performers usually volunteers rather than professionally trained dancers?

Comment: "Unison," "blend," and "mirror" all suggest cooperation and togetherness.

Question: Just "witness and cheer"? Sports fans don't experience an emotional gift?

Comment: Some performances during past Olympic opening ceremonies have been serious and historical.

Comment: He must know he's irritating some readers here, right?

Question: Is there really a total transformation or switch from cooperative to competitive virtues? Or is the same spirit present throughout the Olympics?

Question: If one is totally replaced by the other, doesn't that undermine Brooks's claim about the importance of simultaneously accepting contradictions?

Comment: It seems like Brooks is contradicting himself.

Comment: Brooks's verb phrases suggest intense physical activity.

Comment: The image of the pinnacle suggests there's room for only one at the top.

Comment: The repetition of the sentence structure emphasizes the balance of opposites.

Question: How does the idea of the noble loser work with Brooks's image of the pinnacle?

Comment: Brooks's pairings of "opposites" are not as neat here, which helps support his argument about allowing contradictions to coexist.

Comment: While "victory" and "defeat" are antonyms, "friendship" and "glory" are not. And "fellowship" and "status" are not mutually exclusive desires.

Question: But would the festival be even more moving if it weren't crassly commercial?

Comment: These examples show that contradictions can coexist but not that their coexistence makes people or institutions better or more enduring.

Comment: Brooks hasn't really proved his point yet about contradictions being good.

Comment: In his Olympics examples, Brooks doesn't really stress the importance of opposites being present at the same time.

Question: Does being "two-faced" enhance our chances for survival?

Comment: Brooks doesn't give a concrete example of someone who truly sees or accepts only one side. Maybe he knows human beings are more complex than that.

Comment: This example doesn't seem as strong or interesting as the business examples.

Comment: This sounds like an exaggeration.

Comment: Write your own comment on this card and say it aloud whenever it naturally fits into the group analysis of the text.

Comment: Write your own comment on this card and say it aloud whenever it naturally fits into the group analysis of the text.

Question: Write your own question on this card and ask it whenever it naturally fits into the group analysis of the text.

Question: Write your own question on this card and ask it whenever it naturally fits into the group analysis of the text.

Modeling Critical Reading

Here's what a critical rereading of David Brooks's "The Olympic Contradiction" might look and sound like. My annotations are in the right margin, and the words and phrases they refer to are underlined in the article text. You'll notice that the annotations correspond to possible appropriate places for the cue card comments and questions. The italicized text between the article's paragraphs represents what I say during the think-aloud I conduct with the class. You'll probably want to keep this version of the text hidden from your class, at least until the end. Display an unmarked version of Brooks's article (or the article you choose to use), so you and the students can annotate the text together during your own discussion. Remember, students with Annotation Cue Cards will be chiming in, too.

"The Olympic Contradiction" by David Brooks
The *New York Times*, July 26, 2012

Abraham Lincoln said that a house divided against itself cannot stand. He was right about slavery, but the maxim doesn't apply to <u>much else.</u> In general, the <u>best people</u> are contradictory, and the <u>most enduring</u> institutions are, too.

Whoa—that's a pretty strong claim.

What does Brooks mean by "best"? Most successful? Most admirable?

Really? I'm not sure that I'm ready to accept this generalization. There are probably many other examples of destructive internal divisions that Brooks is deliberately overlooking here. What about Dr. Jekyll and Mr. Hyde? I wouldn't call him one of "the best people."

The Olympics are a good example. The Olympics are a <u>peaceful celebration of our warlike nature.</u>

Oxymoron or paradox?

This isn't the primary way I'd characterize the Olympics. How about a celebration of human achievement, endurance, persistence, and beauty? While the Olympic motto "Faster, Higher, Stronger" might suggest an element of competition (or just excellence), it certainly doesn't suggest war, and the Olympic rings clearly represent solidarity and cooperation.

The opening ceremony represents <u>one side</u> of the Olympic movement. They are a lavish celebration of the <u>cooperative virtues</u>: <u>unity, friendship, equality, compassion and care</u>. In Friday's ceremony, there'll be musical tributes to the global community and the Olympic spirit. There will be <u>Pepsi commercial–type images</u> of the people from different backgrounds <u>joyfully</u> coming together. There will be <u>pious</u> speeches about our <u>common humanity and universal ideals</u>.

> *Do they represent only one side?*

> *Strong image—Brooks sounds a bit jaded. Is he a cynic?*

Hmm . . . Now Brooks sounds like he's exaggerating and maybe gently mocking what he sees as the cooperative virtues. Brooks's references to "Pepsi commercial-type images" and "pious speeches" make it sound as though he finds the opening ceremonies a little ridiculous or unrealistic. The word pious *connotes self-righteousness—is that really the tone of the opening ceremonies? In Brooks's characterization, this celebration of unity and friendship seems naive and overly optimistic. But I'm not sure that the opening ceremonies are always focused on virtues like "equality, compassion, and care"—or when they are, that this focus is naive and simplistic.*

And there will be <u>a lot</u> of dancing. Because we're <u>social, semi-herdlike creatures</u>, we take a <u>primordial pleasure</u> in the sight of a large number of people moving in <u>unison</u>. Dance is physical, like sports, but, in many ways, it is the opposite of <u>sports</u>. In dance, the purpose is to <u>blend</u> with and <u>mirror</u> each other; in sport, the purpose is to come out ahead. Dancers perform for the audience and offer a gift of emotion; athletes respond to one another and the spectators are just there to <u>witness and cheer</u>.

> *Does he mean too much dancing?*

> *Aren't these performers usually volunteers rather than professionally trained dancers?*

> *"Unison," "blend," and "mirror" all suggest cooperation and togetherness.*

> *Just "witness and cheer"? Sports fans don't experience an emotional gift?*

I see that Brooks is trying to entertain me here and maybe win me over with humor. OK, calling humans "semi-herdlike creatures" is funny, and the image of a large number of people moving in unison at the opening ceremonies is definitely comical. But I don't know that that kind of group movement typically qualifies as dance, or that dance of any kind can be called the opposite of sports. And Brooks is on really shaky ground when he says that dancers perform for the audience while athletes respond to one another.

Dancers, especially at the opening ceremony, <u>smile</u> in <u>warmth</u> and <u>friendship</u>. No true sport is ever done smiling (this is the problem with <u>figure skating and competitive cheerleading</u>).

After the opening ceremony is over, the Olympics <u>turn into</u> a celebration of the <u>competitive virtues</u>: <u>tenacity, courage, excellence, supremacy, discipline and conflict</u>.

Brooks knows he's getting in a little jab here at what he must see as pseudo-sports (dance, figure skating, and cheerleading) and probably hopes his light tone makes the joke excusable. It doesn't really work for me because this doesn't feel like a reliable or authentic description of dance. This could be a problem later on for Brooks's argument if he doesn't present the cooperative aspects of the Olympic games credibly.

The <u>smiling</u> goes away and the <u>grim-faced</u> games begin. The marathoner <u>struggling</u> against exhaustion, the boxer <u>trying to pummel</u> his foe, the diver <u>resolutely focused</u> on her task. The purpose is to be tough<u>er</u> and bett<u>er</u> than the people who are seeking the same <u>pinnacle</u>.

Brooks seems to have more respect for the competitive virtues. Doesn't feel even-handed.

If the opening ceremony is <u>win-win</u>, most of the rest of the games are <u>win-lose</u>. If the opening ceremony mimics <u>peace</u>, the competitions mimic <u>warfare</u>. <u>It's</u> <u>not</u> about the brotherhood of humankind. It's about making sure our country beats the Chinese in the medal chart.

Some performances during past Olympics have been serious and historical.

He must know he's irritating some readers here, right?

Is there really a total transformation or switch from cooperative to competitive virtues? Or is the same spirit present throughout the Olympics?

If one is totally replaced by the other, doesn't that undermine Brooks's claim about the importance of simultaneously accepting contradictions?

Brooks's verb phrases convey a sense of intense physical activity.

The comparative adjectives and image of the pinnacle suggest there's room for only one at the top. Does this still make the Olympics contradictory, "a peaceful celebration of our warlike nature"?

These two antithetical sentences capture Brooks's central thesis about embracing contraries. The repetition of the sentence structure further emphasizes the balance of opposites.

"It" refers to the competitions.

Through fierce competition, sport separates the elite from the mediocre. It identifies the heroes and standards of excellence that everybody else can emulate (a noble loser can serve as well as a talented winner). The idea is not to win friendship; it's to win glory. We get to see people experiencing the thrill of victory from the agony of defeat and judge how well they respond.

How does the idea of the noble loser work with Brooks's image of the pinnacle?

In sum, the Olympic Games appeal both to our desire for fellowship and our desire for status, to the dreams of community and also supremacy. And, of course, these desires are in tension. But the world is, too. The world isn't a jigsaw puzzle that fits neatly and logically together. It's a system of clashing waves that can never be fully reconciled.

Brooks's pairings of "opposites" are not as neat here, which helps support his argument about allowing contradictions to coexist. While "victory" and "defeat" are antonyms, "friendship" and "glory" are not. And "fellowship" and "status" are not mutually exclusive desires.

While Brooks's tone is still playful, his argument is becoming more serious and his jokes have a sharper edge to them. Saying that the games themselves are about "making sure our country beats the Chinese in the medal chart" is going a bit far. The contrasts he draws between the opening ceremonies and the rest of the games also feel a little heavy-handed. Brooks is on firmer ground when he moves from the exaggerated, external contrasts he's created to our conflicting internal desires. I'm more persuaded by his claims when he backs off the humor.

The enduring popularity of the Olympics teach the lesson that if you find yourself caught between two competing impulses, you don't always need to choose between them. You can go for both simultaneously. A single institution can celebrate charitable compassion and military toughness. A three-week festival can be crassly commercial, but also strangely moving.

Brooks doesn't address the issue of hypocrisy. Is that a concern for him?

But would the festival be even more moving if it weren't crassly commercial? These examples show that contradictions can coexist but not that their coexistence makes people or institutions better or more enduring.

F. Scott Fitzgerald famously said that the mark of a first rate intelligence is the ability to hold two contradictory thoughts in your mind at the same time. But it's not really the mark of genius, just the mark of anybody who functions well in the world. It's the mark of any institution that lasts.

Is this a cynical view? Does being "two-faced" enhance our chances for survival? Or does Brooks have something more sophisticated and admirable in mind?

A few years ago, Roger Martin, the dean of the University of Toronto's management school, wrote a book called "The Opposable Mind," about business leaders who can embrace the tension between contradictory ideas. One of his examples was A.G. Lafley of Procter & Gamble.

Some Procter & Gamble executives thought the company needed to cut costs and lower prices to compete with the supermarket store brands. Another group thought the company should invest in innovation to keep their products clearly superior. Lafley embraced both visions, pushing hard in both directions.

This is more complex than the switch from cooperative virtues to competitive virtues Brooks discusses in his description of the Olympics. In his Olympics examples, Brooks doesn't really stress the importance of opposites being present at the same time.

Sounds more like Fitzgerald's idea of intelligence. This seems to be about brain capacity, not functionality.

Brooks's language is more moderate here; I notice he repeats the helping verb can *to suggest possibilities rather than certainties. It's interesting that he modifies F. Scott Fitzgerald's claim about contradictions and intelligence into a claim about contradictions and longevity. Here's where I need more convincing again. Being the best is not the same as lasting the longest, and I think Brooks downplays the differences between excellence and endurance.*

The world, unfortunately, has too many monomaniacs— people who pick one side of any creative tension and wish the other would just go away. Some parents and teachers like the cooperative virtues and distrust the competitive ones, so, laughably, they tell their kids that they are going to play sports but nobody is going to keep score.

Brooks makes it clear he thinks this is a bad thing.

Is this a straw man? Brooks doesn't give a concrete example of someone who truly only sees or accepts one side. Maybe he knows human beings are more complex than that?

This doesn't quite seem fair to me. Parents and teachers who do this are probably working with really young kids. Should preschoolers be competitive? Seems like a question of what's appropriate developmentally; it's about the kids' maturity, not the parents' monomania. And "laughably" is a bit harsh.

Politics has become a contest of monomaniacs. One faction champions austerity while another champions growth. One party becomes the party of economic security and the other becomes the party of creative destruction.

Brooks repeats his use of parallelism here, echoing his earlier discussion of opposites in the Olympics. This example doesn't seem as strong or interesting as the business examples.

It sure can appear that way, but is Brooks overstating the case?

The right course is usually to push hard in both directions, to be a house <u>creatively</u> divided against itself, to <u>thrive</u> amid the contradictions. The Olympics are great, but they are not <u>coherent</u>.

What does "right" mean here? The word "thrive" suggests both excellence and endurance. Does Brooks mean this is the most effective or ethical choice or both? The final sentence is pretty reasonable and balanced.

The words "creatively" and "thrive" suggest that Brooks has something higher in mind than functional hypocrisy. He sees embracing contraries as generative, expansive, and enlightened. "Coherent" in this context suggests something that is too neat or narrow.

I once heard former NCTE President Carol Jago describe high school as a place where young people go to watch old people work hard. Carol's point—that we should not be the only ones doing brainwork in our classrooms—is an important one. But we do need to show students exactly what hard intellectual work looks like so they can recalibrate their own effort level, especially when we're trying to break their habit of just reacting to a topic instead of analyzing a text. Our students need to see firsthand what goes on in readers' brains when they care deeply about the power of the written word.

It's also important to remind students of the audience for their annotations: themselves. While we may initially need to read through our students' annotations to be sure they're diligently grappling with a text, annotation should never be busywork. It's a private conversation between a reader and a writer. (To make this point, I sometimes share Billy Collins's wonderful poem "Marginalia" with my classes [1998, 14–16]). We want to help students recognize and develop the critical practices of fluent readers, not commit "readicide" (Gallagher 2009) through excessive meddling with students' reading processes.

Lastly, after we play the doubting game, I remind my students that we were deliberately resisting the authority of the text as a step toward finding our own answer to the question at issue (e.g., "Are internal contradictions good or bad?"). The critical view we "try on" at this stage no more represents our real position than the supportive approach we took during the first reading. We still have some more work to do.

Of course, this kind of against-the-grain modeling takes a good bit of classroom time and works best as a way to introduce students to the concept of what it means to read critically. After you finish the demonstration, be sure to have students compare the plus (+) and minus (–) signs on their Checklist for Listening to a Think-Aloud. Ask students what they notice. Once students understand the differences between the believing game and the doubting game and how to annotate a text, they need to practice these skills on their own.

Descriptive Outlining

For me, that additional work often takes the form of descriptive outlining. Used either in combination with annotation or as a stand-alone activity, descriptive outlining is a terrific—and challenging—way for students to apply the critical understanding they gain from rereading a text to the question at issue that the text addresses. This postreading strategy helps students identify not only a writer's claims but also many of the rhetorical choices he or she makes to support those claims. (See Chapters 3 through 6 for an even closer look at those rhetorical choices.) When college faculty ask students to respond to arguments, they want students to do more than just react to what writers say; they also want students to analyze and evaluate what writers *do* to convey their messages. That's the threshold we want students to cross. Both content and function are important (Bean, Chappell, and Gillam 2014).

You can see why this approach to text structure can present a big hurdle for many kids ("What do you mean what is the writer doing? He's writing"). It helps to do this activity together . . . and to do it a lot.

Start a descriptive outline by asking your students to divide the text into different sections according to their function or purpose; that's the "outlining" part. Finding the introduction and the conclusion are the first steps. I follow the technique used by the California State University's Expository Reading and Writing Course and have my students draw a line after where they think the introduction ends and another line above where they think the conclusion begins. These actions alone can foster interesting class discussions ("How can the intro be four paragraphs?" "Don't you think the conclusion starts after that last transition?"). For less experienced students, I then like to continue the descriptive outlining using a graphic organizer (see the example in Figure 2.1). I might even complete the first few sections for them.

We work through the remainder of the text, "chunking," or grouping, sections together according to rhetorical purpose; that's the "descriptive" part. In contrast to a traditional outline, descriptive outlining examines and explains how a text works—what moves it makes to reach its intended audience. Students quickly find that—unlike the five-paragraph essay—individual "chunks" rarely are contained within single paragraphs in published writing. Instead, a functional section may be several paragraphs long or only a few sentences; it all depends on what the section is trying to accomplish.

This process develops another key rhetorical competency: the ability to discover the best available means of persuasion. Through descriptive outlining, students investigate the various tactics a writer uses to structure a text. They examine multiple strategies in context, charting the progression of claims, evidence, and appeals across the full arc of the argument. Once students understand a writer's game plan, they can more easily evaluate the overall attempt at persuasion.

Consider the sample descriptive outline for "The Olympic Contradiction" shown in Figure 2.1. (For a blank descriptive outline and two student samples, see Appendixes 4, 4a, and 4b.)

The descriptive outline of "The Olympic Contradiction" shown in Figure 2.1 suggests the reasoning behind some of David Brooks's choices and helps me to see that some moves that I might find off-

> Of course, one of the reasons Brooks's article is such fun to use for helping students understand how to play the believing game and the doubting game is that it beautifully performs Elbow's thesis about embracing contraries—that "texts can support multiple and even contradictory interpretations" (1986, 292). Refusing to believe an opposing view (even if we're just trying it on for size) or to doubt our own cherished position leaves us understanding only a part of the picture.

Descriptive Outlining
"The Olympic Contradiction" by David Brooks

Paragraph[s]: 1–2

SAYS: The best people and most enduring institutions—such as the Olympics—are contradictory.

DOES: Challenges the idea that unity and coherence are better than division. Moves from a principle to an example.

Paragraph[s]: 3–5

SAYS: Through its joyful dance numbers, the opening ceremonies represent the peaceful side of the Olympics.

DOES: Elaborates on an extended example—one side of the Olympics. Creates a light and humorous tone.

Paragraph[s]: 6–9

SAYS: In contrast to the opening ceremonies, the rest of the Olympics are about win-lose competition.

DOES: Shifts to a series of examples emphasizing the grim "warlike nature" of the Olympic Games. Changes to a more serious tone.

Paragraph[s]: 10

SAYS: The Olympics—and the world—are made up of competing desires in tension with each other.

DOES: Summarizes a central idea in Brooks's argument.

Paragraph[s]: 11

SAYS: We learn from the lasting popularity of the Olympics that we don't have to resolve internal contradictions. We can accept both sides.

DOES: Turns from a statement of fact about contradictions (they exist) to a suggestion of quality (they're good).

Paragraph[s]: 12-14

SAYS: Although F. Scott Fitzgerald said the ability to embrace contraries is a sign of intelligence, it's actually a sign of effectiveness and endurance. Roger Martin's book shows contradictions are good for business.

DOES: Offers clarification and support for benefits of contradictions.

Paragraph[s]: 15-16

SAYS: Too many people in the world—for example, some parents and politicians—can see only one side of a situation.

DOES: Identifies a problem (monomania) and discusses two harmful instances of it; presents a contrast to accepting contradictions.

Paragraph[s]: 17

SAYS: The right thing to do is to accept and thrive amid contradictions (as the Olympics do).

DOES: Makes a clear and concise closing argument about the positive value of contradictions in "great" institutions like the Olympics.

MAIN ARGUMENT:
Contradictions not only exist in great minds and institutions (e.g., the Olympics) but also contribute to their effectiveness and endurance and should therefore be embraced as a positive quality.

FIGURE 2.1
Descriptive Outline for "The Olympic Contradiction"
(Adapted from Bean, Chappell, and Gillam 2011.)

putting in other genres and contexts are nonetheless effective in this humorous op-ed piece. I have to hand it to Brooks—his sure voice and masterful writing win me over in the end, despite his snarky remarks about dancers.

From Doubt to a Defensible Assertion

Eventually, students need to be able to move beyond believing and doubting to discovering their own stance on an issue. They have to find some answers they can turn into defensible assertions in their own writing.

At this point, students might need to take stock of what claims they're willing to believe so far, which claims they doubt, and which claims they could tweak to better represent their own views. The Believing, Doubting, and Transforming graphic organizer (Figure 2.2, Appendix 5) gives students a tool for capturing their evolving position on an issue.

FIGURE 2.2
Believing, Doubting, and Transforming graphic organizer

Believing, Doubting, and Transforming

Directions: The following activity can help you determine your position on an issue. After reading about an issue, respond to the questions in each section of the three-column chart below.

BELIEVING Which claims, if any, do you believe?	DOUBTING Which claims, if any, do you doubt?	TRANSFORMING What claims could be changed or modified to better represent how you think?

QUICK-WRITE:
What is your position overall?

In the following examples, we can see how these student writers are starting to think about ways to qualify claims. The "Transforming" column in Kayla's graphic organizer (Figure 2.3) on health care reform and Valerie's on gun control (Figure 2.4) both include conditional language that suggests partial agreement with their sources. These students may no longer be willing to give the writer the full benefit of the doubt, but they are willing to see some of the argument's merits or potential.

FIGURE 2.3

Kayla's graphic organizer on health care reform

Believing, Doubting, and Transforming

Health Care

.12·/13

Directions: The following activity can help you determine your position on an issue. After reading about an issue, respond to the questions in each section of the three-column chart below.

Believing	Doubting	Transforming
Which claims, if any, do you believe?	Which claims, if any, do you doubt?	What claims could be changed or modified to better represent how you think?
- The U.S. is one of the few if not the only developed nation in the world that does not guarantee universal health coverage. · Guaranteeing all Americans health care will decrease the quality and availability of health care in U.S. · The cost of health care has become increasingly unaffordable for many working families.	· Health care is the largest industry in the U.S. → It it's that big, why is it so poor? · The cost of our health care is a threat to our economy. → Even though it's the biggest industry in U.S.? ·#6 Pros ·#14 Cons	· 15.4% of the U.S. population did not have health insurance in 2008. → It could've been more convincing if the phrase "did not have" were to change into "could not afford". · People should not be discriminated for being sick → It would have been better if they used stronger word than "discriminated"

Quickwrite:

What is your position overall?

I think that the health care should be a right to every citizens, not just for people's health but also to be fair with the tax payment.

FIGURE 2.4

Valerie's graphic organizer on gun control

concealed Guns

Believing, Doubting, and Transforming

Directions: The following activity can help you determine your position on an issue. After reading about an issue, respond to the questions in each section of the three-column chart below.   Concealed Guns

Believing	Doubting	Transforming
Which claims, if any, do you believe?	Which claims, if any, do you doubt?	What claims could be changed or modified to better represent how you think?
supp•ice • "Shall-issue laws" require police to issue concealed carry permits as long as meets requirements	• carrying a gun in a bar - this could lead to bad things	• If it was phrased like "A gun could be carried in a bar as long as the person carrying the gun is not drinking / doing drugs" then I would maybe concider it being okay at a bar though I cannot be in a bar.

Quickwrite:
What is your position overall?
I would not feel safe with people around me to have a gun just because.

Finding Answers Through Ethos, Pathos, and Logos

After close scrutiny of a text, it can be helpful for kids to pull back and look at the big picture again. Here's where Aristotle's three rhetorical appeals—ethos, pathos, and logos—come into play. Chapter 6 offers a fuller description of ethos, pathos, and logos, but for now, let's take a look at how a basic understanding of these three rhetorical appeals can help students find their own assertions to defend.

Questions about ethos focus on the writer's image or credibility. We can think of this appeal to character as the spokesperson approach in advertising—Michael Jordan uses this product and likes it, we like and trust Michael Jordan, therefore we're willing to try the product, too. The admittedly gender-biased Aristotle notes that "we believe good men more fully and more readily than others" (1984; Book 1, Chapter ii). Celebrities who fall from grace (think Lance Armstrong and Tiger Woods) demonstrate the incredible persuasive power of an admirable ethos. When a spokesperson's image tanks, sponsors can't dump him or her fast enough.

Pathos refers to an appeal to emotion. Teenagers already get the idea that something "pathetic" engenders feelings of pity. From there, it's not much of a leap to Aristotle's more expansive description of the human emotions at work in acts of persuasion. These include anger, calmness, fear, confidence, shame, kindness, unkindness, indignation, and envy (1984). Aristotle says that if we wish to use emotion effectively in our arguments, we need to understand how changing feelings affect people's judgment.

Of course, we also need some proofs for our claims, and that's where logos enters the picture. Just as a speaker or writer's credibility is always an essential component of persuasion (ethos), so too is logic. To achieve persuasion, Aristotle tells us, we must also be able to "reason logically" (1984; Book 1, Chapter ii).

Even at an introductory level, an understanding of ethos, pathos, and logos can help students find answers to critical questions about a text, as the following questions on "The Olympic Contradiction" show. These questions are modeled on the "Thinking Critically" questions from the *California State University Expository Reading and Writing Course*, 2nd ed. (ERWC Task Force 2013). Try having students answer the

A few millennia later, the CCSS likewise validates the importance of logos. For example, one Reading for Informational Text standard for eleventh and twelfth graders calls for students to "delineate and evaluate the reasoning in seminal U.S. texts, including the application of constitutional principles and use of legal reasoning . . . and the premises, purposes, and arguments in works of public advocacy" (NGA/CCSSO 2010, CCSS.ELA-Literacy.RI.11-12.8). The CCSS's anchor standards for reading informational text echo this emphasis on logos, identifying the ability to analyze interactions among various elements of a text and to make inferences as key aspects of college and career readiness (CCSS.ELA-Literacy.RI.11-12.2 and CCSS.ELA-Literacy.RI.11-12.3). Meeting these standards successfully depends upon an ability to identify logical relationships, such as sequencing and cause and effect, and to draw conclusions from evidence.

questions in small groups before debriefing as a whole class. For instance, you might ask an "expert group" to report out on each question set.

Questions About Ethos

- How does Brooks's tone deflect potential criticism? How seriously are we supposed to take him?

- How do Brooks's references to Lincoln and Fitzgerald contribute to his own image as a writer and thinker?

- Read a biography of David Brooks on the Internet. How does his status as a regular columnist for the *New York Times* impact his ethos?

Questions About Pathos

- How might Brooks's reference to "the global community and the Olympic spirit" make his audience feel? What, if anything, does his comment about "Pepsi commercial-type images of the people from different backgrounds joyfully coming together" add to this feeling?

- What is the emotional impact of Brooks's humor? Are any of the jokes offensive?

- How might Brooks's readers feel about his comments on politics and monomaniacs?

Questions About Logos

- What evidence—or proof—does Brooks offer for his claims?

- Do any of Brooks's comparisons seem weak or strained? Are there any false analogies?

- Do any of Brooks's claims about monomaniacs seem unfair or unsupported?

- What counterclaims can you think of to Brooks's assertion that "dancers perform for the audience and offer a gift of emotion; athletes respond to one another and the spectators are just there to witness and cheer"?

- What is the rhetorical function of the semicolon in the preceding example from the article? If you had to use your own words to write out the meaning of this punctuation mark as it's used in this sentence, what would you write?

This is a good time to remind students about stasis theory and the question at issue (see Chapter 1). We tell students that a thesis statement is an answer to a question. When we teach argumentation rhetorically, we help students see that the question their thesis answers is the same question answered by the other writers in the conversation they're joining.

Other Questions for Thinking Critically

- Are you persuaded by Brooks's argument? Why?

- Are some parts of Brooks's argument stronger than others? What are his best points? His weakest?

- Is there anything important that he left out?

- What value, if any, do you see in embracing contradictions?

As students become more comfortable with this kind of critical inquiry, they'll be able to answer more of the questions independently. Ultimately, the answers to these questions not only help students determine their own position on the value of contradictions, but also help students figure out the extent to which they're going to endorse or challenge Brooks's views if they introduce him as a source in their own writing.

Analyzing Arguments Through a PAPA Square and Rhetorical Précis

Two other strategies I use to help students understand how an argument works as a whole are a graphic organizer called the PAPA Square and a template for an analytical summary called a "rhetorical précis." Students who are college and career ready repeatedly ask and answer two key questions: "How?" and "Why?" While they ask other important questions, too—"Who?" "What?" "When?" and "Where?—the ability to discover the function ("How?") and purpose ("Why?") of something is a distinguishing mark of academic preparedness. This is the threshold competency that tells us students are ready to engage complex tasks and texts with sophistication. Both the PAPA Square and the précis emphasize the "How?" and "Why?" of a text, thereby moving students beyond just a summary of main ideas.

The PAPA Square (Figure 2.5, Appendix 6) is a postreading activity that asks students to identify the purpose, argument, (writer's) persona, and audience of a text, as well as the rhetorical choices a writer makes to achieve his or her ends. This is another strategy I learned from Marilyn Elkins, professor of English at California State University, Los Angeles. What Marilyn calls the Rhetorical Square, and we've now been calling the PAPA Square in our high school workshops, was adapted from leading composition scholar Maxine Hairston's *Contemporary Composition* (1986). Hairston identifies four elements of any rhetorical situation:

1. The purpose or occasion for writing.
2. The audience for whom the writing is done.
3. The person or assumed role of the writer.
4. The message or content of the writing. (1986, 78)

PAPA Square

Through a PAPA Square, students analyze the **P**urpose, **A**rgument, **P**ersona, and **A**udience of a text. Around the perimeter of the box, students answer the following questions in response to their own writing: Who is my audience? What is the persona, or public image, that I create for myself through my language choices and tone? What is my thesis or argument? What is my purpose or desired outcome of my argument? (I.e., What would I like my reader to do if he or she is persuaded by me?) In the center of the PAPA Square, students identify the stylistic devices and emotional, logical, and ethical appeals they use to persuade their audience. These may include types of evidence, figurative language, text structures (e.g., cause and effect), and tone. (Adapted from the CSU Reading and Writing Course.)

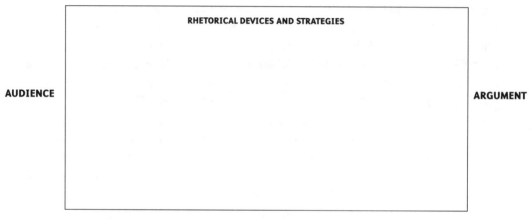

FIGURE 2.5
Blank PAPA Square

Marilyn's brilliant idea was to add rhetorical methods and strategies in the center of the box, converting the graphic into a graphic organizer. Notice how one student's sample (Figure 2.6) shows a developing sense of these elements.

Priya's PAPA Square for "The Olympic Contradiction" (Figure 2.6) shows she hasn't yet done a deep dive into the rhetorical situation, but she'll get there. The thin responses she gives for "audience," "purpose," and "rhetorical methods and strategies" show she has a developing understanding; she is on the continuum from superficial to deep learning. Chapters 3, 4, and 5 suggest several ways to move students beyond this stage.

After students complete a PAPA Square, they can convert their graphic organizer to a paragraph by using the following template for a rhetorical précis from *Reading Rhetorically* (Bean, Chappell, and Gillam 2014, 65):

Sentence 1: Name of author, genre, and title of work, date in parentheses; a rhetorically accurate verb (such as *claims, argues, asserts, suggests*); and a THAT clause containing the major assertion or thesis statement in the work.

Sentence 2: An explanation of how the author develops and supports the thesis, usually in chronological order.

Sentence 3: A statement of the author's apparent purpose, followed by an "in order to" phrase.

Sentence 4: A description of the intended audience and/or the relationship the author establishes with the audience.

To give my students a sense of the finished product, I share a précis I wrote of Mark Antony's funeral oration in Shakespeare's *Julius Caesar* (act 3, scene ii, lines 70–104) —a play many juniors and seniors remember from their sophomore year. Italics indicate the key parts of the précis as described in the preceding directions:

In William Shakespeare's play *Julius Caesar,* Mark Antony gives a funeral oration in which he *suggests that* Caesar was a great benefactor of the Roman people who was wrongfully murdered. Mark Antony *makes this assertion through* an increasingly bitter and ironic characterization of Brutus as a "noble man" and by listing Caesar's many generous acts,

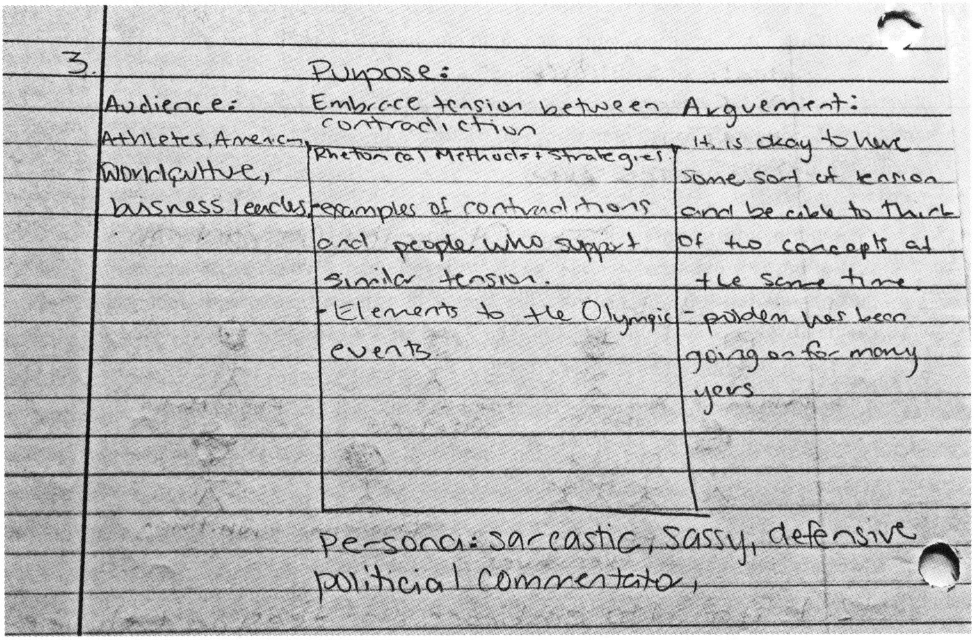

FIGURE 2.6
Priya's PAPA Square

concluding with the legacies Caesar left to the Roman people in his will. Antony's purpose is to incite a riot against the conspirators *in order to* avenge Caesar's death and prevent the conspirators from taking control of Rome. Because the *audience* is emotionally vulnerable and volatile—and is initially sympathetic to Brutus—Mark Antony first pretends to share *his audience's* regard for Brutus before turning the crowd against Caesar's killers.

Now it's the students' turn to try their hand at writing a rhetorical précis. You might ask your own students to write one for "The Olympic Contradiction."

Asking how a text functions—what it does in addition to what it says—is a critical part of reading rhetorically. Students who can identify not only what a texts says but also what it does (the *how*) and to what end (the *why*) have developed the sophisticated literacy and inquiry practices that are the hallmarks of postsecondary success. These activities also prepare students to "cite strong and thorough textual evidence to support analysis of what the text says explicitly *as well as inferences drawn from the text*, including determining where the text leaves matters uncertain" (NGA/CCSSO 2010, 40) (emphasis added). Students who can do this have learned to see more than meets the eye.

Sample Prompt for Argument Essay on "The Olympic Contradiction"

(The prompt is modeled on the style of the California State University English Placement Test [CSU 2009]. The passage is adapted from "The Olympic Contradiction" by David Brooks and has been modified for assessment purposes. You can find the original article in the appendix.)

> *Directions to Students:* **Plan and write an essay on the topic below. Before you begin writing, read the passage carefully and plan what you will say. Your essay should be as well organized and as carefully written as you can make it.**
>
> > **"The world, unfortunately, has too many monomaniacs—people who pick one side of any creative tension and wish the other would just go away. Some parents and teachers, for example, like the cooperative virtues and distrust the competitive ones, so, laughably, they tell their kids that they are going to play sports but nobody is going to keep score.**
> >
> > **Politics has similarly become an arena of monomaniacs. One faction champions austerity while another champions growth. One party becomes the party of economic security and the other becomes the party of creative destruction. In contrast to this rigid single-mindedness, the right course of action is usually to push hard in both directions, to be a house creatively divided against itself, to thrive amid the contradictions."**
> >
> > **—David Brooks, "The Olympic Contradiction"**

Explain David Brooks's argument and discuss the ways you agree or disagree with him.
Support your position, providing reasons and examples from your reading, as well as from
your observations and experience when relevant.

Providing Support at the Threshold

None of this is easy, of course. A key premise behind the idea of threshold concepts is that
we're all novices and outsiders before we pass through that portal into deeper learning. Being a beginner is a normal stage of growth. We can make this stage a lot more comfortable
for our students by reminding them that they're feeling what they're supposed to be feeling
at this point—that some concepts and skills truly are more difficult to master than others.
And that all "insiders" started on the outside. We can also remind them that they've probably already passed through a learning portal in other areas of their lives, perhaps in sports,
music, or technology.

Granted, that portal metaphor can be a bit misleading. The transformation effected by
crossing a threshold is far from instantaneous. On the contrary, the journey from outsider to
insider is often long and laborious, marked by extended time spent on what George Leonard
describes in *Mastery: The Keys to Success and Long-Term Fulfillment* as "the plateau" (1992,
40)—a place where outward progress seems to stall. Leonard's eloquent little book offers
a compelling argument against the "quick-fix, antimastery mentality" that discourages the
sustained effort and routines that ultimately lead to transformative learning (6).

When we teach threshold concepts, we need to let our students know we're asking them
to do something hard. Reading with and against the grain, for instance, "requires a difficult
mix of authority and humility" (Bartholomae and Petrosky 2002, 10). These are not literacy
practices I lightly introduce to my students by saying, "Here's something fun to try that you
might find helpful." I teach those things, too—for example, easy-to-grasp ideas like paragraph hooks or transitions. Mastery of threshold knowledge, on the other hand, requires an
ongoing commitment from students and teachers. It also requires a willingness to change or
reexamine long-held beliefs and practices (Meyer and Land 2003). See Chapter 7 for more
ways to provide support at the threshold.

The Hidden Payoff

So what is the payoff for all this hard work? Our students' ability to read texts more closely?
Yes, absolutely. But there are other benefits that appeal to me greatly as a teacher. Sometimes
we get a good argument going in our classroom, and all of a sudden it's a little *too* good.
Things get heated. Feelings get hurt. Lines get crossed. And we're no longer engaged in just
an academic conversation.

But if students have learned to play the believing game and the doubting game, if they can
identify stasis, and if they're aware of what they're saying and *doing,* we can pull them back
into a safe intellectual space when a controversial or sensitive topic veers too close to the

personal. We can disarm defensive reactions to texts or classmates by reminding students that they know how to postpone judgment and try on different perspectives, if only temporarily. We can tell the student who wants to debate the sanctity of life with the student who wants to debate women's reproductive rights, "You're not in stasis with each other." We can ask students to be mindful of the intent and impact of their words, as well as the surface meaning.

When these rhetorical literacy practices become part of how students relate to other human beings, the learning has been transformative indeed—and the benefits extend far beyond college and career readiness.

Conclusion

John T. Gage says that "the purpose of the scholarly community is to inquire and to share with others the products of inquiry—understanding and knowledge" and defines inquiry as "the active search for answers to questions" (2000, 3). Finding answers doesn't necessarily mean that the answers are already out there, waiting to be discovered. Often, the search for knowledge leads to the production of knowledge; it's a generative, constructive process of knowledge making as much as it's a process of knowledge finding. Finding answers is also about deciding what versions of knowledge or "truth" we find most convincing. To find an answer, we have to make a judgment based on our best critical literacy skills; we have to choose from a continuum of positions or array of alternatives. We also have to know what question we're trying to answer, which is why stasis theory (see Chapter 1) is so helpful.

And often we have to tolerate a great deal of ambiguity and contradiction in our search for understanding.

F. Scott Fitzgerald, David Brooks, and Ender Wiggin would probably agree.

Points to Remember

As you plan your lessons and teach the concepts described in this chapter, you might want to refer to the following list of points to remember:

1. The ability to read against the grain is critical to college and career readiness.

2. Methodological doubting represents no more of an authentic view of an argument than methodological believing. To find their own position on an issue, students need to synthesize both their doubt and their belief.

3. Learning a threshold concept like methodological doubting requires extra effort and support.

4. A descriptive outline captures both the *what* (content) and the *how* (rhetorical function) of a text's structure.

5. Using ethos, pathos, and logos to think critically about a text can help students find answers to the question at issue.

Prompts for Quick-Writes or Pairs Conversations

The following prompts can be used before, during, or after a lesson to help students make personal connections, deepen their understanding, and reflect on their learning:

1. Describe an important decision you've already made. How did you reach this decision? What were your other choices?

2. Describe a time when you had to suspend your belief in something in order to see someone else's point of view. Was it hard to doubt your own position?

3. Describe a time when you read something that caused you to strongly disagree with the writer's viewpoint. What would you say to this writer?

4. Describe your process for annotating a text. What, if anything, do you find difficult about annotation?

5. What does it mean to read with the grain? What do you have to keep in mind during this process?

6. What does it mean to read against the grain? Do you find it easier to read with the grain or against the grain? Why?

7. What's the difference between what a text says and what a text does? How can you figure out what a text is doing rhetorically?

8. Explain the difference between giving your opinion on an issue (e.g., legalizing marijuana) and analyzing a written argument on that issue. Why does analysis take so much effort?

CHAPTER 3

Fostering a Deeper Understanding of the Occasion

Rhetoric has always been concerned with principles of use: How will any piece of discourse be put to use—by particular people in particular times and in particular locations? Thus rhetoric, more than many disciplines, has attended to "situatedness."

—ANDREA LUNSFORD

I f knowing how to read and write rhetorically is the doorway to advanced literacy practices, then understanding—really understanding—what we mean by the *rhetorical situation* is the key. In rhetoric, the concepts of occasion, audience, and purpose represent learning thresholds that require students to cross into new intellectual territory. Sure, these terms are pretty easy to define and memorize, and students can quickly learn to identify basic elements of the rhetorical situation. The familiar SOAPS acronym works well as a good introduction:

Speaker:	Who is making the argument? What is his or her persona?
Occasion:	What is the time, place, and context of the argument?
Audience:	To whom is the argument addressed? What are their interests and concerns?

Purpose: What does the speaker hope to accomplish? What's the desired outcome?

Subject: What is the question at issue?

Purdue's Online Writing Lab (OWL) also offers a user-friendly and nicely updated explanation of the basic elements of a rhetorical situation:

1. A text (i.e., an actual instance or piece of communication)

2. An author (i.e., someone who uses communication)

3. An audience (i.e., a recipient of communication)

4. Purposes (i.e., the varied reasons both authors and audiences communicate)

5. A setting (i.e., the time, place, and environment surrounding a moment of communication) (Sproat, Driscoll, and Brizee 2012a)

But a full appreciation of these concepts requires complex acts of imagination and empathy. To really understand occasion, audience, and purpose, students have to see and feel far more than the words in a text; they have to reconstruct the messy social worlds in which acts of communication take place. While the believing game and the doubting game help students explore the perspectives in a conversation, it's a deep understanding of occasion, audience, and purpose that gets them a seat at the table. Knowing the *when, where, who,* and *why* of an argument allows students to enter academic conversations with skill and confidence.

Threshold Concepts and the Rhetorical Situation

I think part of what is hard for teenagers to understand about the threshold concepts of occasion, audience, and purpose is how dynamic and interdependent they are. Who we are as audience members changes from one situation to the next. (I myself am a much better listener after I've had my morning cup of coffee.) Who we are and what we want as communicators changes, too. Our purpose is immediately shaped by our evolving contexts and relationships, and in fact might be adapted on the fly to respond to a new opportunity or challenge. Crowley and Hawhee explain that each rhetorical situation "occurs in a time and place that can't be wholly anticipated or replicated" (2009, 44). Because teenagers largely write in rhetorical situations superficially characterized by fixed due dates, predetermined rubrics, and teacher-assigned grades, they can have difficulty imagining less predictable conditions.

But writing and reading rhetorically are often all about quick-witted responsiveness. This is what Aristotle means when he talks about the ability to discover the best *available* means of persuasion *in a given situation.* It's that kind of Apollo 13 moment when you face a crisis with only the limited resources at hand and make it work anyway. Remember that scene from the 1995 movie when the NASA engineers had to build a carbon dioxide filter by using only the materials available on the Apollo 13? The challenge upon which the astronauts' lives depended was how to fit a square peg in a round hole: "We got to find a way to make this fit

FIGURE 3.1

The movie *Apollo 13* demonstrates a "square peg in a round hole" moment.

into the hole for this using nothing but that." And they did.

Most teenagers don't start off thinking about the elements of a rhetorical situation as a box of spare parts they must assemble in a do-or-die endeavor. But sometimes the stakes are that high. In Orson Scott Card's novel *Ender's Game* (1977), a perennial student favorite, the Machiavellian Peter tells his sister Valentine he's been studying how rhetoric can alter the course of history: "I've been learning things about patterns in human behavior. There are times when the world is rearranging itself, and at times like that, the right words can change the world" (128). While Peter's opportunism is dangerous, there are many instances when precisely timed combinations of occasion, audience, purpose, and argument have been the vehicles for restored hope or greater social justice. Think of the Gettysburg Address, the St. Crispin's Day speech from *Henry V,* John F. Kennedy's inaugural address, or Martin Luther King Jr.'s "I Have a Dream" speech.

Another way of thinking about occasion, audience, and purpose, then, is that all three are about opportunity: the opportunity to respond to something, to reach someone, or to change something.

Classroom Activity: Analyzing the Rhetorical Situation

To help students understand the many moving parts of a rhetorical situation, I share the Calvin and Hobbes cartoon shown in Figure 3.2.

Like many who came of age in the 1980s, I still miss Bill Watterson's wry and wistful voice in my Sunday paper. In the Mother's Day strip from May 14, 1989, Calvin has written a poem that has a clear argument and purpose (see Figure 3.2). I ask students to read the cartoon together in groups before discussing the following questions:

- What is Calvin's message or argument? What does he say in his poem?
- Who is Calvin's audience? What kind of a person is she? How can you tell? What is their relationship like?
- How does Calvin present this message? What persuasive strategies does he use?
- What is Calvin's purpose in making this argument? What does he want to accomplish?
- What is the occasion or context? What expectations do mothers have on this day?

FIGURE 3.2
CALVIN AND HOBBES © 1989 Watterson. Reprinted with permission of UNIVERSAL UCLICK. All rights reserved.

After lots of practice playing the believing game, most students can easily paraphrase Calvin's argument: I can't afford nice presents because my allowance is too small. They also have a pretty easy time identifying Calvin's mother as his target audience and can usually describe the literary and rhetorical choices Calvin made in writing his poem (e.g., rhyme, logical reasoning, etc.). Purpose presents a bit of a challenge since some students want to give Calvin credit for at least trying to make his mother happy on Mother's Day—even though most recognize that his real goal is to get a raise in his allowance. This gives us a nice opportunity to talk about primary and secondary purposes in acts of communication. And students know exactly what mothers expect or hope for on this special occasion: doting children, breakfast in bed, being treated like a queen, flowers, and candy.

But the real conversation piece in this cartoon is the way the occasion interacts with the other elements of the rhetorical situation. Most students think Calvin's timing is woefully off. In choosing Mother's Day to ask for something for himself, Calvin—students suggest—has blown his opportunity both to please his mother and serve his own interests by disastrously combining purposes made mutually exclusive by the special occasion. However, a few students (often Calvin types themselves) bring the issue of audience back to the foreground. What if Calvin's mother thinks he's cute? What if she's charmed, or at least amused, by his clever egoism? Does his entertainment value—and a mother's unconditional love—compensate for his lousy timing? The back-and-forth discussion we have on the dynamics of this rhetorical situation makes it clear to students that our job is to analyze the *interplay* among occasion, audience, and purpose—not just to identify them.

After we discuss the groups' responses, I share the following "formula" for determining effective attempts at persuasion:

Message/Argument + Means by Which Message Is Expressed + Context/Occasion = Persuasion

Then, I ask groups to decide whether or not they believe all these elements in Calvin's poem add up to an effective act of persuasion. Most students see the occasion as the deal breaker in Calvin's attempt to get a raise. Now I have my opportunity to explain why context matters.

Why Context Matters

Consider the story of virtuoso violinist Joshua Bell playing incognito in a Washington, DC, metro station. In a "stunt" designed by the *Washington Post* to examine how context shapes perception, Bell played for nearly forty-five minutes on a $3.5 million Stradivarius during the morning rush hour. The opening paragraphs from Gene Weingarten's April 8, 2007, story describing this experience foreground the importance of audience and occasion:

> [Bell] emerged from the metro at the L'Enfant Plaza Station and positioned himself against a wall beside a trash basket. By most measures, he was nondescript: a youngish white man in jeans, a long-sleeved T-shirt and a Washington Nationals baseball cap. From a small case, he removed a violin. Placing the open case at his feet, he shrewdly threw in a few dollars and pocket change as seed money, swiveled it to face pedestrian traffic, and began to play.
>
> It was 7:51 a.m. on Friday, January 12, the middle of the morning rush hour. In the next 43 minutes, as the violinist performed six classical pieces, 1,097 people passed by. Almost all of them were on the way to work, which meant, for almost all of them, a government job. L'Enfant Plaza is at the nucleus of federal Washington, and these were mostly mid-level bureaucrats with those indeterminate, oddly fungible titles: policy analyst, project manager, budget officer, specialist, facilitator, consultant.
>
> Each passerby had a quick choice to make, one familiar to commuters in any urban area where the occasional street performer is part of the cityscape: Do you stop and listen? Do you hurry past with a blend of guilt and irritation, aware of your cupidity but annoyed by the unbidden demand on your time and your wallet? Do you throw in a buck, just to be

polite? Does your decision change if he's really bad? What if he's really good? Do you have time for beauty? Shouldn't you? What's the moral mathematics of the moment? (Weingarten 2007)

Phrases such as "mid-level bureaucrats," "middle of the morning rush hour," "nucleus of federal Washington," "each passerby," "quick choice to make," "any urban area," "part of the cityscape," and "of the moment" reinforce the spatial, temporal, and personal significance of context in this description. Context matters. Big time. In this case, the change of venue from concert hall to metro station radically altered the relationship between the artist and the audience, not just in terms of the audience's expectations but also in regard to the artist's. Bell, who has performed worldwide before heads of state and can command fees of $1,000 per minute, admitted he felt nervous about trying to capture his auditors' attention. He was sensitive to the fact that his intended audience was predisposed to ignore him, putting the world-class performer in the unusual position of playing to a resistant crowd in an environment inherently hostile to the appreciation of fine art.

Did Bell succeed in reshaping his context? Were those busy commuters transformed and transported by the sublime? Not in the least. "In the three-quarters of an hour that Joshua Bell played," writes Weingarten, "seven people stopped what they were doing to hang around and take in the performance, at least for a minute. Twenty-seven gave money, most of them on the run—for a total of $32 and change." Some had thrown pennies. You can watch the whole unbelievable scene with your students on YouTube (http://www.youtube.com/watch?v=hnOPu0_YWhw).

But before we jump to the conclusion that Americans are philistines with wacky priorities, my students and I talk about what happens when something is taken out of context. Why does isolating a comment from its original conversation so often lead to trouble? How do we know how to read something if we don't see familiar signposts? Why can we often figure out unfamiliar vocabulary words by using context clues? What happens if the signposts we see (in this case, a subway station, a guy in jeans and a T-shirt, an open violin case) point us to a misreading? And what does timing have to do with it? Through this discussion, we work toward the understanding that all forms of expression—including artistic performances—are socially situated, for good or for ill.

Without appropriate contextualization, the commuters couldn't and wouldn't attend to the genius of Joshua Bell. Weingarten summarizes it nicely: "He was, in short, art without a frame" (2007).

Understanding *Kairos*

Working through examples like this helps students begin to understand that we're calling for far more than a one-sentence response when we ask them to analyze the occasion of a text. Crossing that conceptual threshold is all about moving from surface to depth. To deepen students' developing sense of what we mean by the occasion, setting, or context, I add a critical concept from classical rhetoric: *kairos*.

The ancient Greeks had two different senses of time—chronological time and situational time. *Kairos* was the name given to a circumstantial kind of time, a window of opportunity during which something could happen (Crowley and Hawhee 2009, 45). Unlike *chronos* (or calendar time), *kairos* is about the immediate social space and situation in which arguments must be made, including what's expected in terms of propriety or fitness for the occasion. *Kairos* is also the opportune moment for action, lasting anywhere from a few seconds to several years, depending on the rhetorical situation. George A. Kennedy, an authority on classical rhetoric, refers to *kairos* as knowledge of "when to say what" (1994, 29). For a good sense of *kairos*, look at rapper Eminem's song "Lose Yourself" from the 2002 movie *8 Mile*:

> *Look, if you had one shot, or one opportunity*
> *To seize everything you ever wanted, one moment*
> *Would you capture it or just let it slip?*
>
> *You better lose yourself in the music, the moment*
> *You own it, you better never let it go*
> *You only get one shot, do not miss your chance to blow*
> *This opportunity comes once in a lifetime yo*

FIGURE 3.3
Kairos in *8 Mile*: Marshal Mather's character seizes the moment.

As these lyrics show, a *kairotic* moment can be a turning point, a finest hour, or a crucible. It can also be two roads diverging in a wood or any other special circumstances calling for a time-sensitive response.

What I like so much about adding an understanding of *kairos* to students' concept of a rhetorical situation is the extra attention to particularity that it brings. *Kairos* is all about a precise combination of timing and action; it's about recognizing or creating just the right moment to make the right move, and in order to do that, students have to be able to tell one unique moment from the next. They have to be aware of when things change.

As Crowley and Hawhee explain, "*Kairos* draws attention to the mutability of rhetoric, to the ever-changing arguments than can be found in connection with a particular issue" (2009, 47).

This doesn't mean we sit idly by, waiting for fateful moments. Instead, *kairos* involves an ability to see opportunity in any given rhetorical situation. Glen McClish, professor and chair of the Department of Rhetoric and Writing Studies at San Diego State University and my colleague on Cal State's English Placement Test Development Committee, explains it this way:

> Think about *The Music Man*. When con man Harold Hill arrives in River City, he looks for some way to sell his band concept to the unsuspecting townspeople. When he learns that a pool table has been delivered, he transforms that mundane occurrence into a moment of great urgency (exigence) that opens the door for the need for the band. Hill is persuasive not because he recognizes a truly historical moment just as it arrives, but because he knows how to make something important out of something small—it is his invention process that is salient here. In other words, *kairotic* moments aren't necessarily presented to us by fate to recognize like rare birds—we make them from the bluejays and crows around us. Fate isn't the agent with *kairos*, the rhetor is. And, as teachers of rhetoric, this is exactly where we want agency to be.

> For Plato, *kairos* is "the immediate social situation in which solutions to philosophical problems must be proposed" (1990, 56).

Understanding that they have the capacity to create their own rhetorical opportunities from their immediate circumstances can be deeply empowering to students.

Introducing *Kairos* to High School Students

How can we help teenagers get acquainted with this rather complex concept? Humor works well. In the 1988 film *Who Framed Roger Rabbit,* there's a terrific scene in which the title cartoon character is handcuffed to hard-bitten P. I. Eddie Valiant for an extended period of time (Figure 3.4). Roger's on the run and Eddie doesn't have keys to the handcuffs, so the two undergo all manner of awkward contortions until the exasperated Eddie finally takes a handsaw to the handcuffs. When Eddie asks Roger to hold still, Roger easily slips out of his cuff, saying, "Does this help?" Eddie is incensed:

| Eddie: | D'you mean to tell me you could've taken your hand outta that cuff at any time?! |
| Roger: | No. Not at any time. Only when it was funny. |

The clip is great for helping students see how the success of a joke depends on what Crowley and Hawhee call "the *kairos* of its delivery" (2009, 45). Humor is all about temporal contingencies.

FIGURE 3.4

In *Who Framed Roger Rabbit*, Roger understands the importance of *kairos* in humor.

Newspaper articles are another excellent way to introduce students to *kairos*. When reporters write about periods of broad cultural change, for instance, they're writing about *kairotic* moments. Consider the following excerpt from a story on gay marriage that appeared in the *San Jose Mercury News*. The article ran in my local paper on March 24, 2013, with the headline "Time Could Be Right for Gay Marriage." The text is loaded with the language of *kairos* (in bold):

A little over nine years ago, when **then**-San Francisco Mayor Gavin Newsom decided to flout California law and hand out marriage licenses to gay and lesbian couples, it provoked such a local and national furor that even his own political party and his Catholic neighborhood base wanted to tar and feather him.

At the time, Democratic presidential candidate John Kerry couldn't distance himself enough from Newsom's gay rights stunt. No state had yet to legalize gay marriage. Opinion polls firmly and consistently showed the majority of Americans, including in California, opposed same-sex marriage. **There was not a civil rights lawyer in the country ready** to challenge gay marriage in a conservative U.S. Supreme Court.

But now, as the Supreme Court **this week** takes on gay marriage **for the first time in history**, attitudes on this generation's most contentious civil rights issue have **shifted dramatically since** couples lined up at San Francisco City Hall to take part in Newsom's **short-lived** wedding ceremonies.

"I thought perhaps **it would happen in my lifetime**," Newsom, California's lieutenant governor, said of the Supreme Court deciding gay marriage. "**But I never imagined it would happen within a decade**." (Mintz 2013; emphasis added)

By highlighting the time markers in this excerpt, students can more clearly see how changes in temporal and social contexts have shaped this issue.

Questions Students Can Ask About *Kairos*

Asking questions about *kairos* not only gives students a better understanding of the rhetorical situation but also encourages deeper reading. The following questions require students to extend their thinking about the time, place, and particularities of arguments (note that it's not necessary for students to use the word *kairos* in order to apply its principles). You might try having your students ask and answer these questions in response to texts like Washington's Farewell Address, Roosevelt's Four Freedoms speech, the Preamble to the Constitution, or the United Nations' Universal Declaration of Human Rights:

- What's special about this moment? How can I tell?

- What opportunities for persuasion do I see in this rhetorical situation?

- What would surprise this audience at this time? Why do I think this?

- What evidence do I see, if any, that the writer(s)/speaker(s) knew the time was right to make this argument?

- Are there any special rules or manners the writer(s) or speaker(s) is/are expected to follow? How do I know?

- How frequently does the opportunity to make this kind of argument come along?

- What can the speaker or writer do to create a rhetorical opportunity?

- What could the speaker or writer do on this occasion that he or she couldn't do later on?

- What happens if the speaker or writer isn't successful in his or her attempt to persuade the audience? Can he or she get another chance? How high are the stakes?

Recognizing the Language of *Kairos*

Sentence templates like the ones in Graff and Birkenstein's (2010) *"They Say/I Say"* work well as both reading strategies and writing strategies. Students who recognize the kind of moves writers make through their language choices not only have an easier time understanding the arguments of other writers but also have an easier time making their own readers understand them.

Words and phrases like the following are cues that *kairos* is an important part of the arguments people are making about an issue:

At this point . . .

It's now too important . . .

We need to move as quickly as we can . . .

X increases the urgency . . .

X is a timely development . . .

X is outdated . . .

Last X years . . .

X is an interesting development . . .

At this point on the time line . . .

A new degree of urgency . . .

X has evolved/changed . . .

X is record setting . . .

X is the highest/lowest on record . . .

X is on the wrong side of history . . .

X is trending now . . .

My time will come . . .

This is my year . . .

It's not my time . . .

X is/has perfect timing . . .

The turning of the tide . . .

A landmark case . . .

In light of recent events . . .

Fresh/stale ideas . . .

New reality . . .

New normal . . .

X is a game changer . . .

X signals a new era in . . .

> Teaching students to watch for time-based signal words or transitions ("time markers") is another way to alert them to how *kairos* functions in a text: *then, since, before, after, yet, during, first, second, finally, last, recent(ly), current(ly), previous(ly), subsequent(ly), next, later, earlier, new, older, now, prior, long ago,* and so on.

Becoming aware of the language of *kairos* helps students see that transitions are not just logical; they're also temporal. They mark liminal moments within a text, the turning from one idea to the next. Signal words like those above likewise point to transitional moments in the social world outside a text.

Kairos and Decorum

Not only does *kairos* convey a unique sense of place and time, but it also conveys a sense of decorum and propriety. These are not words we often hazard using with teenagers. If I asked my sophomores to show more decorum and propriety, they might make an initial effort to sit up straighter before devolving into giggles and snide remarks. A more appropriate word for this idea is probably, well, "appropriate." When rhetoricians use the word *decorum,* they aren't talking about a narrow concept of good manners but rather, as Catherine R. Eskin puts it, the idea that "there are times for particular actions that must be chosen with care and experience" (2002, 105). What's appropriate for one occasion may not be appropriate for another.

Teenagers can certainly talk about the expectations surrounding an occasion. How many times have we heard someone say, "This is not the time or the place"? (I tend to say this to my own children whenever we're on the brink of public embarrassment.) And because it includes this sense of what's appropriate for a given situation, *kairos* also helps students to deepen their understanding of the relationship between speaker or writer and audience. Neglecting decorum, whether it calls for our best etiquette or most relaxed behavior, can harm our ethos.

FIGURE 3.5
South Korean president Park Geun-hye (L) shakes hands with Microsoft founder Bill Gates before their meeting at the presidential Blue House in Seoul on April 22, 2013. AFP PHOTO / Lee Jin-man /Getty Images.

Here's an example. During his 2013 meeting with South Korean president Park Geun-hye, Bill Gates was photographed shaking the president's hand while keeping his other hand in his pocket (see Figure 3.5). The casual attitude Gates's posture suggested generated a storm of criticism, especially from South Koreans who saw his behavior as disrespectful to their president. I share the photograph with my students and then ask what they think:

1. Does Gates seem to be too casual for the occasion?

2. How would you feel if you met a head of state? How would you know how to act?

3. Is it OK to act in a way that's different from what people expect? Why or why not?

4. Who is Gates's audience here? President Park Geun-hye? The media? South Koreans? Americans? All of the above?

5. What does it mean if the same occasion involves different audiences and purposes?

6. How do we decide what's appropriate or effective behavior?

7. Would it bother you to see a groom with his hands in his pockets while saying his wedding vows? What about a singer who puts her hands in her pockets while singing the national anthem?

Here's what some of my students said:

1. "In my opinion, Gates did act a little casual . . . he should have taken his hand of his pocket and stand up straight to make it seem more respectful."

1. "No, Bill Gates is not a political figure and he also is of a higher class of people. He meets people like this often. As well, he is making eye contact and that's what matters."

2. "If I would have met a head of the state, the chances are that I would feel nervous and excited that I cannot control myself, I'll keep shaking the president's [hand] with my both hands for five minutes."

2. "I would act respectful and be in my best behavior."

3. "It is OK to act in a way that different then what people expect because you don't always have to do what people want. However, it is probably best to act appropriately."

3. "I believe it is OK to act in a way that's different from what people expect because you're just being you, not trying to be something you're not."

4. "Gates's audiences are the media, South Koreans, Americans and everyone around the world who are interested in politic[s] and internation[al] relation[s]."

5. "It means the outcome is going to be different. There might be different points of view."

6. "We decide [what's appropriate] based on the 'norm.'"

7. "It would bother me seeing a groom with his hands in his pockets because he is showing no respect. He is basically implying he doesn't care like if he's being forced to do it."

7. "Yes, this is inappropriate decorum because marriage happen[s] only once in a lifetime, therefore, a groom should take serious responsibility and act appropriately."

7. "[A singer] should have good posture/straight and keep her hand on the sides or one on her chest, as one does when someone is singing the National Anthem."

7. "All humans make mistakes but in a huge event or occasion, there are times when acting properly is very important."

> It's important to point out that working against an audience's expectations can be a strategic move in its own right. Humor, of course, often depends on an incongruity between occasion and conduct (think Mr. Bean or Lucille Ball). But even writers who have a serious purpose might find it useful to create a disruption in their arguments by doing something that seems situationally inappropriate, like using profanity or slang.

Ultimately, I want students to be able to transfer the insights they gain from this kind of *kairotic* analysis to the choices they make about how to communicate appropriately in different contexts.

Classroom Activity: "*Kairos* Analysis"

Because *kairos* is so particular and unpredictable, focusing on it when analyzing arguments necessarily brings out the subtleties and nuances of a rhetorical situation. A *kairos* analysis is a search for the unique. And that move from the general to the specific is exactly what takes students beyond the threshold into deeper learning.

The following *Kairos* Analysis graphic organizer (Figure 3.6, Appendix 7) is one way to help students see what's special about a particular occasion. In this activity, students identify the time, place, and social expectations of a rhetorical situation, as well as the time markers in a text. They then reflect on whether or not they think the writer made the most of the rhetorical opportunity presented by the occasion. In other words, does the argument show a sense of "right time" and "right measure"?

Figure 3.7 shows a *Kairos* Analysis sheet I completed for Mark Antony's funeral oration in *Julius Caesar* as a teacher model. I agree with adolescent literacy researchers Doug Fisher and Nancy Frey that teachers need to model expert thinking (2010)—even though we might expect novice performances from our students.

Kairos Analysis

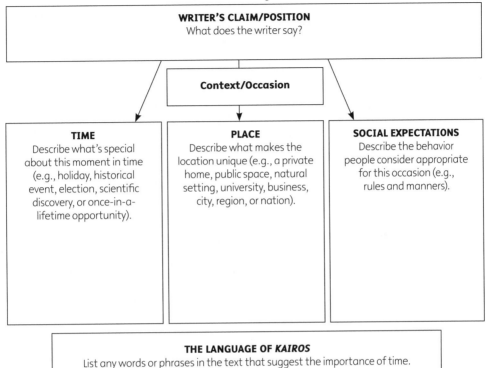

WRITER'S CLAIM/POSITION
What does the writer say?

Context/Occasion

TIME
Describe what's special about this moment in time (e.g., holiday, historical event, election, scientific discovery, or once-in-a-lifetime opportunity).

PLACE
Describe what makes the location unique (e.g., a private home, public space, natural setting, university, business, city, region, or nation).

SOCIAL EXPECTATIONS
Describe the behavior people consider appropriate for this occasion (e.g., rules and manners).

THE LANGUAGE OF *KAIROS*
List any words or phrases in the text that suggest the importance of time.

Quick-Write: How would you describe the *kairos* of this text? How do time, place, and social expectations impact the writer's argument? Do you think the writer has chosen the best opportunity to make his or her argument?

FIGURE 3.6
Kairos Analysis graphic organizer

Each rhetorical situation calls for a particular type of response—in the case of my example *Kairos* Analysis, a funeral oration. But in this scene from *Julius Caesar*, the *kairos* also opens the door to a different kind of rhetoric. Mark Antony is able to incite a rebellion instead of just delivering a staid eulogy, because the very disorder and unpredictability of the moment create an opportunity for a game-changing argument.

The purpose of this activity is to help students dig into the details of the occasion. After students understand the basics of naming an occasion (e.g., "the March on Washington," "the Battle of Agincourt," "the Ides of March," "Mother's Day," etc.), they're ready to analyze

Kairos Analysis
Mark Antony's Funeral Oration

WRITER'S CLAIM/POSITION
What does the writer say?

Mark Antony argues (by implication) that Caesar was a great benefactor of the Roman people who was wrongfully murdered.

Context/Occasion

TIME
Describe what's special about this moment in time (e.g., holiday, historical event, election, scientific discovery, or once-in-a-lifetime opportunity).

The day is the Ides of March, and the great emperor Julius Caesar has just been killed. Brutus has already explained to the restless crowd why Caesar's death was necessary and now gives Mark Antony the opportunity to make a funeral speech on behalf of his dead friend. Mark Antony at first treats the occasion like a funeral, saying, "I come to bury Caesar."

PLACE
Describe what makes the location unique (e.g., a private home, public space, natural setting, university, business, city, region, or nation).

The place is the Roman Forum, now crowded with a throng of citizens. Rome is the center of the world's most powerful empire at this time. The emotional crowd had been yelling, "We will be satisfied!" but is now sympathetic to Brutus. Mark Antony has to make himself heard in this large, noisy public space, so he calls out, "Friends, Romans, countrymen, lend me your ears."

SOCIAL EXPECTATIONS
Describe the behavior people consider appropriate for this occasion (e.g., rules and manners).

Mark Antony knows that this is a special kind of funeral oration; he's not supposed to praise Caesar too much but is still allowed—"under leave of Brutus and the rest"—to publicly mourn Caesar and speak of his "glories" as appropriate.

The crowd expects Mark Antony to support Brutus and to be solemn but not angry.

THE LANGUAGE OF *KAIROS*
List any words or phrases in the text that suggest the importance of time.

Marc Antony points out the citizens' past love for Caesar as a contrast to their current acceptance of his death. "You all did love him once, not without cause: what cause witholds you then to mourn for him"

Quick-Write: How would you describe the *kairos* of this text? How do time, place, and social expectations impact the writer's argument? Do you think the writer has chosen the best opportunity to make his or her argument?

The kairos of this scene is especially intense and unpredictable. A great and shocking historical event has just happened: the public assassination of the Roman emperor Julius Caesar by his friends. The place is important because Caesar was killed in the Roman Senate and the crowds gather in the Roman Forum to hear what happened, making it all very public and political. Mark Antony knows that the crowd is emotionally vulnerable and volatile right now and can easily be manipulated, so it's a good time to turn the Roman citizens against Caesar's killers—before Caesar's death is fully accepted.

FIGURE 3.7

My *Kairos* Analysis for Mark Antony's funeral oration

how the dynamics of the occasion impact the effectiveness of an argument.

Going Deeper into the Rhetorical Situation

As this discussion of *kairos* shows, there's more to the rhetorical situation than can be captured by SOAPS (page 52). Indeed, the very definition of *rhetorical situation* has been debated by rhetoricians. Bitzer's 1968 essay "The Rhetorical Situation" is a good place to start for folks who want to know more about the contested history and particularities of this concept (my use of the term is more general and flexible than Bitzer's). One way that Bitzer differs from some other scholars is that he sees "exigence" as a key characteristic of rhetorical situations that determines how we respond. According to this view, something has to be happening in the world that's worth talking about—and that calls forth and shapes arguments. In other words, we have to fit our response to the exigencies and constraints of that need. Bitzer's description of a rhetorical situation includes the following basic elements:

> Try this modification for students who have crossed the threshold into a deeper understanding of the rhetorical situation: Replace "Context/Occasion" with "*Kairos*" in the formula for evaluating the effectiveness of arguments.
>
> Message/Argument + Means by Which Message Is Expressed + Kairos = Persuasion
>
> In this more advanced understanding of the components of persuasion, kairos involves knowing how to select the means or strategies by which a message is expressed with maximum effect based on the particular situation.

Exigence: "An imperfection marked by urgency; it is a defect, an obstacle, something waiting to be done, a thing which is other than it should be"

Audience: "Those persons who are capable of being influenced by discourse and of being mediators of change"

Constraints: "Persons, events, objects and relations which are parts of the situation because they have the power to constrain decision and action needed to modify the exigence" (1968/1999, 221)

According to Bitzer, when there is an exigence, or problem, that can be helped by speech or writing, we have a rhetorical opportunity. The problem itself gives rise to rhetoric. In Bitzer's view, exigence is "the organizing principle" that determines not only the target audience but also the desired outcome (Bitzer 1968/1999, 221).

Later scholars, however, tend to see the relationship between need and response as reciprocal and multidirectional. Sometimes we argue in response to a need, and sometimes we create a need by arguing. My guess is that most of the time we're probably doing both.

Here's an example. The first time in my post-student life that I ever wrote for a public forum was on September 12, 2001. Like many people at the time, I felt a strong need to respond to the events of 9/11. My letter to the editor was published by the *Orange County Register* the following day.

Then in the summer of 2011, I was invited by an editor from the *Orange County Register* to contribute a follow-up letter as a special "9/11: Then and Now" letters feature commemorating the tenth anniversary of the tragic events. Although I didn't initially feel the urgency, or as Bitzer might say, "defect," in the rhetorical situation in 2011, I was asked to respond anyway, and I found that I had something to say.

Here are both letters, as published together in 2011:

SEASIDE (formerly of Placentia) Jennifer Fletcher

THEN, Sept. 13, 2001: The suffering of those families in New York so far outdistances the kindest intentions of strangers that even our deepest expressions of sympathy are meaningless in comparison to their grief. We don't feel what they feel; their dead—though our countrymen and women—are not our dead. Only those who lost family members on the hijacked planes will wake up tomorrow and understand that life will never be the same. I understand that the American people want justice. I recognize that the United States government has an obligation to protect American citizens.

This is not yet the time for healing, certainly not the time for forgiveness. But when those times come, I hope that Americans will look beyond acts of terrorism as merely the inhuman crimes of madmen—which, on many levels, they are. I hope Americans will also ask important questions about how these horrifying acts of war fit into a larger tradition of violence among nations.

I hope that whatever military response our government deems necessary is accompanied by sincere and compassionate efforts to promote international understanding.

Organizations like the Peace Corps and the Fulbright Program are important starting places. Through work or study abroad, we have the opportunity to promote cross-cultural empathy. In the many conversations that will follow today's tragedy, I hope that there will be many voices of compassion.

NOW: In 2001, I wrote of my hope that our response to this horrific tragedy would include compassionate efforts to promote international understanding. Ten years later, that hope is more fervent than ever.

Learning from other cultures requires a certain comfort with vulnerability, yet 9/11 forever changed our perception of risk. It's not only harder to get through airport security now; it's also harder to kiss our families goodbye.

But taking those risks can be healing. On Sept. 15, 2001, I moved with my husband to the United Kingdom for a year of study abroad. Living in London's multicultural East End, within walking distance of the city's largest mosque, was the most reassuring experience I could have had following the tragedy. Being a newcomer broke down my defenses.

Last year, I was inspired to see how the Defense Language Institute in Monterey embraces this idea of cultural learning as risk-taking. At its annual open house, the DLI's students (military personnel) perform with their teachers (native speakers). I watched soldiers in Middle Eastern clothing dance hand in hand with their Afghan instructors, listened as Marines recited Iraqi poetry—vulnerable in the best way.

Images like these give me great hope. It takes courage to be hurt this badly and yet choose to remain open. With certain kinds of healing, there also comes a softness, an empathy that can make the grief more bearable.

When it comes to exigence and *kairos*, I think the take-away learning for high school students is that real-world conversations don't happen in a vacuum. When the need and the moment change, the conversation does, too.

Kairos and Exigence at Work

Have you seen real estate listings that proclaim, "It's the right time to buy!" or "It's a great time to sell!"? How about advertisements that say, "Supplies are limited—don't wait! Act now!"? Like emotional and logical appeals, appeals to opportunity and urgency can help move audiences to action. Who wants to face charges of being "too slow on the draw," "on the wrong side of history," "out of touch," or "behind the times"? One of my master teachers—a stickler for due dates—would tell the unfortunate student who attempted to submit late work that he was "a day late and a dollar short." All are accusations of a failure to attend to the time sensitivity important to both *kairos* and exigence.

After the opportune moment passes, it's too late. Think of the expressions we use to describe when a particular moment or opportunity passes. That ship has sailed. The horse has already left the barn. The train has left the station. We excuse a joke that falls flat by saying, "You had to be there." When the stories broke about Lance Armstrong's use of banned substances in cycling, Armstrong's fall from grace was a hot topic that found its way into many classroom discussions throughout the fall and winter of 2012–2013. But by late spring of 2013, Armstrong was old news. Claiming that a topic is "relevant," "trending," "timely," or "an idea whose time has come" are all invocations of *kairos* and exigence.

We can ask students to bring in advertisements, news headlines, tweets, and social media posts that signal *kairotic* moments or make appeals to exigence, like the following:

"A Time of Transition" (*National Catholic Reporter*)

"Park on brink of making history at U.S. Women's Open" (*Monterey County Herald*)

"We can all help make it better—today, not tomorrow." (U.S. Department of Education tweet)

These kinds of examples are easy to find. Noting the abundance of rhetorical exigencies that surround us, Bitzer observes, "the world really invites change" (1968/1999, 225).

Kairos and Stasis Theory

How does *kairos* impact the kinds of questions we ask about conversations? A shift in stasis, or point of disagreement, often creates a shift in *kairos*. Gerard A. Hauser explains that the Greek word *stasis* "refers to a point of suspended animation" (2002, 130). In rhetoric, stasis represents a fixed point upon which arguments hinge, the *"clash of ideas that differ about the same thing"* (Hauser, 2002, 131; original emphasis). From this clash emerge the questions at issue to be decided (see Chapter 1 for examples). After old questions have been answered, new ones are formed, and the conversation continues in a different direction. For instance, a *USA Today* front-page article titled "Human Embryos Cloned for Stem Cells" from May 16, 2013, contained this concluding paragraph:

> "This study shows that human cloning can be done," said Richard Doerflinger of the U.S. Conference of Catholic Bishops, which opposes research that destroys embryos, arguing that it treats human beings as products. "The more important debate is whether it should be done." (Vergano 2013, 1A)

We can almost hear the implicit time marker "now" in that last sentence: "The more important debate [now] is whether it should be done." As questions of fact are replaced by questions of policy, a different *kairotic* moment, marked by changing concerns, develops in the ongoing conversation on stem cell research. The new arguments ricochet off from the old into a fresh rhetorical opportunity.

Seeing the Writing Situation as a *Kairotic* Moment

Understanding *kairos* can help students see the writing situations they encounter as opportunities, not assignments. This is especially important with on-demand essays. When I would score essays with my colleagues for our District Writing Exam, I took to heart the annual admonishment of our table leader to "reward the students for what they do well." Because I was scoring essays holistically, I didn't deliberately look for ways I could ding students on their poor grammar, faulty logic, or weak support. Instead, I was looking to match the overall quality of the essay that a student had produced with a description from a particular score category. What this meant was that the less effective choices students made—such as an overly general hook in a funnel introduction ("From the dawn of time . . .") or a three-part, formulaic thesis statement ("The diction, syntax, and imagery . . .")—were simply lost opportunities. They didn't give me a chance to reward the student for something done well.

After explaining the importance of not letting a chance to persuade a reader slip by, I ask my students to reread their own essays, looking for any "lost opportunities." My goal is to give the writers more time and white space for what really counts. Once we're all comfortable with this idea, we start crossing out phrases or sentences in their writing that are too vague, weak, clichéd, or redundant to do the writer much good. The following student sentences are examples of the kinds of "lost opportunities" we've found:

> "All writers use diction to express their ideas."
>
> "For this analysis, paragraph 3 of the article will be discussed."
>
> "The writer's imagery creates a picture in the reader's mind."
>
> "The writer uses language that grabs the reader's attention."
>
> "The irony makes a big statement."
>
> "From the dawn of time, people have had problems."
>
> "Throughout history there are many different interpretations to be made."

By identifying and eliminating empty statements like these, I'm trying to train my students not to waste their shot at making a successful argument. We don't want to try our readers' patience by making them read anything that doesn't help our cause.

Kairos and the Teaching Profession

Does *kairos* really matter in an educational context characterized by the Common Core, district pacing guides, and standardized tests? I believe it does. We ignore *kairos* to our peril. Here are some *kairos*-blind assumptions I held as a brand new teacher in the mid-1990s. I assumed the social world described in my credential program would be the social world I'd experience for the duration of my career. I took my district's culture and policies for granted. I presumed that my small class sizes (20:1 for ninth graders!) would continue to be part of my teaching reality. I looked forward to my yearly salary increases and my growing retirement savings. As a twenty-three-year-old new to the profession, I had no expectations of change. Had I read the rhetorical context of my profession more *kairotically*, I might have anticipated some of the sweeping changes to come.

Being attentive to *kairos* means we watch for those moments when the landscape shifts. If you've ever had a proposal dismissed by colleagues or administrators who said, "We tried that and it didn't work," take heart—the old roadblocks may no longer be there. Thinking *kairotically* means we don't assume we know the lay of the land until we make a new survey of the terrain. Understanding *kairos* helps us not only respond to change but also to create it.

I believe veteran teachers are masters of the *kairotic* moment. Adept at improvisation or "winging it," experienced teachers know how to capitalize on the "teachable moment"—or what rhetoricians might think of as "the reachable moment." When we practice gradual release of responsibility or differentiated instruction, for instance, we're responding to changes and particularities in our classroom *kairos*.

Conclusion

We are all beginners at some point in our learning on any topic. We have to start with the simple before we can move to the complex. When it comes to understanding occasion, audience, and purpose, ultimately, we want our students to move from passive recognition to active practice.

As for all threshold concepts, what makes *kairos* a threshold concept is its complexity. On the one hand, *kairos* is "a principle of adaption or accommodation to convention, expectation, predictability" (Miller 2002, xii). On the other hand, *kairos* represents "not the expected but its opposite: the uniquely timely, the spontaneous, the radically particular" (Miller 2002, xiii). Being able to hold these two opposing views of *kairos* in their head at the same time while applying the principles of both is what irrevocably changes the way students think.

Moreover, when we add *kairos* to students' understanding of occasion, we deepen their sense of responsiveness and responsibility. It's a way of turning up the heat and raising the stakes. We don't do this before they're ready, but when they are ready, we want them to feel the pressure of the moment, to know when they have that one shot to seize what they want.

> Notice the connection to *kairos* in the following Common Core Standard: "CCSS.ELA-Literacy.CCRA. SL.6 *Adapt* speech to *a variety* of contexts and communicative tasks, demonstrating command of formal English *when indicated or appropriate*" (NGA/CCSSO 2010; emphasis added). Teaching our students to assess contexts and tasks rhetorically empowers them to choose from a variety of conditionally effective responses. This sort of skillful adaptation, whether expected or unexpected, is exactly what constitutes *kairos*.

Points to Remember

As you plan your lessons and teach the concepts described in this chapter, you might want to refer to the following list of points to remember:

1. Each rhetorical situation is unique and calls for a customized response.

2. When we teach students to think rhetorically about arguments, we teach them how to figure out what kind of response each unique situation calls for.

3. It is even more important to teach students how to analyze the interactions among parts of a rhetorical situation than to identify them.

4. Threshold concepts like occasion, audience, and purpose require new ways of thinking and seeing the world.

5. Successful arguments depend upon a successful combination of message, persuasive strategies, and context or occasion.

6. The classical concept of *kairos* helps students understand the dynamics of an opportune moment for persuasion.

7. Rhetorical knowledge includes knowing an array of literacy strategies that can be applied to any task, genre, discipline, or context.

Prompts for Quick-Writes or Pairs Conversations

The following prompts can be used before, during, or after a lesson to help students make personal connections, deepen their understanding, and reflect on their learning:

1. Have you or has anyone you know experienced a once-in-a-lifetime opportunity? If so, what made that moment so special? If not, what once-in-a-lifetime opportunity would you like to experience?

2. How do people know the "supreme moment" to propose marriage? Describe a "perfect" wedding proposal you've heard about. What elements of time, place, and occasion made this the right opportunity to propose marriage?

3. Describe a time when you or someone you know turned a bad situation into something good. What can we do to change how people view or respond to their circumstances?

4. What does the expression "to make lemonade from lemons" mean? Do you believe that we can find opportunities for change in any situation? Why or why not?

5. Describe a time when you waited for just the right moment to make a special request, such as a raise at work, a favor from a friend, or a special privilege from your parents. How did you know when you had a good opportunity to make your request?

6. What do you think of when you hear that some product you can buy is "available for a limited time only"? Does this advertising strategy persuade you? Why or why not?

7. What do you think will be the next big thing in music, technology, fashion, or sports?

CHAPTER 4

Fostering a Deeper Understanding of Audience

Let us now consider the various types of human character, in relation to the emotions and moral qualities, showing how they correspond to our various ages and fortunes.

—ARISTOTLE

Everything may be an argument, but not everyone is in the audience. One AP English Language and Composition class website I came across asked students to identify the audience for Stephanie Ericsson's frequently anthologized essay "The Ways We Lie." Out of thirty responses, twenty-nine students identified "everyone," "anyone," or "everybody" as the audience for Ericsson's article. Variations on this answer included "anyone who lies," "all her readers," "the general public," "mainly everyone," and, most broadly, "the whole of the human population," "the entire world," and "every single human." The outlier was the student who said Ericsson didn't have an audience in mind but just wrote to organize her own thoughts.*

If *audience* is truly such a catchall term, then why are we even asking our students this question? Don't we and they already know the answer? The practical side of the rhetorical tradition tells us no, we can't easily identify the intended audience of an argument unless we are part of the original conversation, and even then we might have to do some detective work to suss out who in the room is really being targeted.

Who's in the Audience?

For Aristotle, effective rhetoric is about speaking to the unique needs and experiences of highly specific audiences. What's more, in the classical tradition, the contingencies of audience ultimately determine the different types and purposes of rhetoric. Whether a speech answers a question of fact, judgment, or policy depends on who the listeners are. The roles and responsibilities of audience members also vary. According to Aristotle, a listener must either be "a judge, with a decision to make about things past or future, or an observer [who offers praise or criticism]" (1984; Book I, Chapter 3).

Aristotle and other ancients, such as Cicero, saw major differences between audiences based on factors like age, emotion, rationality, social status, past experience, education, and values (e.g., young men were supposed to be quick tempered and impulsive, whereas old men were supposed to be cautious and cynical). Aristotle especially wanted his students to figure out the different kinds of motives—like self-preservation, revenge, power, or ambition—that could influence different audiences (1984; Book 1, Chapter 2). This precise attention to listeners' characteristics, motives, and tasks doesn't jibe with a view of an audience as "everyone."

It's no surprise the Common Core also expects precision. In the writing standards for eleventh and twelfth grade, the CCSS requires students to identify and respond to distinctions in audience:

> Develop claim(s) and counterclaims fairly and thoroughly, supplying the most relevant evidence for each while pointing out the strengths and limitations of both in a manner that anticipates the audience's knowledge level, concerns, values, and possible biases. (NGA/CCSSO 2010, CCSS. ELA-Literacy.W.11-12.1b)
>
> Develop and strengthen writing as needed by planning, revising, editing, rewriting, or trying a new approach, focusing on addressing what is most significant for a specific purpose and audience. (NGA/CCSSO 2010, CCSS.ELA-Literacy.W.11-12.5)

The ability to anticipate an audience's knowledge level, concerns, values, and possible biases involves a good deal of detective work that won't happen if we assume the audience is "everyone." For the record, my students tend to overgeneralize audience, too. I once asked a class who was the audience for an article we'd read on fast food and had a student answer,

*"The Ways We Lie" was originally published in *Utne Reader* in 1991. According to its website, *Utne Reader* is a digest "of independent ideas and alternative culture. Not right, not left, but forward thinking." The magazine is known for lively, well-crafted writing on emerging cultural trends and for reprints from cutting-edge publications. *Utne Reader*'s focus on intellectual debate can be seen in a 1992 *New York Times* article linking the magazine to a "comeback for the literary salon." Ericsson's original audience would include the participants in this "salon."
See the following links for more information:
http://www.nytimes.com/1992/04/13/books/an-attempted-comeback-for-the-literary-salon.html
http://www.utne.com/about.aspx#ixzz32I3Eg1Ls

"Anyone who eats." This doesn't mean that our students aren't capable of nuanced thinking; it just means that distinguishing nuance in audience is a new skill for them. And to be fair, many of us don't learn to make these distinctions until we're writing for our jobs or for publication, and we have to think through how our boss, coworkers, clients, or editors are going to view what we say. I know I didn't. Our challenge as teachers is how to give our students a sneak preview of the rhetorical demands of the postsecondary world.

Audience in the Twenty-First Century

In the modern age, the real-world distinctions in audiences become even more complex as speakers and writers attempt to engage increasingly diverse audiences. As Kenneth Burke (1969) notes, modern rhetors know they even have the opportunity to carve out audiences. In contrast to the Aristotelian notion of a stock audience (e.g., "young playgoers"), Burke sees audience as something the media can shape and choose.

Radio stations certainly get this idea. One oldies station made me chuckle the other day with the following attempt to claim me as a listener: "If you're still hanging on to your AOL email address, then *this* is *your* station." I'm not sure my thirteen-year-old niece even knows what AOL is. (I do still have an AOL account, by the way.)

Newspapers understand the complexities of audience, too. Have you seen this Internet joke about how the media will report the end of the world?

Headlines for the Apocalypse:

USA Today: WE'RE DEAD.

Wall Street Journal: Dow Jones Plummets as World Ends.

Rolling Stone: The Grateful Dead Reunion Tour.

Sports Illustrated: Game Over.

Lady's Home Journal: Lose 10 Pounds by Judgment Day with Our New "Armageddon" Diet!

TV Guide: Death and Damnation: Nielson Ratings Soar!

Each of the mock headlines is strategically pitched to a different audience, cleverly making the point that the style and substance of a publication depends on its audience and purpose. The headlines reveal the expectations and interests of their audience, the writer-reader relationship, the strategies used to reach a target market, and even something of the setting in which the articles will be read. Will these stories be read by busy people on the go? Or by folks at home in bed after a long day? (Assuming there's still time to read before the apocalypse.) The strategic brevity and clarity that characterizes *USA Today,* for instance, serve readers' needs for quick, easy news. The homey image and casual voice of *Ladies' Home Journal,* on the other hand, suggests a cozy rapport between writers and readers.

Learning About Audience Through Newspapers' Profiles

Newspapers, in fact, are a great starting point for helping students learn about nuances in audience. I once attended a workshop on media training in which the facilitator—a vice president of a big public relations firm—told us to remember that we are never talking to a reporter when we're interviewed for a newspaper article; we are talking to that newspaper's readers. In other words, our audience is not the person sitting in front of us asking questions but is instead the thousands of readers we have to imagine critiquing our answers. And if we're going to stay out of trouble, we'd better know who those readers are. A quick scan of the comments section after an article in the online edition of a newspaper illustrates the potential dangers.

Fortunately, the papers make knowing who their readers are fairly easy because they publish their audience profiles. You might have to dig around in a paper's website a bit, but you can usually find this information by following links for potential advertisers—often under headings like "Market" or "Media Kit." For example, here's the market description that the *Orange County Register* offers advertisers (this is the same Orange County of *Real Housewives* and *The OC* fame):

> Orange County, CA is located in Southern California (Los Angeles DMA) and continues to be one of the most desirable counties in the entire United States. There are 34 cities within Orange County and 9 beaches. Orange County is the 6th largest county by population in the U.S. . . .

Orange County ranks 5th nationally in total retail store expenditures.

- 97% shopped at a department store in the past 3 months.

Orange County has the lowest unemployment rate in Southern California.

Orange County adults are digitally savvy:

- 90% own a computer, smartphone or tablet.

- 63% shopped online in the past year.

- 48% use online social networking regularly.

- 37% own a Smartphone.

Notice how this description of what the website calls "upscale Orange County" provides a detailed analysis of the newspaper's audience. I might add—having grown up in Orange County—that this characterization of the region's affluence is somewhat misleading, demonstrating Burke's point about communicators carving out the audiences they desire. The fact that I don't see things the same way as the *Register* may mean I'm not part of its target audience.

Newspaper websites can also provide important information about what an audience is looking for. The September 2011 ABC Publisher's Statement, for example, lists several reasons why people read small-circulation community publications. Because these kinds of publications offer information that isn't found anywhere else, residents look to community papers for news about the following:

Youth and prep sports

City government

Recreational programs

Schools in their neighborhood & community

New businesses coming to the area

Police & fire activity

Community celebrations

Local shopping & dining (ABC Publisher's Statement, September 2011)

The ABC Publisher's Statement also includes readership data linking audience to purpose: "97% purposefully look for discounts, deals, sales, and coupons in their own cities and neighborhoods" (2011).

Headlines and op-ed letters are another indication of the interests, values, and priorities of a newspaper's readership. I like reading the letters to the editor in my small, local paper, the *Monterey County Herald,* because I often see names of people I know. With a circulation of only about 25,000, the *Herald* runs front-page stories on such divisive social issues as a new exterior paint color for the Embassy Suites Hotel.

Comparing the audience profile of a small-town paper like the *Monterey County Herald* to the audience profile of the *Register* or the *San Francisco Chronicle* or the *New York Times* makes clear to students that there's no such thing as a general reader when it comes to how newspapers see their market share. The activity I describe in the next section helps students see this point.

> A Word of Caution: While the comments section after an online article can reveal a great deal about a publication's readers (or, at least, those readers most likely to post comments), reader comments can often be inflammatory or offensive. Remind your students that they are looking for evidence that reveals the particularities of the paper's audience. They're not engaging in a debate with these people.

Comparing Newspaper Audience Profiles

Directions to Students: Choose two newspapers to compare for this activity. Try to find papers that represent different markets or that serve different needs—for instance, a large, urban paper and a small, local paper. Or you could choose two papers from the same city that represent different political views—for instance, one conservative and the other liberal. Once you've selected your two newspapers, visit the papers' websites to get a better sense of their reader profile. Look at the kinds of articles published by each paper. View the advertisements. Read the opinion pages. Scan the comments sections after a few articles. Then, if possible, find the newspapers' "media kits" or links for potential advertisers to see what the newspapers say about their readers. Imagine you are thinking about buying ad space in each paper. How will you know if your ad will reach your target audience?

Now answer the following questions:

1. What do the newspapers' articles, advertisements, online comments sections, and reader profiles or "media kits" (if available) tell you about the characteristics, values, and interests of their audiences?

2. What kind of advertisers would you expect to buy ad space in each paper?

3. How large is the circulation for each paper? (Hint: Search the page that's for advertisers.)

4. What are some of the similarities and differences between the two newspapers' audiences?

Julia, a star volleyball player from Salinas, California, demonstrated a sound understanding of audience differences in her comparison of the *New York Times* to the *Salinas Californian,* especially as those differences relate to rhetorical purpose:

> The *New York Times* is tailored to a United States and even an international audience whereas the *Salinas Californian* only reaches the local audience of Monterey County. Therefore, both audiences are looking for very different traits in the papers themselves. The *New York Times* needs to provide a comprehensive look at the major issues and headlines across the United States, but the local audience of Monterey County wants to see human interest stories about their neighbors and reports of violence within the city, for example.
>
> Advertisers hoping to reach a broader audience would target the *New York Times* and those hoping to reach the people of Monterey County would target the *Salinas Californian*. For example, the *New York Times* might publish an advertisement for a cruise line while the *Salinas Californian* would publish an ad about a job site in Salinas that needed construction workers.

Comparing newspaper profiles makes it clear that real-world publications are driven by their readers' needs and interests.

Anticipating the Audience's Values

In addition to reader characteristics like income level, educational attainment, and interests, newspaper audience profiles—and the content of the papers themselves—can also reveal quite a lot about the values of their readers. A comparison of the *Orange County Register* to the *Los Angeles Times,* for instance, suggests that the *Register*'s readers are more politically and socially conservative than the readers of the *Times*. When we ask students to anticipate an audience's values, we're asking them to play the believing game with other people's beliefs. Once again, students might have to postpone their own judgments if they are going to sincerely try to understand an issue from someone else's perspective. Glen McClish, my colleague in the Cal State University system, offers the following questions to help students think about how an audience's values impact rhetorical attempts at persuasion. Students respond to these questions at various moments during their reading of a text.

> What do you have to believe/value/care about to get past the first line/paragraph/page of this text? [Ask after the introduction.]
>
> Who is going to check out right here? [Ask in relation to a specific claim or assumption.]
>
> How does the reader attempt to bring in people who value X here? [Supply a relevant value.]
>
> Who's not going to be able to read this? [Ask in relation to a specific claim or assumption.]
>
> What is implied here and why is it so important to the audience? [Ask in relation to a key inference students must make.]

When it comes to writing their own texts, these same kinds of questions can help students think about how they might convince their audience that they share, or at least deeply respect, their audience's values, beliefs, and interests. Showing our audience that we share their interests, Kenneth Burke says, helps them to identify with us (1969).

Classroom Activity: Analyzing the Audience for Gerald Graff's "Hidden Intellectualism"

Once students understand how much one audience can vary from another, it's time for them to apply their knowledge to a full text. The following activity takes some frontloading, but it's worth it.

When it comes to understanding the audiences of texts, teachers have an enormous advantage over students. Our life experiences, wide reading, college educations, and many other factors give us an edge that we can use to our students' benefits. We're the ones who can put faces to names. We know the backstories of the texts, the writers' personal histories, the axes to grind, the industry secrets. We can be the ones to give flesh and blood to our students' abstract notions of a text's audience.

So—when I teach American Book Award–winner Gerald Graff's essay "Hidden Intellectualism," I give my students a little sketch first. Graff's essay was originally published in a work of educational scholarship, *Clueless in Academe: How Schooling Obscures the Life of the Mind* (2003), although he later revised it for the popular student textbook *"They Say/I Say"* (2006). Graff's *Clueless in Academe* is published by Yale University Press.

"Do you know how hard it is to get something published by Yale University Press?" I ask my students.

They usually nod.

I drive the point home: "Let me tell you—really, really hard. Keep in mind that Graff is professor of English and education at the University of Illinois at Chicago and the past president of the Modern Language Association."

When I saw Graff at the MLA Convention in San Francisco in 2008, he was rubbing shoulders with the likes of Stanley Fish, Judith Butler, and Patricia Bizzell. I tell my students that in the weird world of academic celebrity, these people are rock stars. And the MLA Convention is like the Grammy Awards—only instead of pop stars in evening wear, you have a bunch of academic sophisticates with New York suits and haircuts. So despite his folksy approach and his central argument about demystifying academia, Graff is an insider writing for insiders. That's his audience.

I also frontload my students with Graff's central claims from the introduction to *Clueless in Academe*:

> Academia makes its ways of thinking look harder and more confusing than they really are.
> Educated people need to know how to play the argument game, but academia hides its rules for playing. (2003, 1–3)

Now we read the text. The following excerpt represents a particularly interesting section to analyze in terms of audience. To read the full essay, see the appendix to Graff and Birkenstein's *"They Say/I Say,"* third high school edition (2014). For this first reading, I ask my students to think about the following questions: What problem does Graff describe in "Hidden Intel-lectualism"? What causes this problem? Who does Graff see as responsible for this problem? What does he want them to do about it? (The answers to these questions reveal some of the particularities of Graff's audience.)

"HIDDEN INTELLECTUALISM": FIRST READING

> Everyone knows some young person who is impressively "street smart" but does poorly in school. What a waste, we think, that one who is so intelligent about so many things in life seems unable to apply that intelligence to academic work. What doesn't occur to us, though, is that schools and colleges might be at fault for missing the opportunity to tap into such street smarts and channel them into good academic work.
>
> Nor do we consider one of the major reasons why schools and colleges overlook the intellectual potential of street smarts: the fact that we associate those street smarts with anti-intellectual concerns. We associate the educated life, the life of the mind, too narrowly and exclusively with subjects and texts that we consider inherently weighty and academic. We assume that it's possible to wax intellectual about Plato, Shakespeare, the French Revolution, and nuclear fission, but not about cars, dating, fashion, sports, TV, or video games.
>
> The trouble with this assumption is that no necessary connection has ever been established between any text or subject and the educational depth and weight of the discussion it can generate. Real intellectuals

turn any subject, however lightweight it may seem, into grist for their
mill through the thoughtful questions they bring to it, whereas a dullard
will find a way to drain the interest out of the richest subject. That's why
a George Orwell writing on the cultural meanings of penny postcards
is infinitely more substantial than the cogitations of many professors on
Shakespeare or globalization.

Students do need to read models of intellectually challenging writing—
and Orwell is a great one—if they are to become intellectuals themselves.
But they would be more prone to take on intellectual identities if we
encouraged them to do so at first on subjects that interest them rather than
ones that interest us. (Graff 2010, 198–199)

After discussing the gist of Graff's argument—that college professors are overlooking students'
intellectual potential because scholars don't value street smarts—we then reread the text
together, looking not only for *what* the text says but also for *how* it says it. This time, I ask
students to pay special attention to Graff's pronouns, point of view, references, and assumptions to see what they show about his target audience. For this next reading, I give students
a special version of the text to annotate.

"HIDDEN INTELLECTUALISM": SECOND READING

Everyone [*What does Graff mean by "everyone"?*_____] knows
some young person who is impressively "street smart" but does poorly
in school. What a waste, we think, that one who is so intelligent about so
many things in life seems unable to apply that intelligence to academic
work. [*Whose voice is this?*_____] What doesn't occur
to us, [*Who does Graff mean by "us"?*_____] though, is
that schools and colleges might be at fault for missing the opportunity to
tap into such street smarts and channel them into good academic work.
[*What do schools and colleges want?*_____]

Nor do we consider one of the major reasons why schools and
colleges overlook the intellectual potential of street smarts: the fact
that we [*What is the referent for the pronoun "we"?*_____
_____] associate those street smarts with anti-
intellectual concerns. We associate the educated life, the life of the
mind, too narrowly and exclusively with subjects and texts that we
consider inherently weighty and academic. [*What does this suggest
about what professors value?*_____] We
assume that it's possible to wax intellectual about Plato, Shakespeare,
the French Revolution [*What do these references suggest about Graff's*

*audience?*_____], and nuclear
fission, but not about cars, dating, fashion, sports, TV, or video games.
[What assumptions does Graff suggest professors share?
_____]

   The trouble with this assumption is that no necessary connection has
ever been established between any text or subject and the educational
depth and weight of the discussion it can generate. *[How does this
statement appeal to its audience?* _____] Real
intellectuals turn any subject, however lightweight it may seem, into grist
for their mill through the thoughtful questions they bring to it, whereas
a dullard will find a way to drain the interest out of the richest subject.
That's why a George Orwell writing on the cultural meanings of penny
postcards *[What does this reference suggest about the age and education
level of Graff's audience?* _____
_____] is infinitely more substantial than the cogitations
of many professors on Shakespeare or globalization.
   Students do need to read models of intellectually challenging writing—
and Orwell is a great one—if they are to become intellectuals themselves.
But they would be more prone to take on intellectual identities if we
encouraged them to do so at first on subjects that interest them rather than
ones that interest us. *[Who does Graff see as "us" and "them"?*
_____] (Graff 2010, 198–199)

Now we're ready to complete the Audience Analysis activity. Figure 4.1 shows one student's
analysis of Graff's essay. (See Appendix 8 for a blank version.)

Audience or Reader?

The importance of audience is a key difference between a traditional literary approach to texts
and a rhetorical approach. In his discussion of Aristotle's distinctions between poetry and
rhetoric, Wayne C. Booth explains that "only in studying rhetoric proper must we trouble
about the peculiarities of audiences and the adaptation of our case to fit those peculiarities"
(1983, 92–93).
   This rhetorical emphasis on audience "peculiarities" reveals the difficulty high school students
face when they read texts—literary or otherwise—out of an anthology. Unlike newspapers or
scholarly journals, anthologized reading selections bear few traces of their original contexts—
which is why it's so easy for students to confuse audience and reader. They're reading the text,
so they must be part of the audience, right? And if so, then the audience is anyone who reads
the article, or is interested in the topic, or can relate to the experience . . . in other words,
everyone. Without context, students can't trouble about particularities.

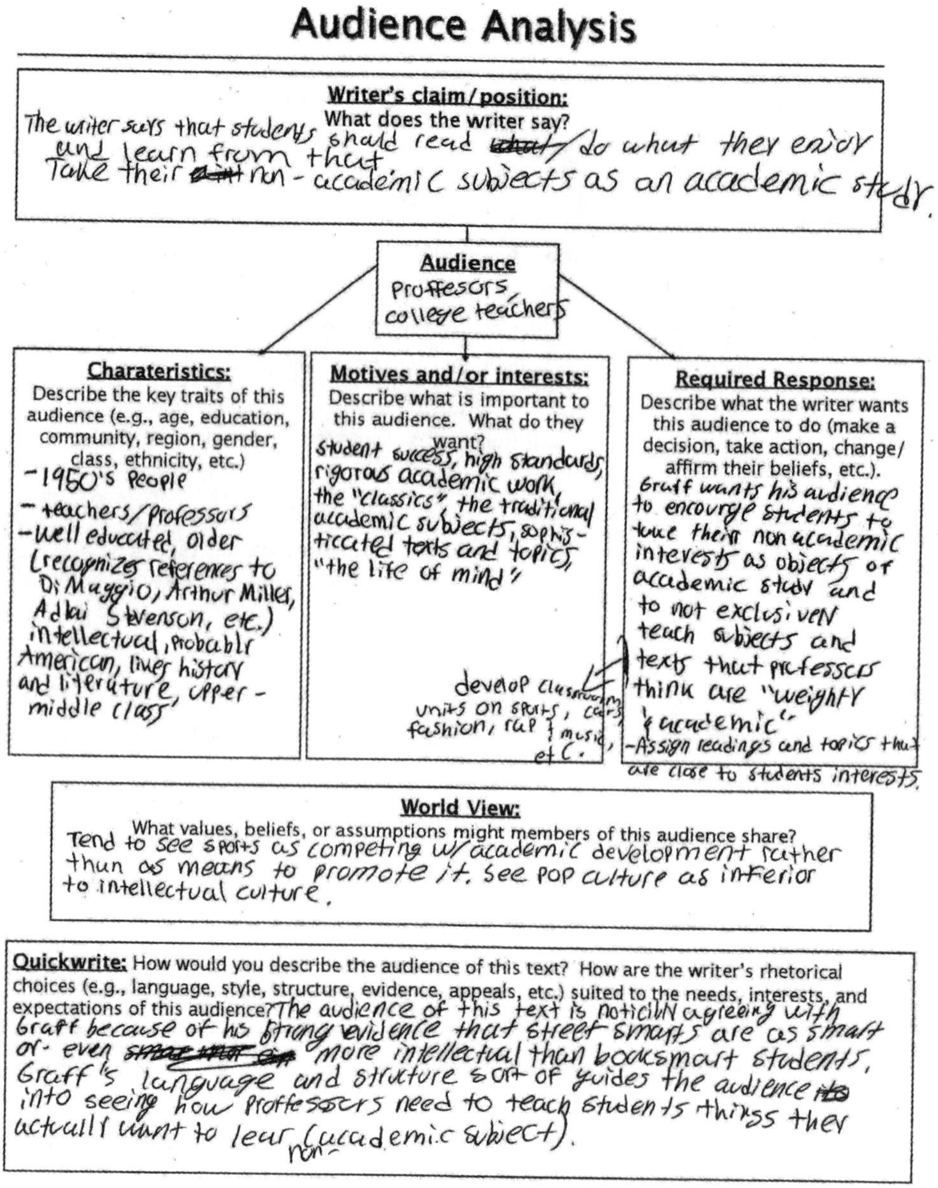

Audience Analysis

Writer's claim/position:
What does the writer say?

The writer says that students should read ~~that~~ /do what they enjoy and learn from that. Take their ~~that~~ non-academic subjects as an academic study.

Audience
Proffesors, college teachers

Charateristics:
Describe the key traits of this audience (e.g., age, education, community, region, gender, class, ethnicity, etc.)

- 1950's People
- teachers/professors
- well educated, older (recognizes references to DiMaggio, Arthur Miller, Adlai Stevenson, etc.) intellectual, probably American, likes history and literature, upper-middle class

Motives and/or interests:
Describe what is important to this audience. What do they want?

student success, high standards, rigorous academic work, the "classics" the traditional academic subjects, sophis-ticated texts and topics, "the life of mind"

develop classroom units on sports, cars, fashion, rap + music, et c.

Required Response:
Describe what the writer wants this audience to do (make a decision, take action, change/affirm their beliefs, etc.).

Graff wants his audience to encourage students to take their non academic interests as objects of academic study and to not exclusively teach subjects and texts that professors think are "weighty & academic"
- Assign readings and topics that are close to students interests.

World View:
What values, beliefs, or assumptions might members of this audience share?

Tend to see sports as competing w/ academic development rather than as means to promote it. See pop culture as inferior to intellectual culture.

Quickwrite: How would you describe the audience of this text? How are the writer's rhetorical choices (e.g., language, style, structure, evidence, appeals, etc.) suited to the needs, interests, and expectations of this audience? The audience of this text is noticibly agreeing with Graff because of his strong evidence that street smarts are as smart or even ~~smarter or~~ more intellectual than booksmart students. Graff's language and structure sort of guides the audience ~~its~~ into seeing how proffessors need to teach students things they actually want to lear (non-academic subject).

FIGURE 4.1

Audience Analysis for "Hidden
Intellectualism"

When we ask students to recontextualize an article or short story in an anthology by im-agining—or actually researching—the audience of its original publication, we breathe social life back into what teenagers often see as dead texts. This can be as simple as asking students

what kinds of products might have been advertised in the publica-tion that first printed the article or story: Luxury cars? Diapers? Bail bonds? Cosmetic surgery? Weight loss pills? Perfume? Resort hotels? Smartphones? Dating services? Denture cream? Their answers reveal a lot about how they see the text's readers. Early editions of Victorian fiction can be fun because the original publications often did contain pages of advertisements, a convention that master graphic novelist Alan Moore playfully acknowledges in his neo-Victorian work, *The League of Extraordinary Gentlemen* (2000).

> While there are times when we can use the words *audience* and *readers* or *audience* and *listeners* interchangeably, we don't want students to substitute sweeping generalizations for a rigorous audience analysis.

Classroom Activity: Rewriting Texts for Different Audiences

One way to help students see differences between kinds of audiences is to take a message intended for one recipient and rewrite it to suit a different reader and context. For instance, an e-mail complaining to a close friend about an awful dining experience at a restaurant could be rewritten as a formal letter of complaint to the restaurant's customer service department.

I created the following activity, Translating for Outsiders (Appendix 9), to help my students distinguish between the "insider" and "outsider" audiences they may already be negotiating in their lives. Turns out, this kind of rhetorical "code switching" is a big part of academic literacy. In *Clueless in Academe,* Graff argues that not only should students be able to parlay their out-of-school interests into good academic work, but also that scholars should know how to explain their research in everyday language. "Translating academic ideas into nonacademic terms is already internal to successful academic communication itself," Graff claims, offering the maxim "Dare to be reductive" (2003, 11).

Translating for Outsiders

Directions to Students: Think of a subject that makes you feel like an expert, or insider. This might be your favorite sport, a style of music, a video game, anime, graphic novels, a hobby, a job, or "digitalk," like texting. Then use special "insider language" to express each of the ideas in the following chart. Feel free to use slang, dialect, emoticons, abbreviations, or jargon to express your ideas. Then translate exactly what your insider language means for an outside audience in the final column.

What subject are you an "expert" on? _____

How would you say each of the following ideas if you were talking with other experts, or insiders, about your subject? (For example, how would a surfer describe the perfect wave to another surfer?)

IDEA	INSIDER LANGUAGE	OUTSIDER TRANSLATION
That's good.		
That's bad.		
That's frustrating.		
Hello		
Goodbye		
That's scary.		
That's funny.		

The following example is from a tenth-grade boy, Bryan, an expert in online gaming:

IDEA	INSIDER LANGUAGE	OUTSIDER TRANSLATION
That's good.	clutch	You win in a cool way
That's bad.	noobs	Someone that uses guns that other people don't use
That's frustrating.	trolling	People that mess around when you're serious
Hello	S'up bro	Hello, hey, hi
Goodbye	rage quit	When you quit in the middle of a game when you lose
That's scary.	hackers	People go in your account
That's funny.	whining	When kids that play whine about you cheating

Bryan also wrote a paragraph using his insider language:

> The online gaming world is just crazy. Once your in the game it's war.
> People try hard, and other people are noobs. The try hard start doing 360,
> trick shots, quick scoping, and till the end they clutch it. The other people
> are noobs, trol around, hack people, and start whining, so they rage quit.
> Try hards and noobs are two different things that people love to do in this
> game which makes people get mad.

This next example comes from one of my students who considers herself an expert in soccer.

IDEA	INSIDER LANGUAGE	OUTSIDER TRANSLATION
That's good.	(scoring)	pass, shot ball across the goal line
That's bad.	"dummy"	player lets ball go through his or her legs
That's frustrating.	(grunting noise)	something is wrong
Hello	"What's up?"	Hi team, what are you doing, what drills are you practicing?
Goodbye	"Later"	seeing those people or individuals at a later time
That's scary.	(Red or Yellow Card)	being or caution of being rejected from game due to unsafe actions, or physically or emotionally harming another player intentionally
That's funny.	"LOL"	laugh out loud

Analyzing the Audience for a Book

I reinforce the idea of differences in audience by asking a few simple questions about each book I read with my students. After completing a full-length work, we talk about the rhetorical moves the book makes to reach its intended audience. Unlike a magazine or newspaper article, a book has to do all the heavy lifting of capturing its audience's attention by itself. I help students see this work by asking these questions:

> What does the back cover description show about the audience?
>
> Does the book include a preface or introduction? Why or why not?
>
> What other kinds of books are this book's readers likely to read?
>
> What is the book's "competition" (i.e., What texts are competing for the same audience)?
>
> What kind of publisher is most likely to print this text?

With all the classroom activities I describe, it's important to remember that these are exercises to help teach a complex concept. They're intended as mini-lessons to build conceptual understanding, not an end in themselves. The point is to help make the complexities of audience visible to students so they can effectively apply this concept with whole, authentic texts.

Thinking of a book as a product that has to reach its intended market brings a whole new understanding to the reader-writer relationship. The only job I've ever been fired from was my brief stint as a fifteen-year-old telemarketer for a market research firm. Trying to recruit participants for focus groups and surveys was hard, humbling work. But cold calling people on those contact lists taught me a lesson that has important implications for determining the market or audience of texts: who is on the call list depends on the product.

Classroom Activity: The Back Cover Book Description

Another fun way to help students practice understanding the unique needs and expectations of an audience is to have them write a back cover description for a favorite book. While a back cover description shares some traits with a book review, it is usually much more focused on capturing the interest of a specific market.

> *Directions to Students:* Choose one of your favorite books. This could be fiction, nonfiction, a graphic novel—whatever you really enjoyed reading. Then imagine you are an editor with the book's publisher and that you have been assigned the job of writing the description for the back cover. The back cover is what a potential buyer usually reads before purchasing a book, so this is your opportunity to reach your target market and convince those readers that this is the book for them.
>
> Include the following in your back cover book description:
>
> > Need, problem, subject, or demand the book addresses
> >
> > What the book offers
> >
> > The book's purpose
> >
> > The audience for the book
> >
> > Key selling points

Student Sample

Clare's back cover book description for Ursula K. Le Guin's *The Left Hand of Darkness* shows her sensitivity to audience by inviting potential readers to imagine themselves on a journey with the sci-fi novel's main characters:

> Take a journey through time and space, and enter the world of Winter. A world where the population has no definition of gender, they are neither man nor woman, but can choose and change their sex. Ursula K. Le Guin has introduced audiences to a world unlike our own, and has created a society that strives on communication called mind speak. This novel has won both the Hugo and Nebula Awards for the best science fiction novel of the year, and has made science fiction a part of literature. Travel with Genly Ai and Estraven as they embark on a voyage through the Hainish universe to try to bring unity amongst the different planets.

Clare's invitations to "take a journey" and "travel with Genly Ai and Estraven" show that she's directly talking to the readers Le Guin herself is trying to reach.

Breathing Social Life into Texts by Reading Prefaces

Like the back cover, the preface to a book often gives an excellent sense of the relationship a writer has with his or her readers—at least, the relationship as the writer imagines it. In the preface to the bound edition of his novel *Little Dorrit* (1855–1857/1999), for instance, Charles

Dickens says to his readers that he is "deeply sensible of the affection and confidence that has grown up between us" (vii). He also notes that "some of my readers may have an interest in being informed whether or no any portions of the Marshalsea Prison are yet standing" (see Figure 4.2) and gratifies their curiosity on this point by revealing what he's personally discovered about the remnants of the jail (vi). These comments reveal a genuine responsiveness on Dickens's part to his audience. He's clearly addressing real individuals—some of whom he's either spoken to or corresponded with—and is trying to please them. By sharing these kinds of real-world examples with our students (even if that world existed 160 years ago), we can help bring a written conversation to life.

FIGURE 4.2
The outer wall of the Marshalsea Prison in London
Photo by Jennifer Fletcher

Analyzing Target Audiences

Students can further explore the nuances of audience by considering circles of intimacy. Within an ongoing conversation, there are multiple levels of participants. Some are at the very heart of the issue; some may be more on the periphery. Distinguishing these differences is an additional way to help students move from an overly generalized to a far more nuanced understanding of audience.

In the case of Gerald Graff's "Hidden Intellectualism," the inner circle would be occupied by those scholars who read *Clueless in Academe* (2003), the middle circle would be occupied by college writing instructors and their students who encountered the essay in *"They Say/I Say"* (2006), and the outer circle would include high school teachers and their students who read "Hidden Intellectualism" in *"They Say/I Say,"* third high school edition (2014). Appendix 10 provides a reproducible graphic of concentric circles.

Directions to Students: Use the concentric circles below to chart the levels of intimacy of participants in an ongoing conversation on an issue. Place those folks at the heart of the issue in the very center. Then identify other participants in this conversation according to their level of involvement. For instance, for a conversation that originates from a conference presentation, you might place the original panelists or speakers in the first circle, then the people in the room, then the readers of the journal that published the conference paper, then the scholars in the field, then the students of those scholars, and so on.

Hint: To find the names of other scholars in a field who are part of a text's audience, check the names in a writer's works-cited list. If the writer is listening to those folks, chances are he or she is speaking to them, too. Endnotes are an additional clue to who's in the audience. In works that have endnotes, the scholars who are cited are typically the ones who agree or disagree with the author. Endnotes are thus a kind of transcript of a scholarly debate.

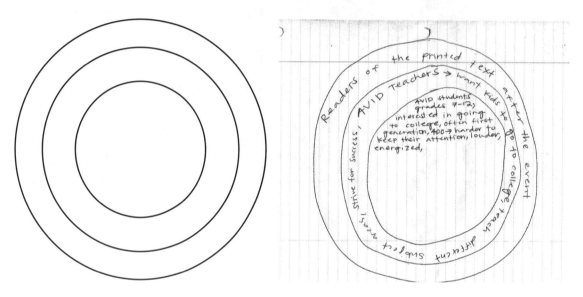

FIGURE 4.3

Analyzing Target Audiences graphic organizer student sample (For the speech that inspired this example, please see Chapter 5.)

Writing for an Audience

As students shift from being readers to being writers, understanding audience becomes an even more complex task. They now must apply what they know about analyzing audience in other writers' works to the choices they'll have to make in their own writing. This is hard stuff. Peter Elbow and Pat Belanoff make the difficulty clear in their discussion of the different kinds of audiences student writers encounter:

Sometimes you know your audience, for example, your parents or a particular committee or group of friends. Perhaps your audience is your classroom partner or friend.

But sometimes you don't know your readers. You may have to write a letter to an organization or an application to a bureaucracy and not have a clue who will actually read it. You may be writing an essay of application to law school, medical school, or some other special program and have little sense of who the admissions people are and what they'll be impressed by. Sometimes you know who your readers are but not what they're like. That is, you may write something for a particular newspaper or magazine that gets all sorts of readers with all sorts of views and feelings. (2000, 190)

In my experience, the only audience that tends to really count with students is the person who's giving them the grade. Other potential readers typically don't matter. For instance, here's what my students say about peer review:

- "[Conducting peer evaluations] is less effective to me because sometimes other students' critique is not as credible as the teacher's feedback."

- "I often times find that when I talk about [my writing] with a friend, they have different views and when I try to incorporate their thesis along with mine, it often confuses my paper and makes it harder to understand."

- "I get confused [after discussing my writing with a partner] and find reasons for their claim instead of mine."

- "The only opinion I listen to is the teacher's or someone with a higher degree than my peers."

- "Conducting peer evaluations using a score guide is not useful for me because in the past when I have done peer revision, I'd feel that the people who are peer reviewing and correcting others' essays, they do not help me at all. The only feedback that I would receive would be 'good job' or 'I really liked your paper.' "

I want to change this. I don't want my students to see me as their only audience or to see my opinion—or their own—as the only opinion that counts. In addition to seeing their peers as part of their discourse community, I also want students to know that they are writing to the writers whose texts they've read. The fact that so many of my students feel confused by the perspectives of others means they haven't yet crossed the threshold of being able to negotiate the many voices in a real academic conversation.

Engaging Authentic Audiences

Remember the point I made earlier about a deep understanding of audience requiring sophisticated acts of imagination and empathy? Before students typically have the opportunity to write for real-word audiences (outside of social media), they have to practice imagining what it's like to write for real, complex individuals . . . and not just their teachers or themselves. The writing of students who haven't yet developed this imaginative capacity often smacks of inauthenticity.

Consider this. Something funny happens to some kids' brains when they sit down to write an argument essay: They become remarkably prim and proper. Maybe it's performance anxiety or the stress of writing in academic English, but they say things I *know* they don't believe. Something about writing an academic argument induces them to endorse surprisingly priggish viewpoints for the sake of the assignment. Ban the wearing of jeans to school? "Yes!" Add a sin tax to sugary sodas? "Please do!" Raise the driving age to twenty-five? "By all means!" It's a rare teen that authentically advocates for more propriety and fewer freedoms, and yet when I read high school students' college placement tests, they often sound like a cross between George Will and Michael Bloomberg.

I think the problem these kinds of inauthentic responses point to is a lack of engagement with a real audience and rhetorical situation. My guess is that the students (often rightly) see the writing situation as calling for a perfunctory demonstration of written language proficiency, not critical thinking or communication skills. In other words, students figure out that it doesn't matter what they really believe. They're perfectly happy to game the test by taking on a position they don't genuinely support because they're not actually communicating their ideas to anyone.

A real audience makes a world of difference. For instance, I was more afraid of showing my drafts of this book to my friends and colleagues than to my editor (sorry, Jill!). What would Tammy and Silva think of the classroom activities? What would John and Ernie think of the rhetorical theory? What if I didn't get it right? Having to account for myself to real people whom I deeply admired was a daunting prospect.

Unlike my own generation, twenty-first-century students often do have extensive experience writing for authentic audiences because of social media; they just need help transferring this experience to academic tasks and contexts. A quick scan of teens' posts in Facebook, Twitter, Tumblr, and Instagram reveals that kids are highly attentive to genre and image in this context—an attention I think we can use to our advantage as teachers. For instance, we can ask our students how they choose which photos of themselves they share. What kind of look do they want to present? How would they like other people to describe them? What kinds of posts draw the most positive responses? How do they know when it's appropriate to be funny or sarcastic or serious in a post? What is not OK in online behavior? How is a tweet different from a status update? How do they know what kind of tone or language to use with different social media? Have they seen the style of posts, blogs, or tweets change during the time they've been using social media? If so, what might explain this change?

Crossing the Threshold

Teaching our students to think deeply and rhetorically about audience can help pull them out of the pit of egocentrism that many teen writers fall into. Being self-absorbed is part of the adolescent profile, and I don't begrudge high school students their day in the mirror. But I do want them to know that self-absorption doesn't work when it comes to academic writing.

Many a time I've given my students corrective feedback on their essays only to have them say, "Oh, I know—that's just how I write." I'm most dismayed when students say this in response to my observation that they haven't capitalized the start of their sentences or used periods at the end. Writing for an audience means it's not just about how *you* write; it's about how *your audience reads.*

Classroom Activity: The Personal Letter of Recommendation

Letters of recommendation make this point abundantly clear. What motivation does someone reading a reference letter have to indulge the idiosyncrasies of the writer? That's why I like to assign students the task of writing a letter of recommendation for themselves as an exercise in writing for an audience with little time and less patience. The formal language and tone of a recommendation letter and "one-shot" nature of its occasion further direct students to pay attention to what the target audience needs and expects: in this case, a quick and compelling case for why the subject of the recommendation should be hired, admitted, chosen, funded, or whatever.

This assignment has the added side benefit of giving students a heads-up to what references could possibly say about them—something that helps me when those requests for letters of recommendation start to pour in down the road. I'd rather my students make the discovery that they're a little thin in the accomplishments department than for me to make it.

Questions to Ask About the Audience We're Writing For

Here's a bit of genius: Teachers, of course, have to write for audiences every day. It's called lesson planning. Several years ago, the California Reading and Literature Project developed a terrific tool to help teachers match their literacy strategies to their students' needs: the Textual Analysis Template. After reading a text they plan to share with their classes, teachers use the template to identify any language or content that might present challenges to their students.

Look at the following questions on reading comprehension from the Textual Analysis Template :

Will students be motivated to read about this topic?	YES	NO
Is there a need to develop prior topic knowledge?	YES	NO
Is the text structure difficult?	YES	NO
Will the language level present a challenge to my students?	YES	NO

Is the main idea difficult to identify?	YES	NO
Will students need help relating details to the main idea?	YES	NO
Is the writing dense with information?	YES	NO
(CRLP 2005, 29)		

Aren't these some of the same questions we want students to ask themselves about what they write? This template, in essence, is an audience analysis and can be converted to a student tool for essay planning with just a few modifications:

Will my audience be motivated to read about my topic?	YES	NO
Does my audience already know a lot about my topic?	YES	NO
Will any of the words I need to use be difficult for my readers?	YES	NO
Will my main idea be difficult for my audience to understand?	YES	NO
Will my readers have to deal with a lot of new information?	YES	NO

The idea behind both sets of questions is that the teacher/writer will use this information to suit the instructional/rhetorical approach to the needs of the audience. See? I take this as further evidence that teachers are master rhetoricians. When allowed to practice their craft unhampered, teachers can out-adapt, out-modify, and out-improvise anyone.

Group Project: The Magazine Playlist

This quick activity borrows from the concept of Pandora's Music Genome Project to identify songs and artists that would appeal to a target audience. It's the old "If you like that, you'll probably like this" idea. Used as a warm-up to help students collaboratively explore the particularities of a magazine's readers, The Magazine Playlist could serve as the introductory activity for The Mock Rejection Letter (see page 95). First, organize students into small collaborative groups. Then, distribute to each group a different magazine for the students to analyze. The best magazines for this activity are those with a distinctive style and readership, such as *Sports Illustrated, Rolling Stone, Seventeen, National Geographic, Surfer, Vibe, Esquire, The Source, Motor Trend, Anime, Country Weekly,* or *Vogue*. This activity also works well as a whole-class discussion. If it's OK with your school's technology policy, you might even invite students to generate ideas by searching their own playlists on their electronic devices or by visiting sites like Pandora or iTunes.

Directions to Students: **Working in groups of four or five students, create a music playlist that would likely appeal to readers of your selected magazine (your teacher may assign you a specific publication or may allow you to choose one of your own). Start by carefully examining the table of contents, advertisements, images, special features, and articles in your magazine. Pay special attention to what readers say in the "Mailbox" or "Letters" section in** your magazine. What can you infer about the values, interests, tastes, and life experiences of the magazine's readers? What songs and artists do you think this audience would like?

Create a music playlist that you think this magazine's audience would enjoy. Include a minimum of seven tracks, and be ready to share with the class. See the example playlist below:

Magazine Playlist for *Seventeen:*

"22" by Taylor Swift

"What Makes You Beautiful" by One Direction

"Beauty and the Beat" by Justin Bieber

"Treasure" by Bruno Mars

"Good Time" by Carly Rae Jepsen

"Heart Attack" by Demi Lovato

"I Love It" by Icona Pop

My students have a lot of fun with this activity. I loved the playlist one group created for *National Geographic:*

"African Djembé" by African Drums

"Drums of Defiance" by Visca

"A Night in Havana" by Sao Benitez

Symphony No. 9 by Beethoven

"Laagan" by Kanth Kaler

"Appalachian Spring" by Aaron Copland

"Akita Ohako" by Shogetsu Watanabe

I like to have the students choose one spokesperson from the group to share both their audience analysis and their playlist. If I think students haven't quite gone far enough in their analysis—for instance, maybe they've just said *Seventeen* is a magazine for teenaged girls—I try to push them to compare their publication with a similar magazine that meets a different niche in the same market. For example, I might ask them to consider how the fashion-oriented *Seventeen* is different from the celebrity-oriented *Twist,* even though both magazines target overlapping audiences of the same age and gender.

Classroom Activity: The Mock Rejection Letter

My favorite experiences as a high school teacher included when students brought me a piece of writing and asked, "How do I get this published?" Oftentimes it was a poem, but I've also seen fantasy fiction, letters to the editor, and play scripts that my students hoped to one day see in print. I love this stage in writers' lives, and I'm very protective of young hope. I also want to gently prepare students for actually getting their work published if they choose, and for me, that starts with a realistic understanding of their intended audience, or "market." Even students who have no interest whatsoever in getting published can benefit from a real-world look at the relationships between writers and readers.

As a way of trying on the perspective of a particular audience in the publishing world, I ask my students to write a mock rejection letter. This is role-playing and creative writing, not academic writing, but it has a point. While few of our students will ever need to master this genre, writing a rejection letter from the perspective of an editor can be a helpful exercise in understanding the complexities of audience, because the editor must explain *why* the submission is not suitable for the intended readers.

Because this activity also calls for students to take on the role of an editor at one of their favorite magazines, it can be a nice way to bridge students' in-school and out-of-school literacies.

The Mock Rejection Letter

Directions to the Teacher: Bring several copies of popular magazines to class or arrange to have your students look at magazines online. The best magazines for this activity are those that make clear the distinctive interests, values, and characteristics of their readers. If possible, you may also (or alternatively) want to have your students search for submission guidelines for publications online.

Directions to the Student: Imagine you are an editor of a popular magazine and that you have to write a rejection letter to an aspiring writer who has submitted an article that is clearly *not* suitable for your publication. Your letter must explain why the writer's work is not a good fit for your audience, but be careful not to discourage the writer. He or she could turn out to be a fantastic contributor down the road. Your goal is to inform this potential contributor about what your audience is looking for so that he or she can do a better job next time.

Step 1: First, you'll need to do a little research on your selected magazine. Look over a print or online issue of the magazine to get a sense of its style and content. Then see if you can find any guidelines for writers who want to submit articles to this publication. Many magazines share their submission guidelines online.

For instance, the submission guidelines for the teen magazine *Cicada* describe its readers as "intelligent and sophisticated" and says they "can handle complexity with respect to theme, characterization, and plotting." The website for *Cicada* further notes that it's especially looking for humorous stories, including "satire, lighthearted romance, deadpan humor, black humor, screwball comedy, humor with heart, contemporary realism with absurdist overtones . . . whatever makes you smile, even if it's through your tears" (2013).

Cicada's submission guidelines offer more helpful tips:

The magazine is for readers ages fourteen to twenty-three.

The editors like to see first-person experiences of interest to teen and young adult readers.

Poems can be up to 25 lines.

The magazine also publishes alternative comics and graphic narratives.

Visit *Cicada*'s website for more information: http://www.cricketmag.com/22-Submission-Guidelines-for-CICADA-magazine-for-teens-ages-14+.

Step 2: Next, imagine what might be wrong with a submission to your magazine that could cause you, the editor, to reject it. Is the topic not interesting to your readers? Is the style not appropriate? Is the article more suited to a different publication? You'll need to invent a reason for rejecting this imaginary article. For example, a scholarly study on the history of the clarinet—with footnotes—would probably be rejected by *Rolling Stone*.

Step 3: Write a mock rejection letter declining to accept the writer's article for publication. In your rejection letter, be sure to explain what readers of this magazine are looking for so that the writer has a better idea what to do next time. Include the following:

The kinds of topics that appeal to readers of this publication

An example of a successful article (include the author and title)

A description of the style of writing readers of this publication enjoy

The reason why readers buy or subscribe to this publication

The problem(s) with the imaginary article—be creative and have fun!

See the sample mock rejection letter that follows (note: this is *not* an actual letter from *Cicada*!):

Submissions Editor

Cicada Magazine

Carus Publishing

70 E. Lake Street

Suite 300

Chicago, IL 60601

July 5, 2013

Dear Ms. P. Lana Head,

Thank you for sending your article on how to choose the best life insurance policy to *Cicada* magazine for publication consideration. We have read it with interest and agree that this is a timely and important topic for many people. Your comparison of different policy rates is especially instructive.

Our readers, however, are teens and young adults who are probably not interested in purchasing life insurance at this time in their lives. While *Cicada* does welcome articles on real-world experiences, this particular topic is more suitable to an older audience, and we regretfully have to decline your submission. You may want to try a publication that targets working adults or parents, like *Readers' Digest*.

If you would like to revise your article for *Cicada,* please keep the following guidelines in mind. *Cicada* is a literary magazine that publishes serious or funny fiction or nonfiction by young writers for young writers. Popular topics include teen relationships, family dynamics, travel and other new experiences, and magical adventures. Our audience is made up of passionate readers who enjoy creative, thought-provoking, personal, funny, and edgy writing in a wide style of genres, including historical fiction, fantasy, mystery, poetry, and firsthand accounts of teen life. See Molly Fessier's poem "Reasons" in our 2011 issue for a good sense of the kind of work we publish.

Our young readers subscribe to *Cicada* because they want to be inspired—to live and to write!

Perhaps a personal story on the challenges of paying for college would be more appropriate for our audience?

Thank you again for considering *Cicada* as a home for your work.

Sincerely,

The Submissions Editor

It's great fun reading the letters the students write. Reyna's superb rejection of an imaginary submission to the hip-hop magazine *The Source* shows her skill in style imitation as well as her astute understanding of *The Source's* audience.

Reyna Chavez
The Source Magazine
The North Star Group
28 W 23rd Street

Neighborhood: Flatiron

New York, NY 10010

July 24, 2013

Dear Mrs. Hernandez,

Thank you for submitting your article on how to choose the healthiest makeup products to protect your skin and yet still make it look as ravishing as the other brands. I assure you that we read it with interest and we definitely agree that it is best to inform the public in order to help them keep their beauty confidence by using makeup without damaging their skin.

Our readers, however, are mostly adult or young adult men who will most likely would not be interested in knowing this since they do not use make up. *The Source* looks for articles that cover hip-hop music, politics, and culture. Unfortunately, the topic you chose for our magazine is not applicable for the group of audience we try to target, therefore we dreadfully must decline your submission. For your best interest, try publicating where they target females mostly teenagers and above, like *Seventeen Magazine*.

If you want to take a look at your article once more for *The Source,* make sure to remember the following guidelines for your best interest. *The Source* is a magazine that as I mentioned previously, focuses on covering hip-hop music, politics, and culture. Some great topics for our magazine include revelations of new songs and collaborations, scandals with rappers or athletes, sports, and celebrities political actions or views. Taking into consideration, our audience is mostly male aged sixteen-to-thirty, have an interest in current music industry and definite interest in hip-hop or rap music, and likely to also have interest in American popular culture. Take a look at John Weber's entertainment article "HipHop Got Jokes: Rappers in Comedies" for further comprehension of the type of work we publish.

Our readers follow *The Source* because they want to get informed about what is going on in the Hip-Hop and rap world. A personal life story of a hip-hop/ rapper artist of how he or she gained fame and the challenges he or she faced to get to where they are would maybe be in more interest for our audience?

Once again, Thank you for considering *The Source* as your option for submission of your work.

Sincerely,

Reyna Chavez

Cindy's letter also gave me a good understanding of her ability to analyze the audience of a text:

Submissions Editor

Sports Illustrated Kids

802 N. Bound Street

Suite 300

Los Angeles, Ca 60603

July 22, 2013

Dear Mr. Gabriel Rios,

As the Submission Editor for the *Sports Illustrated Kids* magazine I would like to inform you that your article has been read. I appreciate your interest on informing our audience about important supplements that help keep our body healthy especially the athletes; however that is not our purpose.

Sports Illustrated Kids magazine likes to inform the audience about healthy diets and active lives and although supplements are important we are not trying to send that message to our audience. Our audience is between ages 7–15 and we do not believe this is an adequate age for a kid to worry about the way their body looks or to consume something they do no need for their age.

I would like to thank you for your interest and recommend that you try publishing your article in another magazine, perhaps a health magazine would be ideal since your article contains a lot of health information.

If you are still interested in publishing an article for our magazine I would recommend you to write a childhood story that could motivate our audience, we look for inspiration, humor and optimism.

Thank you for your consideration.

Sincerely,

The Submission Editor

As a formative assessment, The Mock Rejection letter tells me not only how well students are able to understand the audience of a text they read, but also how well they are able to meet audience expectations in the texts they write. One of my students, Robert, clearly understood the topics that appealed to readers of *Rolling Stone* but had trouble writing his letter in a style appropriate to business communication. His abrasive tone and casual diction told me he hadn't quite crossed this learning threshold yet. In my feedback to him, I reminded Robert that editors seek a good relationship with readers and potential contributors and use respectful and encouraging language in declining a submission.

Writing a mock rejection letter shows students that what works for one audience might not work for another—something that can help take the sting out of the different disciplinary standards that students have to contend with in their academic lives. Instead of feeling that a history teacher just doesn't appreciate their creativity or feeling that they're not "flowery" enough for their English teacher, students who understand how audience impacts rhetorical choices can tell themselves, "It's not personal—that's just how they write in that subject."

Revising Through the Lens of Audience

One former principal I know shared a brilliant strategy for revising writing through the lens of audience. After writing a newsletter to her staff, she'd then read through it from the perspectives of her most curmudgeonly teachers, asking herself which parts of her letter were likely to cause the most trouble—and with whom. What would Mrs. Dutcher think about this? How about Mr. Walton? Her goal was to continue revising through the perspective of her audience until she had a newsletter that would offend the fewest teachers.

Students can also try this technique. In something of a virtual version of peer review, I ask my students to pick three friends and then write feedback on their essay/poem/letter from the points of view of each of these friends. The idea here is not to get actual feedback from real readers but to test how well a writer knows specific audience members' tastes, interests, and viewpoints. It's about anticipating an audience's reaction.

Another way to practice revising through the lens of audience is to ask students if there are any parts of their writing they'd want to omit or change if they knew they'd have to read their writing aloud before a particular group. When I was a graduate student, I had the chance to present a paper on Charles Dickens's novel *Dombey and Son* (1846–1848/2008) at the annual Dickens Universe at the University of California, Santa Cruz. A kind of summer camp for scholars, the Dickens Universe brings Victorianists together from around the world for a week of shared inquiry. These folks are uber insiders, leaders in the field of nineteenth-century British literature. When I shared a draft of my paper with my adviser, he warned me that I was telling my audience things they already all knew. "You can't say that to an expert audience," he cautioned me. Really? I didn't know. I've since learned, however, that my own radar will go off if I'm about to say something to a live audience that is redundant, boring, weak, or irrelevant. I find I simply want to skip those parts (and I usually do).

> **Directions to Students:** Imagine you have to read your paper aloud in front of a live audience. Are there any parts you would want to skip? Practice reading your paper aloud to yourself or to your family or friends. What parts of the paper are fun and interesting to read? Are there any parts you didn't like reading aloud? Could your paper be improved by changing or omitting those sections?

Distinguishing Writer Needs from Reader Needs (or How to Tell When a Funnel Introduction Is Too Wide)

Revising through the perspective of an audience helps students distinguish between moves that are just a crutch to get the writer going and moves that genuinely attempt to communicate some meaning to real people. Take the funnel introduction, for example. I'll admit, I've taught many a ninth and tenth grader how to write a funnel introduction, because, well, darn it, they needed to start somewhere. The old "question hook" ("Have you ever wondered . . . ?") or general statement about a topic seemed like a good way to help young writers find a foothold as they began drafting their essays. But when it came time for me to read those essays, I found I always skimmed over the wide end of the funnel because those sentences didn't contribute anything to the student's argument. Those handholds generally had more to do with the writer's needs than the reader's needs.

Thinking more rhetorically and strategically about audience can help students avoid gaping funnel introductions in their essays. Maybe you've seen the funnel introduction that looks like this:

Fossil-fuel-based transportation is a fact of life in the modern world.

Of the many means of oil-powered transportation available to us, cars are by far the most popular.

This popularity has devastating environmental consequences when it comes to the gas-guzzling SUVs we see everywhere on our roads and highways.

Or this?

The Industrial Revolution brought radical changes to our power sources for transportation.

Fossil-fuel-based transportation is now a fact of life in the modern world.

Of the many means of oil-powered transportation available to us, cars are by far the most popular.

This popularity has devastating environmental consequences when it comes to the gas-guzzling SUVs we see everywhere on our roads and highways.

Or even this?

**Throughout human history, people
have needed to get around.**

**This need was behind many of the radical changes
to our power sources for transportation
brought about by the Industrial Revolution.**

**Fossil-fuel-based transportation is now
a fact of life in the modern world.**

**Of the many means of oil-powered trans-
portation available to us, cars are
by far the most popular.**

This popularity has devastating
environmental consequences
when it comes to the gas-
guzzling SUVs we see
everywhere on our
roads and
highways.

If student writers are addressing an audience that's engaged in the same conversation they're entering—in this case, whether or not SUVs harm the environment—then they can assume that they share some common ground and knowledge with their readers. They can get right to the point. There's no need to rehearse the whole history of human transportation.

The funnel introduction with a "question hook" poses a similar problem in terms of audience. When students open an essay with a question that begins, "Do you ever wonder . . . ?" I ask them to think about the following:

> Is this really a question you'd ask your audience?
>
> Would you say this to someone's face in a conversation?
>
> How do you expect your audience to respond?

Considering the Reader-Writer Relationship When Revising

Chapter 6 offers a deeper explanation of the choices writers make in creating an image of themselves, but I think it's worth noting here that many of those choices have a profound impact on the reader-writer relationship. For instance, writers who haven't crossed the threshold into a more rhetorical and nuanced understanding of their audience often give in to feelings of hostility or exasperation when worked up over a topic—without considering how their tone affects their reader. I think of the young writers who, audience-blind, complain about people who "have no clue" or who "don't realize [insert critically important point negligent reader has overlooked]." I remember one young writer's paper I read: I had just been entertaining a counterargument to the writer's thesis when she anticipated me and cut me off. "Let's not be foolish!" she chided in her essay. A line like this can make the reader suddenly feel like Mr. Dick in Charles Dickens's *David Copperfield.* Then there was the student who, angry over another writer's position, forgot her own audience entirely and lashed out at the writer, "Tell someone who cares!"

My goal in teaching about audience is to sensitize students to the rhetorical kick of their language choices, especially when it comes to how they present their own persona to their readers. Attending to *kairos* helps (see Chapter 3); when students know they may have only one shot at reaching their audience, they're more likely to guard against losing their cool. Extended practice playing the believing game can also help young writers develop restraint.

What Do We Mean by Real-World Audiences?

As they engage an increasing variety of real-world conversations, it's important for our students to continue writing for academic audiences, too. The kinds of authentic audiences that students have access to as teenagers—peers, parents, school board members, teachers, newspaper editors, blog readers, and so on—are not the same audiences that students will address in academic disciplines in higher education or in their careers. Thus, while we want students to have the opportunity to reach some real readers now, we also need to prepare them to reach other readers down the road. There's an apprenticeship period for students when they're learning the moves they might eventually be called on to make if they go on to present at conferences or submit their work for publication. As undergraduate research opportunities continue to increase (and they sure seem to be on the rise), more students will have the opportunity to write for authentic academic audiences earlier in their postsecondary lives.

Disciplinary Differences in Audience

A final benefit that comes with developing students' critical awareness of audience is this: Students find it easier to negotiate disciplinary differences in academic essay structures and conventions. Have you heard this one before? "Why can't you teachers make up your minds about what you want? My history teacher, science teacher, and English teacher all tell me different things about how to write." Students typically don't see their teachers as different audiences situated in different contexts. They see us as capricious eccentrics who require different written language conventions from one class to the next just to make teenagers' lives difficult. Students tend to identify different content areas by teacher personality, not by disciplinary distinctions in ways of thinking and communicating.

Once skilled in audience analysis, however, students understand, as Gerald Graff explains, that "the Arguespeak of literary studies, philosophy, or history is very different from the Arguespeak of mathematics or chemistry, which is different in turn from the Arguespeak of the social sciences, economics, or computer science" (2003, 22). That's a critical insight that students find on the other side of the threshold.

Conclusion

When we're joining a conversation already in progress, we need to take extra care to listen for the way past voices, concerns, and counterclaims are invoked by writers or speakers. An audience is a sound archive, a composite record of not everyone in general, but everyone involved in a very specific discussion.

For high school students, crossing the threshold to college and career readiness is all about going beyond the superficial. As students develop a deeper understanding of audience, they mature from writing essays that might show little awareness of audience and purpose, to writing that is generally appropriate for its audience (although a bit simplistic), to writing that makes skillful use of rhetorical choices to effectively communicate with its intended audience. Most teens need explicit modeling and mentoring in this journey toward greater rhetorical sophistication—help we can provide by making visible the particularities of audience.

Points to Remember

As you plan your lessons and teach the concepts described in this chapter, you might want to refer to the following list of points to remember:

1. Understanding audience is an act of imagination and empathy.

2. Audiences are specific to unique rhetorical situations.

3. The audience for a text can include both the original readers as imagined by the writer and later communities of readers.

4. Different audiences have different values, motives, interests, experiences, traits, and tasks.

5. Writers need to speak to their readers' unique needs and experiences.

6. The choices writers make to satisfy their audiences are also shaped by purpose and occasion.

7. New forms of communication can empower writers to select their "best" audience.

8. Rhetoric is deeply interested in the social situations that shape acts of communication.

9. Prethreshold learning is an important development stage that should not be treated derisively.

10. Mini-lessons can help make the complexities of audience visible to students so they can effectively apply this concept with whole authentic texts.

Prompts for Quick-Writes or Pairs Conversations

The following prompts can be used before, during, or after a lesson to help students make personal connections, deepen their understanding, and reflect on their learning:

1. Why does the thought of a text or e-mail being sent to the wrong person make us cringe? What is so embarrassing or troubling about a message meant for one audience being sent to another?

2.   What kinds of texts make you feel like an insider or expert? What kinds of texts make you feel like an outsider or novice? Why?

3.   Describe a reading experience when you felt you were not part of the intended audience for the text. What was the text? What made you think the writer didn't have someone like you in mind when he or she wrote it? What did you do to try to understand the text anyway?

4.   Who is the audience for your favorite music artist? Describe the interests, values, likes, dislikes, and key characteristics of the people who typically listen to this artist. Feel free to note exceptions and variations.

5.   What are the different audiences you engage through social media (e.g., friends, family, coworkers, teachers, etc.)?

6.   What are some common spaces to communicate online? How are the audiences for these spaces different from each other?

7.   How do you decide what online audiences and contexts are safe for you?

8.   What are the differences between public information and private information?

9.   What does it mean to write for the public?

CHAPTER 5

Fostering a Deeper Understanding of Purpose

Each of the main divisions of oratory has . . . its own distinct purpose.
—ARISTOTLE

The purpose of all writing is to communicate—but to what end? While we can't predict all the reasons our students will need to write in their post-school lives, we can help them learn about the different kinds and combinations of purposes writing accomplishes. We can also prepare students to recognize that tug on their conscience or intellect that tells them it's time to have their say. "Writing well does not begin with teaching students how to write," Kelly Gallagher reminds us, "it begins with teaching students why they should write" (2011, 7).

Lloyd Bitzer talks about an urgent sense of need, or exigence, that motivates and shapes attempts at persuasion (see Chapter 3). In response to or in anticipation of a specific exigency, we make arguments to impact what our audience knows, believes, values, feels, or does. Sometimes the outcome we seek is a change from the status quo; other times it's an affirmation. But when we earnestly enter an argument, we do so with a specific purpose in mind.

The Three Ends of Rhetoric

One of the biggest differences between a rhetorical approach to texts and a traditional literary approach is rhetoric's explicit emphasis on purpose. We can talk about the ways literature enlightens and entertains us, but when Aristotle talks about the three ends of rhetoric, he has something highly specific in mind. Rhetoric's eminently practical focus means that rhetorical acts of communication target real audiences, situations, and outcomes—outcomes that Aristotle sees as entirely dependent on context.

To introduce this idea, I ask my students to consider how the purpose of each of the attempts at persuasion pictured in Figures 5.1, 5.2, and 5.3 is shaped by its rhetorical situation.

FIGURE 5.1
Student revolutionaries calling for people to join the June Rebellion in *Les Miserables* (2012)

FIGURE 5.2
Atticus Finch defending Tom Robinson in *To Kill a Mockingbird* (1962)

FIGURE 5.3
Abraham Lincoln dedicating the Gettysburg National Cemetery in *Abraham Lincoln: Vampire Hunter* (2012) (The epic moment doesn't appear in Spielberg's historically-minded film from the same year, so I make do with an image from the gothic mash-up.)

Students usually need just a minimal amount of backstory to get the gist of each of these scenes. We review the idea of exigence (an urgent need that calls for a rhetorical response) and discuss, in each case, the "thing which is other than it should be" (Bitzer 1999, 221):

Exigence for Figure 5.1: A people disempowered

Exigence for Figure 5.2: A man falsely accused of rape

Exigence for Figure 5.3: A nation deeply divided

Once they understand the context for the three images—postrevolutionary France, a southern courtroom in the 1930s, a Civil War burial ground—I ask my students to think about the purpose of each type of rhetoric depicted. What's the goal of a call to arms? What's the outcome of a trial? What's the function of a dedication ceremony? And why are the time and place of these different rhetorical acts important?

Now we're ready to look at the framework provided by the classical tradition.

In the *Rhetoric,* Aristotle describes three kinds of rhetoric that relate to different purposes (1984; Book I, Chapter 3): deliberative, forensic, and epideictic. Each of the three kinds of rhetoric has its own setting, methods, and time province. Deliberative, or "political," rhetoric aims at establishing the benefits or drawbacks of a proposed future course of action and urges people to do something or not do something in response to a question of policy (e.g., Should we pass this law or not?). Its setting is often a public forum, senate, or assembly. Forensic rhetoric aims at achieving justice and either attacks or defends someone in response to a question of fact (e.g., Did the accused commit the crime or not?). Its setting is often a court of law. Epideictic, or "ceremonial," rhetoric aims at establishing the honor or dishonor of someone or something and offers praise or blame in response to a question of quality (e.g., Is this person admirable or not?). Its setting could be a sacred space, a gravesite, or any formal gathering place.

The special "kinds of time" that Aristotle associates with each branch (1984; Book I, Chapter 3) further enhance the connection between purpose and context:

1. Deliberative/political rhetoric: a decision about the future

2. Forensic rhetoric: a judgment about the past

3. Epideictic/ceremonial rhetoric: a performance in the present moment

Look again at the scenes from the three films pictured in Figures 5.1, 5.2, and 5.3 to see how they relate to deliberative, forensic, and epideictic rhetoric. Keep in mind that rhetorical acts can have multiple purposes.

My purpose in this chapter is to share a helpful framework from the classical tradition that's seldom taught in high schools but that can offer teachers and students a deeper understanding of what it means to use a rhetorical approach to texts. As it turns out, high school students already encounter these three ends of rhetoric whenever they read or write any of the following:

Policy recommendations, voter ballots, or proposals (deliberative rhetoric)

> Cause and effect essays, mock trials, essays that assign blame for a problem (e.g., childhood obesity), or science lab reports (forensic rhetoric)
>
> Commencement speeches, recommendation letters, funeral orations, inaugural addresses, job applications, and essays on heroes or role models (epideictic rhetoric)

When we make this framework visible to students, we help them to be more strategic readers and writers.

"It's All Greek to Me"

Admittedly, I had some reservations about how these ancient Greek concepts would play with twenty-first-century teenagers. Some of my colleagues had their doubts, too. One early reviewer of this book put it bluntly: "Are you going to use these terms with high school students? Don't make me vomit." OK, maybe we don't need to use the Greek or Latin terms. When I taught AP literature at Buena Park High School, I would concede to my students that they didn't really need to know *chiasmus* and *zeugma* even though the words were on their literature terms list. They didn't even need to know *parallelism* per se as long as they could recognize the move and describe it: echo, repetition, mirror, shadow, whatever. My students were welcome to invent their own labels for literary devices provided they could accurately identify what the writer was doing and *why* he or she was doing it.

In fact, not knowing the terminology can sometimes help students avoid performing a lit terms or rhetorical devices scavenger hunt in place of a critical analysis. That's a metaphor! That's an allusion! That's pathos! That's a false analogy! These enthusiastic reactions are great in what Kelly Gallagher calls "first-draft reading" (2004, 53), but we need to help our students move beyond locate-and-name to more complex cognitive tasks as they progress through a full rhetorical reading of a text.

I like the student-friendly terms composition scholar George Hillocks offers in place of the Aristotelian terms for the three ends of rhetoric: policy, fact, and judgment. In *Teaching Argument Writing: Grades 6–12,* Hillocks calls argument "the heart of critical thinking and academic discourse" and "the kind of writing students need to know for success in college and life" (2011, xvii). Hillocks's book offers lots of ways for students to comprehend, critique, and create the kinds of arguments that have been translated from Aristotle's deliberative, forensic, and epideictic rhetoric categories.

Regardless of what terms we choose, the key idea to share with students is that a writer's sense of purpose is shaped by the particularities of the rhetorical situation—especially audience, occasion, and exigence.

Let's look at each of the three ends of rhetoric in greater detail.

Deliberative Rhetoric

Whether we call it policy, political rhetoric, or deliberative rhetoric, it's clear that a special class of communication is concerned with making group decisions about a community's future well-being. Proficiency in this branch of rhetoric is essential to democratic participation. When a state assembly debates a proposed budget, a community discusses how to renovate its public parks, or a school site team explores how to increase parent involvement, they're participating in the kind of rhetoric that Aristotle saw as the basis of shared governance. Deliberative rhetoric makes a direct appeal to the interests of the audience with an eye to promoting its security, prosperity, and happiness.

Twenty-first-century examples of deliberative rhetoric abound. For instance, I recently watched a documentary at the Monterey Bay Aquarium on collaborative efforts to conserve marine habitats. The film, *Ocean Frontiers: The Dawn of a New Era in Ocean Stewardship* (Green Fire Productions 2012), tells the stories of several communities of diverse stakeholders—including fishermen, scientists, shippers, civic leaders, and tourism professionals—who worked together to create policies that would have both environmental and economic benefits. Notice how the following descriptions of these efforts, taken from the film's website, bear traces of deliberative rhetoric. (You can watch clips from the documentary at http://ocean-frontiers.org/the-film/.)

An Ocean Blueprint for Florida Keys

The coral reefs of the Florida Keys are America's most popular marine destination, home of myriad sea creatures, magnet of sport fishers, divers and sightseers. Lately they are also America's showcase of marine conservation zoning, providing refuge, recreation, and livelihoods, through a collaborative plan developed by all concerned.

Iowa Farmers & Gulf of Mexico

The Mississippi Delta—terminus of America's mightiest river, nursery of one of the nation's premier fisheries, and lately an unfortunate poster child for ecological disaster—is getting help from an unlikely team of people, in an unlikely place. More than a thousand miles upstream, in the cornfields of Iowa, farmers are changing their ways to send cleaner water and new life to the nation's beleaguered Delta.

Port Orford Fishermen Protect Ocean & Way of Life

In a small fishing community on the coast of Oregon, the people of Port Orford are taking control of their destiny, by conducting their own brand of conservation. They are using local science to inform their fishery management, and protecting upstream forests to save their salmon—a farsighted perspective that considers both their links to the land, and the future of their children.

The real-world, forward-thinking purpose of deliberative rhetoric—and the strong sense of exigence that motivated these discussions—is readily apparent in these examples.

> **The aim of deliberation is to discover "what is most useful to do" (Aristotle 1984; Book I, Chapter 6).**

SAMPLE DELIBERATIVE WRITING PROMPT

High school students can practice purpose-driven communication when they engage questions of policy. The following sample prompt, for instance, asks students to deliberate over the expediency of establishing a law that would require toy manufacturers to make a majority of their products gender-neutral. Modeled on the California State University's English Placement Test, this style of prompt offers a generally plausible argument supported by a few dodgy claims so that students can reason their way through the expediency or inexpediency of the policy recommendation. While I like to have students respond to real writers as often as possible, I find I sometimes need to write the passage myself, so that I can embed it with the kinds of brainwork I want students to do. When I do this, I disclose to students that I'm the author—although the views I express are not always my own.

(By the way, prompts that present fairly dodgy arguments with a little bit of reason tacked on work, too. This alternative sort of prompt challenges the thinking of a student who might have been ready to dismiss the writer's ideas out of hand but then suddenly finds himself or herself in agreement.)

Directions to Students: **You will have forty-five minutes to plan and write an essay on the topic assigned below. Before you begin writing, read the passage carefully and plan what you will say. Your essay should be as well organized and as carefully written as you can make it.**

> Gone are the days when toy stores were a kaleidoscope of primary colors—an indistinct mix of blocks, books, puzzles, bead kits and bouncy balls, jump ropes and jacks meant to appeal to an equally diverse mix of youthful shoppers. Walk into any toy store today, and you see a world rigidly divided between pale pinks and dark blues, the aisles devoted either exclusively to princesses and fairies or to weapons and action figures. This forced and false choice between "girls' toys" and "boys' toys" denies children the carefree youth that is their birthright. By compelling young children to conform to gender stereotypes, we limit the exploration and creativity that are essential to healthy development. For this reason, toy manufacturers should be required by law to make a majority of their products gender-neutral.
>
> —Jennifer Fletcher

Explain the argument that Fletcher makes and discuss the ways in which you agree or disagree with her analysis and conclusion. Support your position by providing reasons and examples from your own experience, observations, and/or reading.

Suggested Sources for This Topic

Sweet, Elizabeth. 2012. "Guys and Dolls No More?" *New York Times,* **Dec. 21.**

Orenstein, Peggy. 2011. "Should the World of Toys Be Gender-Free?" *New York Times.* **Dec. 29.**

Kanazawa, Satoshi. 2008. "Why Do Boys and Girls Prefer Different Toys? Why Girls Like Barbies and Boys Like Trucks." *Scientific Fundamentalist.* **Apr. 17.**

GoldieBlox and Rube Goldberg. 2013. "Princess Machine." Video advertisement. http://www. youtube.com/watch?v=IIGyVa5Xftw.

Figure 5.4 shows one student's essay in response to this prompt.

FIGURE 5.4

Sample student essay on gender and toys

Should Toys be Gender-based?

"Why do all the girls have to buy pink stuff and all the boys have to buy different color stuff?" —Riley on Marketing. Boys and girls toys have been a controversial topic for ages. What leads girls to play with dolls and boys to play with trucks has interested researchers into observing the fine line between what is socially acceptable and what is not. I feel that children's toys should be made more gender-neutral in order to allow kids to possess positive life skills and expand their interests instead of conforming to society.

To start, I believe children are missing out on important life skills by only experiencing certain abilities. By only being allowed to practice certain areas, children do not recieve all of the skills they will need later on. For example, a female who never played with building blocks or Legos may struggle in the future when she tries to go into engineering. Or a male who wants to be a chef but never played "kitchen" because it was too girly. I think that if children used gender-neutral toys, they would be able to recieve more skills for their future life. Another point is that toys are not just for boys, or vice versa. Many girls enjoy playing with model cars whereas some boys are interested in cooking and family life instead. The term tomboy, a female who pursues activities more typical of boys is proof to this case. Children who are involved in different toys should be able to purchase the items they want without feeling insecure because it was made for the opposite sex. Children should be able to

walk into a store and see "rather than floors dedicated to Barbie dolls and action figures, merchandise is now organized by types and interests," stated by Peggy Orenstein. Conclusively, I think kids would have healthier lifestyles if they experienced a wider variety of activities.

Addressing the obvious concerns, I will concede that children have certain preferences for specific toys, due to brain wiring and social influences. Why waste time pointlessly debating when the kids won't care? The child's mind is hooked up to practice skills that would traditionally be used to train them for their future roles. To this day, due to the wiring of the child's mind, kids will still continue to gravitate towards their specific, gender-based toys. Secondly, toy marketing has a huge impact on children's behavior. A child will not purchase a toy for simple reasons such as "the box is pink" or "but girls play with that," due to the ideas that marketing and peer pressure have pushed onto children on what is deemed appropriate and what is not. A child's peers are often very important to them and they will struggle to do everything they can to fit in with their friends. Altogether, children will have certain preferences due to brain wiring and for the sake of being accepted by society.

Conversely, children would have a healthier mind-set if the majority of their toys were gender-neutral. Studies have shown that there are many, many toys that appeal to both genders, such as stuffed animals and books, amongst other things. Instead of having seperate isles devoted to girls

Understanding Forensic Rhetoric

Forensic rhetoric also pervades our culture, especially on Court TV and in dramas like *CSI* or *Bones*. Concerned with wrongdoing, motives for wrongdoing, and the laws or unwritten principles that determine culpability, forensic rhetoric occurs not only in legal contexts but also in many academic contexts where questions of causality or responsibility are critical. The whodunnit purpose of forensic rhetoric, for instance, motivates scientific inquiry into such problems as the cause of colony collapse in honeybees. Forensic rhetoric asks, What's behind this? Whereas deliberative rhetoric tends to use lots of examples to support claims, forensic rhetoric favors logical proofs, as the following sample writing prompt shows. See Figure 5.6 for a student sample.

Sample Forensic Writing Prompt: Cause and Effect Essay

Directions to Students: Write a three- to four-page argument essay analyzing a sequence of lethal cause-and-effect relationships in either Jack London's "To Build a Fire" ([1908] 2007) or Jon Krakauer's *Into the Wild* (1996). Your purpose is to establish the extent to which the main character is responsible for his own death. In your analysis, address counterarguments to your thesis, justifying why your view of the cause-and-effect relationships is more likely than an alternative. What evidence can you produce to persuade your reader that each event somehow contributed to the next? How do these events implicate or exonerate the main character?

As you write your essay, keep the following notes in mind:

Causal relationships can be difficult to establish. You may want to qualify your claims with modal verbs and moderate adverbs.

Distinguish among results that are possible, probable, or conclusive consequences of specific events.

Play the doubting and believing game to imagine other possible reasons and outcomes.

Use signal words to cue your reader to the relationships among events.

Keep in mind that signal words such as *therefore, thus, hence,* and *consequently* signal a high degree of proof; use these words with qualifiers or modals if there is room for uncertainty in your claims.

Avoid extreme claims (*always, never, all, none, absolutely,* etc.) unless you can support them convincingly.

Include direct quotations in your essay.

Test the logic of your thesis.

Students can also use the graphic organizer in Figure 5.5 and Appendix 11 to generate ideas.

For students who might need help recognizing and using the language of cause and effect, I offer a word bank: *effects, impact, influence, outcome, consequence, product, result, because, originate, catalyst, reaction, trigger, motivate, inspire, impel, encourage,* and so on.

FIGURE 5.5

Forensic Rhetoric:
Accusation and Defense

Directions: Use the following graphic organizer for forensic analysis

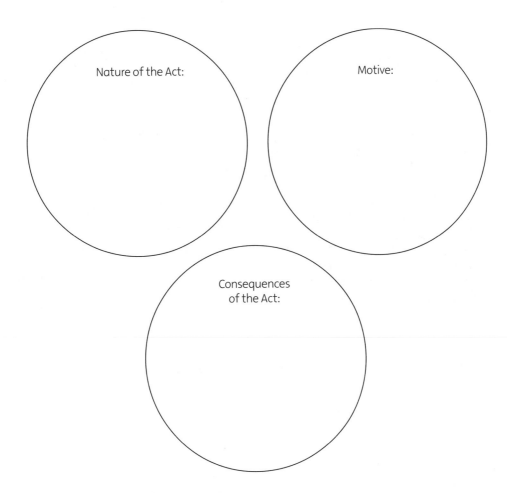

Nature of the Act:

Motive:

Consequences
of the Act:

A sample student essay is shown in Figure 5.6. The example shows excellent control of syntax and diction. It also shows the markers of emerging proficiency in academic argumentation. Both this essay and the one on gender and toys by the same thirteen-year-old writer (Figure 5.4) flip-flop a bit—a classic sign of a writer who's just beginning to learn how to negotiate multiple perspectives and address counterarguments. As she matures in this genre, this student will be able to more skillfully signal her own position on an issue when citing other writers.

"To Build a Fire" Persuasive Essay

"To Build a Fire", by Jack London, is a short story about a man and his dog, traveling in the wilderness in sub zero weather, struggling to survive. London weaves a tragic tale with inner meanings of how a man's own faults will be his demise. At the end of the story, the main character dies of cold, but whether or not he was the cause of his own death remains debatable. I believe that the man in London's "To Build a Fire" is responsible for his own death, due to the facts that he was unprepared and careless while he traveled.

To begin, the main character set off into the woods very unprepared. He did not listen to the old-timer at the beginning of the trail who warned him of traveling alone through dangerous weather. However, the man didn't take heed of the old-timer's advice and proceeded to call the old-timer "rather womanish." The man then continued his travels without a "trail-mate", which he instantly regretted later when he was so numb he needed someone to build a fire for him. In addition, the main character traveled too lightly, with nothing but a bundle of matches and a sandwich. The main character quickly began freezing to death, and, as he was out of supplies, could not do anything to save himself. In conclusion, the man was unprepared and irresponsible, which makes him responsible for his own death.

On the other hand, the man was a very quick and alert traveller. First, he was a smart man, and knew how to cross the frozen springs and where the hidden ice traps were. He had a good amount of survival skills and the basic know-how to being in the wilderness. The man knew the basics to staying warm and had mittens and other warm gear on him. Also, he was knowledgable about the land, and keenly observant. He paid attention to every detail along the trail, and when his "spittle had crackled in the air... undoubtedly it was colder than fifty below" or when he fell in ice water it was useless to run because "the circulation of wet and freezing feet cannot be restored by running when it is seventy-five below." Finally, the man knew how to build fires, and just how to set up the pile of sticks, twigs, and branches so it would burn. All in all, the main character was logical and smart, and did all he could to prevent his death.

Nevertheless, the man was responsible for his demise as he was too thoughtless and careless to keep himself alive. For example, during his travels, he tried not to stop and recuperate. The man wouldn't allow his body to get the rest and warmth it needed, a fatal error. To elaborate, the main character also built a fire under a tree burdened with snow. Another careless mistake on his part. The tree, jostled by the man, had loosened its hold on the snow covering its branches, "and it descended without warning upon the man and the fire, and the fire was blotted out!" Next, when the man tried to start another fire, this time out from under the trees, he used the whole bundle and "it flared into flame, seventy sulphur matches at once!" The man wasted all his matches, his last shot at survival, in one try, which proved worthless when he dropped the blazing matches into the snow where they extinguished with a finality. Conclusively, the man inevitably sealed the deal on his own death by being, overall, careless.

Altogether, Jack London's "To Build a Fire" has spun a thrilling tale on survival in which I feel that the main character is responsible for his own death. He was poorly prepared and too reckless to have been able to survive his journey. I think that he should have taken the time to find a traveling partner and have thoroughly been ready. Perhaps, if the main character had listened to the old-timer, he would have been able to reach his boys' after all.

FIGURE 5.6

Sample student essay on "To Build a Fire"

Understanding Epideictic Rhetoric

Epideictic rhetoric might seem to be the most antiquated of the three ends of rhetoric—after all, how long has it been since schools trained students in making funeral orations?—but the ceremonial function of rhetoric is probably the one students experience most often. From their parents' and teachers' lectures about the differences between wrong and right, to the inspirational stories of sports heroes, to movie and video game reviews, to comments on Yelp (or, heaven forbid, www.ratemyteacher.com), students have extensive exposure to judgments of virtue and vice.

For instance, driving to work, I heard a commentary by Frank Deford on National Public Radio about how baseball legend Pete Rose should enter the Hall of Fame alongside legend-in-the-making Ichiro Suzuki. Deford argued eloquently for the establishment of Rose's honor as a player, despite his dishonorable history as a team manager who placed bets on games. Notice the words *appropriate, shrine, damage, dishonored, deserves, proper,* and *lovely* in this example of epideictic rhetoric:

> It would also be so appropriate at that time for baseball to finally show some mercy to Pete Rose and let him enter the shrine with Suzuki. The drug cheats have put Rose's offense in perspective. He did not damage baseball one iota as a player, and his misdeed as a manager now appears as small beer alongside how those druggies dishonored the game, distorted history and robbed their fellow players. . . .
>
> If anyone deserves a pardon after all these years, before the petals fall, it is Rose, and for him and Suzuki to go together through that curtain—that noren—would be both proper and lovely. (2013)

Epideictic rhetoric is about a celebration or condemnation of a particular person, event, or cultural experience. While speakers might reference the past or future, the focus is on the present moment and the ties that bind us as living communities. The purpose of epideictic rhetoric is to strengthen our sense of shared values.

EPIDEICTIC RHETORIC AND CAREER READINESS

You can't get much more real-world than the insurance industry—something my husband knows all too well after twenty years of working as an auto and property claims manager. When I saw the letter my husband's company had sent its employees during Employee Stock Option Week, I knew that epideictic rhetoric was alive and well in the modern business world. The letter was a ceremonial affirmation of the company's worth and values. What follows is a paraphrase:

Dear Fellow Team Member and Shareholder:

We are pleased to report that our stock value increased significantly over the past year. As team members, we should all be proud of our contributions to this collective increase in share value. This positive result should encourage us to continue working hard to provide excellent service to our customers, overcome business challenges, and expand into new markets while remaining focused on our core values.

Please join us in celebrating our company's achievements and recognizing each other for the contributions we made to our company's success.

Sincerely,

Your Vice President

My husband shared that this same kind of ritualistic praise also happens annually when performance bonuses are awarded.

Although business schools will likely never use the term *epideictic rhetoric,* this genre is clearly part of the management toolkit . The secret of many a CEO's success is precisely this ability to rally employees around a shared vision and purpose, to praise achievements, and to censure faults.

Sample Epideictic Writing Prompt

Aldous Huxley's frequently taught novel *Brave New World* (1932) presents an excellent opportunity for students to practice their skills in praise and censure. The following epideictic prompt also includes extra practice in the doubting and believing game, since students are required to write two essays for this assignment—one arguing for the virtues of the World State of the novel and one arguing against its vices. Both essays (and much of imaginative literature) fit George A. Kennedy's general description of epideictic rhetoric as "any discourse that does not aim at a specific action but is intended to influence the values and beliefs of the audience" (1994, 4).

Directions to Students: The ability to read and write rhetorically includes the ability to entertain multiple perspectives. Persuasion often demands the ability to see both sides of an argument. This means that skillful rhetors must practice both "the believing game" and "the doubting game."

For this assignment, you will write two argument essays. The first essay must praise the World State as represented in Aldous Huxley's *Brave New World* as an ideal, master-planned community; the second essay must condemn or criticize the World State as an oppressive dystopia. Consider how issues such as social stability, personal freedom, art, culture, standards of living, sustainability, morality, education, and self-determination relate to your arguments for and against the World State. Be sure to look at what the characters say, too. Your purpose is to influence the values and beliefs of your audience. Each essay should be two to three pages in length and include examples from the novel, your experiences and observations, and outside reading.

When we have an epideictic assignment like this or similar ones that answer questions of quality, I help my students brainstorm some language they can use to praise or criticize their subject:

The Language of Praise

helpful, beneficial, supportive, productive, encouraging, constructive, hopeful, generative, reassuring, instructive, empowering, invigorating, inclusive, informed, and so on.

The Language of Blame

harmful, hurtful, destructive, damaging, corrosive, detrimental, enfeebling, enervating, debilitating, isolating, exclusionary, ignorant, and so on.

Notice that *positive* and *negative* are left off these lists; instead, these overly vague terms find themselves on my "Dead Words" list. See Chapter 6.

I also use the following prewriting activity (see also Appendix 12) to help students develop their arguments.

Epideictic Rhetoric: Ways to Praise

Directions to Students: According to Aristotle, praise can be deserved for being the first, the last, the only, the best, and the most consistent. He tells us we can praise something or someone by generating examples and by making positive and negative comparisons. The following prewriting exercise can help you think of support for an epideictic argument.

Subject for praise (X): _____.

Examples of Exceptionality
Directions: Complete all that apply.

1. X is/was the only _____ to _____.
2. Every _____ is/was_____by X.
3. X is/was the first to _____.
4. X is/was the last to _____.
5. X is/was/has the largest _____.

Positive and Negative Comparisons
Directions: Use Aristotle's model language to write your own comparisons.

1. X is/was better than Y. _____.
2. X is/was the best _____.
3. Y is/was worse than X. _____.
4. X is/was more consistent than Y. _____.

Here is my teacher example of ways to praise exceptionality using the Monterey Bay Aquarium as my subject. Try having your students create their own examples of positive and negative comparisons:

Subject for praise: The Monterey Bay Aquarium.

Examples of Exceptionality
Directions: **Complete all that apply.**

1. The Monterey Bay Aquarium is the only aquarium to have tuna on permanent exhibit in North America.

2. Every restaurant that participates in Seafood Watch was directly influenced by the Monterey Bay Aquarium's education and advocacy efforts.

3. The Monterey Bay Aquarium was the first aquarium to successfully exhibit Great White Sharks.

4. The Monterey Bay Aquarium was the first aquarium to successfully exhibit a living kelp forest.

5. The Monterey Bay Aquarium has the largest living exhibit of deep sea animals anywhere.

Classroom Activity: "A Lifetime of Learning"

Looking at models of the three different types of rhetoric and responding to deliberative, forensic, and epideictic writing prompts gives students a developing sense of how different rhetorical purposes lead to different choices in style, structure, and content. The goal at this point is to help students see the diverse range of meaning-making options available to writers.

A key step toward deepening students' understanding of how purpose functions in rhetorical situations is to analyze a text in context. I like to use texts whose backstories I know well since it's the unique details of audience and occasion that determine a writer's purpose. One of my favorite texts to use for a Purpose Analysis is a keynote address given by poet and American Book Award–winner Diana Garcia at the March 22, 2011, AVID Writers Conference at Cal State Monterey Bay. Garcia's collection of poems, *When Living Was a Labor Camp* (2000), offers a rich reflection on life in the migrant labor camps of California's San Joaquin Valley.

In addition to Garcia's superb writing skills and national renown, her keen understanding of the interests and experiences of the teenagers who were attending the conference made her a particularly inspiring speaker. AVID, or Advancement Via Individual Determination, is an academic support program aimed at helping underserved middle school and high school students achieve their college dreams. Garcia's audience at the AVID Writers Conference included over 400 high school and middle school students and their teachers, including many low-income and multilingual students from throughout the agricultural communities of the Salinas Valley who would be the first in their families to attend a four-year university.

It helps that I was sitting in the audience that day. It also helps that Diana's office is in the same building as mine. I asked Diana how the rhetorical situation presented by the AVID Writers Conference influenced her purpose. Her answers show us a writer's mind at work:

Jennifer: What do you know about the AVID program?

Diana: I've had AVID students in my college writing classes. Students begin our creative writing course by writing an educational autobiography that describes how their experiences have brought them to this point or almost derailed them. Several students have written about how AVID has helped them. I wish there had been an AVID program in the late sixties to describe to me and explain to me what a college education could offer.

Jennifer: How did knowing who would be in your audience that day influence your purpose and rhetorical strategies?

Diana: I wanted to begin by placing myself within the cultural expectation that girls sit in the backseat—that girls don't achieve. I wanted the students to identify with me. . . . I knew these were middle school and high school students, and I was a little concerned about talking about my single parenthood, but I knew these were adolescents, and I wanted to let them know what other possibilities [exist] if you have the drive and ambition, and you have the courage. I wanted to let them know, "You can do this!"

Jennifer: What did you want to accomplish through your keynote address? What did you want the students to know, feel, do, or believe?

Diana: I wanted to challenge [the AVID students] to face the difficulties of academic success. I wanted to inspire them to strive for more than they thought they were capable of achieving. I wanted to provoke their imaginations so they could envision themselves in this other world, this other country, so very different from the one in which they'd been raised. I also wanted them to trust in the learning curve that failure offers.

When I read Garcia's speech with my students, I emphasize that a keynote address is a purpose-driven genre. The *Oxford English Dictionary* defines a keynote as "a speech intended to set out or summarize the central theme of a conference, convention, etc., or to arouse enthusiasm for a party, cause, etc."—in other words, a speech intended to set a purpose.

I first ask my students to skim "A Lifetime of Learning" silently. (See Appendix 13 for the full speech.) Then we read Garcia's speech aloud to give it a sense of performance. While we read, my students use the Purpose Analysis graphic organizer as a note-taking tool (Figure 5.7, Appendix 14), capturing any insights the oral reading gives them into what Garcia might want her audience to think, feel, and do. I also ask students to highlight any words or phrases in the text that convey a sense of its purpose. For classes that need more scaffolding, I offer the hint that Garcia's speech is both a call to impassioned living and a celebration of what makes life worth living—thus serving two rhetorical ends.

What follows is an excerpt from Garcia's speech. Appendix 13 provides the full speech.

"A Lifetime of Learning"
By Diana Garcia

Take risks. Stay curious. Be ambitious. Learn to recognize opportunities. Learn from your failures. Never give up. If I could sum up a lifetime of learning, my own successes and failures would fall into several of these categories.

Growing up in the 50s and 60s, taking risks for a Chicana in the San Joaquin Valley was not considered acceptable behavior. As a female child, I learned to keep my voice low, my head lower, and my hands folded in my lap. No shouting, no running, no getting dirty. One of my earliest memories was coming to Monterey with my parents, my maternal grandparents, and my brother who was one year younger. I was probably five years old. When we got to the beach, my grandfather, father, and brother got out of the car and climbed down the shore toward the rocky outcroppings.

Mesmerized by the ocean, the waves crashing onto the shore, the powerful thunder they made as they attacked, I tried to get out of the car. My father yelled something about it was too dangerous. I remember thinking, if my younger brother could climb down, why couldn't I? I watched my brother scramble from one rock to the next, bending, stooping, yelling, tossing shells, rocks, and sand into the air. He was having fun. I was trapped between my mother and grandmother in the back seat of the car, safe, and furious. My father called me ungrateful when I refused the handful of sea glass that my brother offered me when they returned. The gift paled in comparison to the adventure he'd had. Even then, I knew that's what I wanted. I wanted my life to be an adventure.

As toddlers, we stumble from our beds in the morning conscious of cool tile beneath our feet, the brush of air along our arms, the way the fine hairs on our cheeks respond to changes in temperature. We race outside and see the intimate immensity of sky and yard. Each moment, each discovery, is fresh and new and brilliant. We know nothing and want to understand everything. We hide in the hollow of a tree trunk and imagine a fantastic world where birds talk a language we understand. We live in an ever-changing present, overwhelmed with what is, aware of how much we need to understand, unafraid of a future because the now is what concerns

Purpose Analysis

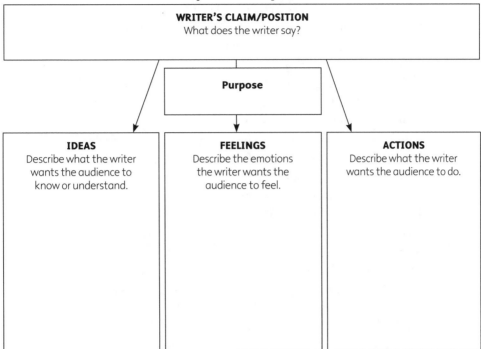

WRITER'S CLAIM/POSITION
What does the writer say?

Purpose

IDEAS
Describe what the writer wants the audience to know or understand.

FEELINGS
Describe the emotions the writer wants the audience to feel.

ACTIONS
Describe what the writer wants the audience to do.

PAST, PRESENT, OR FUTURE
Explain whether the writer wants the audience to make a judgment about the past, understand a statement about the present, or decide a course of action for the future.

Quick-Write: How would you describe the purpose of this text? What do you think the writer hopes to accomplish through his or her argument? Does the argument serve multiple purposes? If so, which one(s) is/are most important?

FIGURE 5.7
Purpose Analysis graphic organizer

us. Life is an adventure . . . and then we forget. Perhaps repetition and familiarity breed insensitivity. Perhaps red marks on math and English homework erode our willingness to take risks. Perhaps we learn that risk can result in failure, that adventure can lead to setback.

I moved to San Diego at age 23, a single mother on welfare. I knew no one, I had no place to live, but I had a job at SDSU. Over the next three years, I worked at Children's Hospital and then the San Diego County Department of Education, each time moving into positions that involved more responsibility, better pay, and better benefits. With several letters of recommendation, outstanding LSAT scores, and a full scholarship, I also went to law school. Never mind that I didn't even have a BA at the time. I knew how to research and how to write: I could do anything.

Here's where the failures began to creep in. I was working full-time during the day at the Dept. of Education and going to law school at night. I saw my son before and after school and during dinner, then I'd drop him at a friend's house while I went to law school. I won the Am Jur award for legal writing and quit my job so that I could accept a position as a poorly paid law clerk for the most prestigious real estate law firm in the county. Within a week I knew I'd made a big mistake. These were wealthy, powerful people working with and for wealthy, powerful people. I was neither. I hated how they talked about Chicano Park and poor people and Mexicans as if I weren't even there. I was invisible. In retrospect, I should have applied to work with one of the immigration rights law firms or with the public defenders' office. I just didn't know. So, I quit. I quit the firm, quit law school, and let regret eat at me each time I saw the list of names of former classmates who had passed the bar exam. . . .

During the day, for three years I worked as a personnel manager for an electronics research, development, and manufacturing firm. I knew nothing about the world of electronics research or personnel management, but I recognized an opportunity when I saw it. I was bilingual, I knew shorthand, and I was a strong researcher and convincing writer. I learned my way around the growing field of computer technology, patent applications, and business licensing. I learned how to put together an employees' handbook and a personnel manual. I learned how to conduct new employee orientations and seminars on patent law documentation procedures.

One day, the president of the electronics firm asked me when I planned to finish my degree. He told me I was ambitious. The first time he called me ambitious I wondered what I'd said or done to make him think so poorly of me. After all, in my culture, to be ambitious means you set yourself above the other members of your community. To be ambitious means that you want to leave that community behind, shake its dust from your heels, and pretend the past never existed.

When he called me ambitious a second time, I thought about how much I respected him. I considered his renown as a physicist and mathematician, the fact that he loved opera and was a wonderful writer. He seemed to think ambition was an admirable quality. I paid attention and went back to college part-time. When the electronics firm lost a major contract and had to lay off a quarter of our workforce, I laid myself off, too. What some people saw as a terrible decision, I recognized as an opportunity. I went back to college full-time.

Probably the biggest risk I took was switching from a major in business psychology to an English major with a creative writing emphasis. Yet, that decision changed my life. After 21 years of going to school part-time, applying for leaves of absence, and generally muddling through a degree program, I finally got a BA.

[*After sharing her story of how she became a writer—a journey that took Garcia from California to Connecticut and back—Garcia closes her keynote address with a special message for her young audience.*]

Perhaps you remember someone telling you when you were five years old, "Stop asking so many questions!" That was a long time ago. Now is the time to be curious. There is so much to know. Often the simplest questions raise the most complicated answers. Learn to relish complexity. When you've exhausted your sources, go and experience for yourself. Be ready to leave familiar surroundings and explore new parts of the world. By the way, learn at least one other language. The world grows smaller each day.

There will always be a new app and new software and the latest and fastest technology to capture your attention. Just remember, don't let technology be a substitute for your life. Life is for living. Remember to be there for those who love you, for those who encourage you, for those who have faith in you.

Finally, remember to breathe. Take long walks through fields of native wildflowers. Turn your face towards a clear sky; pretend you're a suncup in April. Play. Pretend. Imagine.

Your life is an adventure. Don't settle for less.

After we finish the oral reading, I ask my students to compare their Purpose Analysis with a partner's, adding any details or insights their partner may have captured that they missed. Students then compare their amended Purpose Analysis to a teacher-prepared sample (Figure 5.8), again adding any information they may have overlooked.

We close this activity by discussing how Garcia's keynote address combines elements of deliberative and epideictic rhetoric. Through the Purpose Analysis, students see how Garcia's speech serves both as a call to action, making specific recommendations to students about how they should live their lives, and as an affirmation of the values and behaviors that characterize lifelong learning. These two complementary ends—the one exhortative, the other celebratory—work together to set a meaningful purpose for the day.

> **What's important overall for students to see is how a motivational speech like Garcia's uses a significantly different tone and style from other types of rhetoric, such as a forensic analysis of what's causing the decline in reading habits in America. The take-away learning is that rhetorical choices are made based on the purpose a text serves.**

Distinguishing Among Different Purposes for Writing

Beyond Aristotle's three ends of rhetoric, there are other ways for students to think about the kinds of purposes texts serve. Drawing on the classical tradition, Bean, Chappell, and Gillam identify eight rhetorical aims or purposes that writers typically seek to accomplish in academic contexts:

Express and reflect

Inquire and explore

Inform and explain

Analyze and interpret

Take a stand

Evaluate and judge

Propose a solution

Seek common ground (2011, 25–27)

An essay that informs and explains attempts to impact what we know; an essay that evaluates and judges or that seeks common ground attempts to impact what we value; and an essay that proposes a solution attempts to impact how we act. We can imagine the exigence behind each of these aims: (1) ignorance, (2) indifference, and (3) inaction.

Purpose Analysis

WRITER'S CLAIM/POSITION
What does the writer say?
"Your life is an adventure. Don't settle for less."

Purpose
To inspire, encourage, and motivate teen writers

IDEAS
Describe what the writer wants the audience to know or understand.

Garcia wants the teenagers at the Writers Conference to know that failure, risk, ambition, curiosity, opportunity, and persistence are essential to learning and thriving.

FEELINGS
Describe the emotions the writer wants the audience to feel.

She probably wants her audience to feel motivated, empowered, and reassured. Speaking as someone who has "been there," Garcia lets her listeners know that failure is an important part of lifelong learning. She also wants her audience to feel that it's OK to stand up for themselves.

ACTIONS
Describe what the writer wants the audience to do.

Garcia wants the young writers to take chances and to live life fully and passionately. She wants them to have faith in themselves, to be determined, and to take ownership for their own learning.

PAST, PRESENT, OR FUTURE
Explain whether the writer wants the audience to make a judgment about the past, understand a statement about the present, or decide a course of action for the future.

Garcia's speech offers students advice for how to live their future lives.

Quick-Write: How would you describe the purpose of this text? What do you think the writer hopes to accomplish through his or her argument? Does the argument serve multiple purposes? If so, which one(s) is/are most important?

Garcia's overall purpose is to inspire the students at the conference to make the most of their lives and their educations, but she's also trying to set the tone for the day, so that students will appreciate why writing is so important. An additional purpose she has is to reassure those students who might come from backgrounds similar to hers; she wants them to know that she faced multiple challenges that ultimately contributed to her success and her art and that they can persist and thrive in the face of their challenges, too.

FIGURE 5.8
Teacher model of Purpose Analysis for "A Lifetime of Learning"

Writing a Statement of Purpose

Esteemed composition scholar Maxine Hairston (1986) recommends that students write a statement of purpose before they begin composing so that they don't waste time and effort wandering off topic. Teacher-prepared purpose statements can also help focus students' attention when reading complex informational texts. Using the preceding list of rhetorical purposes from Bean, Chappell, and Gillam (2011), I share sample statements of purpose with my students to show them what these might look like:

To inquire into and explore the causes of colony collapse in honeybees

To inform teens and explain the connection between energy drinks and high-risk behaviors

To analyze and interpret the problem of stereotype threat in American culture

To evaluate and judge the benefits and drawbacks of gated communities

To propose a solution to the underrepresentation of women in the STEM fields

It's important to help kids recognize that texts can have primary, secondary, and even tertiary purposes. One difference that real-world writing often does have from school writing is that it resists easy classification by genre or purpose. When we look at published texts, we find writers start heading in one direction only to take us somewhere else by the end. Many times writers have to address one purpose on the way to a bigger goal; they have to inform before they can evaluate or analyze before they can take a stand.

Reading Prefaces and Abstracts

Another strategy for teaching kids about purpose is to alert them to the places in texts where writers typically state their intentions. Raise your hand if you, like me, used to skip reading the preface or abstract to a text in your own high school or undergraduate education. When I was a student, these textual appendages always seemed like extra homework to me. If I'd been assigned a novel or article to read, then, by golly, I was going to read the novel or article and nothing else. I wasn't going to spend my time reading something that "didn't count."

Of course, in retrospect, I see that I missed a critical opportunity to identify a text's purpose before reading—something that would have made my homework easier, not harder. Reading a text's preface or abstract, in fact, is almost like reading its cheat codes. Look at this abstract for a scholarly article from the *Journal of Adolescent Health* on the correlation between energy drinks and high-risk behavior:

"Energy Drinks, Race, and Problem Behaviors Among College Students"
Kathleen E. Miller

Abstract
Purpose

This study examined relationships between energy drink consumption and problem behaviors among adolescents and emerging adults. It was hypothesized that frequent consumption of energy drinks would be positively associated with substance abuse and other risky behaviors, and that these relationships would be moderated by race. . . .

Results

Frequency of energy drink consumption was positively associated with marijuana use, sexual risk-taking, fighting, seatbelt omission, and taking risks on a dare for the sample as a whole, and associated with smoking, drinking, alcohol problems, and illicit prescription drug use for white students but not for black students.

Conclusions

These findings suggest that energy drink consumption is closely associated with a problem behavior syndrome, particularly among whites. Frequent consumption of energy drinks may serve as a useful screening indicator to identify students at risk for substance use and/or other health-compromising behavior. (2002)

The article itself is quite a challenging read but not unrepresentative of the kind of text complexity called for by the Common Core at the senior level (see English Language Arts Appendix A at the Common Core website). However, without a careful study of the abstract first, the article's dense content and specialized language would be almost impenetrable to most teenagers.

For books with prefaces, identifying the purpose usually involves a search for key words and signal phrases. I show my students how prefaces often include phrases like *my purpose* or *this book aims* or *my intention.* Take, for example, this excerpt from the textbook *Rhetorical Grammar: Grammatical Choices, Rhetorical Effects* by Martha Kolln and Loretta Gray:

Rhetorical Grammar brings together the insights of composition researchers and linguists; it makes the connection between writing and grammar that has been missing from our classrooms. It also avoids the prescriptive rules and error correction of handbooks, offering instead explanations of the rhetorical choices that are available. And, perhaps what is most important, it gives students confidence in their own language ability by helping them recognize the intuitive grammar expertise that all human beings share.

This difference in the purpose of *Rhetorical Grammar* is especially important. Too often the grammar lessons that manage to find their way into the writing classroom are introduced for remedial purposes: to fix comma splices and misplaced modifiers and agreement errors and such. As a consequence, the study of grammar has come to have strictly negative, remedial associations—a Band-Aid for weak and inexperienced writers, rather than a rhetorical tool that all writers should understand and control. (2013, xiii)

My students and I look at a passage like this together and talk about what we notice. What words or phrases indicate that Kolln and Gray are trying to solve a problem? What do they say is different about their approach? What do they want for students?

Classroom Activity: Writing a Preface

After analyzing a few prefaces together, I ask my students to try their own hand at writing about purpose in this explicit way. I find this activity works best after students have prepared a final, revised, and edited draft of a research paper or argument essay—although trying to write a preface for a work-in-progress can also be illuminating. Other versions of this assignment include a cover letter, abstract, or rhetorical précis. See Figure 5.9 for a student sample.

Directions to Students: In a preface to your research paper or argument essay, explain to your audience why you wrote this piece and what you hope will be the impact of it. Be sure to directly tell your target readers why the text they are about to read is important. This is your chance to motivate your audience to read what you've written and to offer any insights or explanations that you, as the writer, think might be helpful. As you write, consider the following questions:

Why were you motivated to write about this topic?

Why is your topic important?

What need or problem does your topic address?

What's your purpose?

What do you hope to accomplish through your writing?

What unique contribution does your writing make?

FIGURE 5.9

Cindy's preface

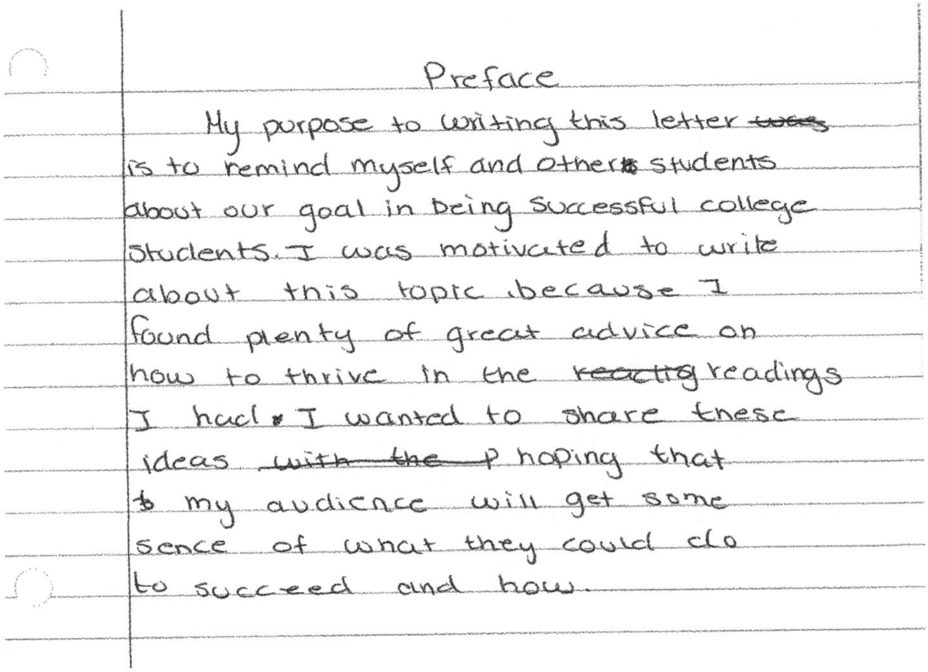

> Preface
>
> My purpose to writing this letter ~~was~~ is to remind myself and other students about our goal in being successful college students. I was motivated to write about this topic because I found plenty of great advice on how to thrive in the ~~reading~~ readings I had. I wanted to share these ideas ~~with the~~ P hoping that my audience will get some sence of what they could do to succeed and how.

Writing a preface is a measure of how genuinely engaged students are with their subject. If they're just going through the motions—in other words, if their purpose is just to get a decent grade—it's going to show. Take away authentic purpose, Hairston says, and you have "a voiceless paper written only to fulfill a requirement" (1986, 81). I tell my students, "You're not practicing how to write when a teacher forces you; you're practicing how to write for real purposes, audiences, and occasions."

Revising Through the Lens of Purpose

"Not fit for purpose." A bit harsh, but this is how I heard a critic describe some data the British government had collected on immigration in a recent news story on NPR. The critic's point—that the data was too general and imprecise to be used for the intended purpose for which it was gathered—is one we want our students to grasp. They also need to know when their evidence and appeals are fit for their purpose and when they're not.

Revising with the idea of what is appropriate or helpful to their purpose can be a transformative experience for students. Instead of worrying over whether what they've written is "correct" or not, students focus on whether or not their writing accomplishes what they want it to accomplish given the constraints of their rhetorical situation. This takes the emphasis off personal feelings and puts it on functionality, making effective writing a matter of what works.

From this perspective, an evaluation of a writer's rhetorical choices all comes down to how well they get the job done. Writing on this connection between ends and means, composition scholar John T. Gage offers the following advice to students:

1. Try to be as clear as possible about what purpose you want your writing to achieve.

2. Use your intended purposes as the test for deciding whether any given part is necessary and whether any additional parts are needed.

3. Make your own sense of purpose clear to the readers too, so that they can follow the parts and the transitions between them as they progress through the writing. (2000, 9)

Gage further reminds students that "the purpose of a composition is its *whole* purpose, the sum of its parts" (2000, 9; original emphasis). Purpose is much larger than rhetorical effects, the accumulation of which work together in the service of the purpose.

Students can practice purposeful revision through Descriptive Outlining (see page 37 in Chapter 2). As a reading strategy, Descriptive Outlining asks students to identify not only what a writer says, but also what he or she *does* in each section of a text. As a revision strategy, Descriptive Outlining directs students' attention to the reasons behind the rhetorical choices they've made. If they don't see a good reason for a particular move they've made—or if they've already made this move several times—then students might want to change or omit what they've written. One of my students, Elliott, says descriptive outlining helps him see "what's adding to the argument and what's just filling up pages." The purpose-focused question students must ask themselves throughout this activity is "What am I trying to do here?"

The following list of verbs can help students think about their aim or intention in each section of their writing:

examines	turns	compares	clarifies
challenges	illustrates	contrasts	interrogates
questions	demonstrates	concludes	critiques
introduces	performs	analyzes	undermines
provides	connects	evaluates	subverts
addresses	integrates	synthesizes	establishes
complicates	relates	summarizes	makes
switches	shows	offers	
transitions	moves	exemplifies	
assumes	describes	documents	

Real-World Purposes and College Readiness

Understanding how authentic rhetorical purposes shape communication can present a significant hurdle for students who are trying to cross intellectual thresholds not only between simplistic and deep learning but also between the worlds of K–12 and higher education. Composition scholar Charles Bazerman explains why: "College students find themselves located in new worlds of literacy. They are moving from the simplified, defined worlds of textbooks and official knowledge into the multiple literacies of different disciplines and professions" (1995, ix). The earlier we can prepare students for this transition, the better.

By directing high school students' attention to authentic writing situations, we're trying to shift their focus from "What do I need to do to get an A?" to "Does this work?" This redirection away from a grade-based purpose to a communication-based purpose is important. One teacher I heard at a workshop expressed it this way: "It's the difference between having to say something and having something to say" (a nice chiasmus for you rhetoric fans). A colleague at San Francisco State University calls writing where the only exigence is a need to pass a class "holding a grade to our students' heads." Giving our students real contexts and purposes for writing not only acts as a performance enhancer but also helps them move further down the path toward independence.

How do we do this? We can start by looking at what *not* to do. In "Beyond 'Is This OK?': High School Writers Building Understandings of Genre," Anne Elrod Whitney, Michael Ridgeman, and Gary Masquelier describe how the "arhetorical" approach used in many high school English classes makes it difficult for students to develop an authentic sense of occasion, audience, and purpose:

> The problem with much writing in schools is how false it is. For example, many students write "literary essays" mimicking journal articles of a type they have never read. They write for unspecified audiences, which really means individual teachers, or they write for teachers or examiners posing as outside audiences, as in "letters to the principal" that are never sent. They write in genres they have never read, or they read without attention to the work as situated in any particular discourse community other than that of the classroom. (2011, 526)

In place of decontextualized, perfunctory writing, we can engage students in meaningful academic conversations. We can help them see that writing starts with reading and that reading starts with listening. In this way, students practice reading as a writer (i.e., learning rhetorical moves from what they read) and writing as a reader (i.e., attending to their discourse community as they write). Many of the activities in this chapter, as well as those in books such as Kelly Gallagher's *Write Like This* (2011), use precisely this combination of mentor texts and attention to the rhetorical situation to foster students' success in postsecondary writing.

Conclusion

Understanding the different kinds and combinations of rhetorical purposes writers achieve begins with understanding writing as authentic communication. From there, students learn that the different rhetorical choices a writer makes are based on what he or she wants a particular audience to think, feel, believe, or do. As they develop a fuller understanding of the reasons *why* writers write, students learn to judge arguments not by what counts for a class but by what works for a specific audience and occasion. They learn to see outcomes in terms of effective decision making, the achievement of justice, and the celebration of our most cherished values—not just a test score or letter grade.

> Reading-based writing provides both mentor texts and rhetorical situations. Often the problem with topic-based writing prompts (rather than text-based prompts) is that there's no easily identifiable model or context for the task students are to perform. If we ask students to write about gun control or sustainability without giving them any readings, for instance, it's difficult for them to know which audience and occasion they're addressing because there are thousands, sometimes millions of different conversations happening on these issues. In other words, it's hard for students to strategize rhetorically about how they want to position themselves if the field is too broad. Starting with a text-based argument allows the students to find and learn from the other writers in that conversation (by checking the works cited, for example) and to get a better grasp of a particular rhetorical situation.

Points to Remember

As you plan your lessons and teach the concepts described in this chapter, you might want to refer to the following list of points to remember:

1. A writer's purpose is shaped by the contingencies of the rhetorical situation, especially the audience and occasion.

2. Writers make choices about their style, structure, and means of persuasion based on their purpose.

3. Aristotle's three ends of rhetoric—deliberative, forensic, and epideictic—can help students see how purpose relates to specific settings and time provinces.

4. Purpose can be a challenging threshold concept for students who haven't experienced authentic writing situations.

5. Learning about where and how writers communicate their purpose in a text—such as in abstracts or prefaces—helps students to be more strategic readers.

Prompts for Quick-Writes or Pairs Conversations

The following prompts can be used before, during, or after a lesson to help students make personal connections, deepen their understanding, and reflect on their learning:

1. Describe a time when you tried to inform someone about something they didn't know or didn't understand. What was missing or inaccurate in your audience's knowledge base that you were trying to change?

2. Describe a time when you tried to change how someone valued something.

3. Describe a time when you tried to change how someone felt about a situation. What emotions did you want your audience to experience?

4. Describe a time when you tried to change someone's actions. How did you want this person or this group to behave differently?

5. Have you ever influenced someone's future plans or actions? How did you do this?

6. Have you ever changed someone's feelings about the present? For example, maybe you helped someone see a negative situation more positively or realistically. If so, how did you do this?

7. Have you ever influenced someone's feelings about the past? For example, maybe you changed someone's opinion about a past event or relationship. If so, how did you do this?

8. Whose lives have you changed? Describe examples.

9. Whom do you influence? Describe examples.

10. Describe something you made or accomplished. What means did you use to achieve your end?

CHAPTER 6

Analyzing and Integrating Ethos, Pathos, and Logos

Persuasion must in every case be effected either (1) by working on the emotions of the judges themselves, (2) by giving them the right impression of the speakers' character, or (3) by proving the truth of the statements made.

—ARISTOTLE

Think of the kinds of questions your students ask you about a big argument essay you've assigned:

How long does it have to be?

Do I have to use direct quotations?

Can I use *I* in my writing?

Do I have to include a works-cited list?

Is it OK to tell a personal story?

Do I have to talk about the other side?

Of course, the very first questions students ask will be "How much is this worth?" and "When is this due?" but when students do get around to asking questions about style and content, how do we know how to answer?

Helping Students Figure Out the Answers

Teaching students to think rhetorically about literacy tasks isn't about teaching them formulas for academic writing; it's about teaching students how to figure stuff out. The whole point of learning about ethos, pathos, and logos is to discover when and how and why real writers use appeals to character, emotion, and logic—and what moves we can borrow from the professionals to use in our own writing.

Consequently, when my students ask me if they have to use sources or if they can include a personal story and use *I* in their academic writing, I give them some detective work to do. I show my students recent scholarly articles and books from English studies (e.g., literature, rhetoric, linguistics, and composition) and challenge them to find their own answers. How are the people who work in this field actually doing their work?

Google Scholar works great if you don't have hard copies of these kinds of mentor texts. Better yet, if your school library subscribes to one of the databases that provides access to the MLA International Bibliography (http://www.mla.org/bibliography), like EBSCO or ProQuest, your students could survey a variety of scholarly texts. It helps to do this as a whole-class demonstration the first time.

> *Directions to Students:* Skim a few articles or books from the field of English studies, paying special attention to *how* scholars in this field make their arguments. You don't have to figure out *what* the scholars are saying at this point; just notice their style and strategies in general. Then answer the following questions with a partner or small group:
>
>> Do English studies scholars currently use the first person pronoun (*I*) in their writing?
>>
>> Do they include anecdotes?
>>
>> Do they support their arguments with evidence? If so, what kind of evidence?
>>
>> Do they document their sources using MLA style?

My students find, often much to their surprise, that twenty-first-century scholars do all these things. I have books on literature, history, language, gender, and culture sitting on my office shelves right now that are full of personal anecdotes related through the first person. Of course, the anecdotes are buttressed by rigorous scholarly evidence, carefully documented in MLA style.

Approaching writing rhetorically is about being aware of what works for a particular audience, occasion, and purpose (not what is intrinsically right or wrong) and knowing when the expectations for that rhetorical situation change. What was true in academic writing forty years ago is not necessarily true today. Learning to recognize the characteristics of a genre that they need to master is one of the most important and transferrable skills students can acquire and is crucial to postsecondary success. When real writers write for work, civic engagement, or publication, they make a close study of successful models of writing in their chosen area to see what passes muster with a given discourse community.

In many ways, the previous three chapters were about helping students figure out what's happening and who's involved in the rhetorical situation. This chapter on ethos, pathos, and logos is about taking students back into the text—whether another writer's or their own—to work out the strategies behind rhetorical responses to different situations.

Enter Ethos, Pathos, and Logos

The preceding section's student questions on style and content are also questions on ethos, pathos, and logos. When students ask if they can include a personal story, they're asking about how ethos and pathos should function in their essay. When they ask if they have to use sources or address other views, they're asking about the importance of ethos and logos to the assignment.

First, a quick review of these terms from Aristotle's *Rhetoric*. Aristotle says that since rhetoric exists in order to affect decision making, a speaker must "not only try to make the argument of his speech demonstrative and worthy of belief; he must also make his own character look right and put his hearers, who are to decide, into the right frame of mind" (1984; Book II, Chapter 1). In other words, speakers must satisfy the intellectual and emotional needs of their audience while establishing their own credibility if they're going to get the outcome they're after. From these requirements are derived the three rhetorical appeals: (1) logos—the "proof" that demonstrates the "truth" of an argument, (2) ethos—the "right" appearance of the speaker's character, and (3) pathos—the "right" frame of mind of the audience.

Pathos, Logos, and . . . Eros? The Three Rhetorical Appeals as Threshold Concepts

When I was a tender undergraduate first bruising myself against the limits of my intellect, I took a course in rhetoric from a brilliant British scholar who scared the wits out of me. One day I mustered the courage to respond to a question he had posed to the class. He had introduced the topic of persuasion and asked if anyone knew the classical rhetorical appeals Aristotle recommended to influence audiences. One eager student volunteered "pathos" while another said "logos." Out of my dim memory I seemed to recall that there was a third appeal that began with the letter *e*.

"Eros?" I ventured.

"No," my professor answered with a slight smile, "but that's interesting."

Another student then provided the correct response, "ethos," and the lecture continued. Knowing that I had given the wrong name for the appeal I intended to identify—that is, persuasion through shared identification with an ethical or admirable character—I began to have serious misgivings about what I'd actually said. The professor soon solved the mystery for me. In concluding remarks he made before a lecture hall of eighty students, he summarized the three appeals and then added, "But as Jennifer reminds us, we should also never underestimate the power of sex appeal."

Although the joke was on me, this incident helped me better understand the potent mix of persuasive appeals at the command of rhetors—a compound that includes humor as one of its most powerful ingredients. It also showed me how much trouble I could get into if I tried to use Greek terms I only understood superficially (or not at all).

For our students, understanding that different means of persuasion not only work on the audience but also work with each other makes up another major threshold competency on their path to college readiness. Being able to see the interactions and tensions among ethos, pathos, and logos in an act of communication requires a good deal of sophistication. When students first start working with these concepts, they often try to keep each appeal in its own box: "*Now* the writer's using logos, but earlier he was making an appeal to emotion." As they develop a fuller understanding of these concepts, however, students

> Like the definitions of *audience, occasion,* and *purpose,* the definitions of *ethos, pathos,* and *logos* are pretty easy for kids to learn. It is harder for them to understand how to integrate and apply these concepts.

are better able to embrace the complex and sometimes contradictory ways these rhetorical appeals function as a whole in arguments. They learn to see the forest instead of just the trees.

It's also a challenge to work out how the appeals connect to other rhetorical concepts. For example, Purdue University's Online Writing Lab (OWL) lists logos, ethos, and pathos under the heading "Aristotle's Rhetorical Situation" (Sproat, Driscoll, and Brizee 2012b; see http://owl.english.purdue.edu/owl/resource/625/03/). In the classical view, pathos relates to audience, logos relates to the text or "word," and ethos relates to the writer or speaker. If it seems like all these terms are almost too close kin to untangle, that's about right. In the following description from OWL, notice how the Aristotelian terms intersect with contemporary understandings of the rhetorical situation:

Logos

Logos is frequently translated as some variation of "logic or reasoning," but it originally referred to the actual content of a speech and how it was organized. Today, many people may discuss the logos qualities of a text to refer to how strong the logic or reasoning of the text is. But logos more closely refers to the structure and content of the text itself. In this resource, logos means "text."

Ethos

Ethos is frequently translated as some variation of "credibility or trustworthiness," but it originally referred to the elements of a speech that reflected on the particular character of the speaker or the speech's author. Today, many people may discuss ethos qualities of a text to refer to how well authors portray themselves. But ethos more closely refers to an author's perspective more generally. In this resource, ethos means "author."

Pathos

Pathos is frequently translated as some variation of "emotional appeal," but it originally referred to the elements of a speech that appealed to any of an audience's sensibilities. Today, many people may discuss the pathos qualities of a text to refer to how well an author appeals to an audience's emotions. Pathos as "emotion" is often contrasted with logos as "reason." But this is a limited understanding of both pathos and logos; pathos more closely refers to an audience's perspective more generally. In this resource, pathos means "audience." (Sproat, Driscoll, and Brizee 2012)

You can see why grappling with how these concepts correspond to one another is both enriching and challenging for students. Trying to isolate one component in an argument can be like trying to pull one thread from a spiderweb. My goal is to move students through the frustration and confusion to a place where they're comfortable with complexity.

In their work on threshold concepts, Meyer and Land describe a period when learners "oscillate between superficial and more sophisticated understandings" of a concept (2003, 1). I see this clearly in my own students when we first start to work with the concepts of ethos, pathos, and logos. Students generally understand that these three appeals represent different ways to persuade audiences, and they can define the terms pretty readily. They also have

FIGURE 6.1

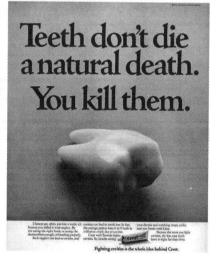

FIGURE 6.2

FIGURE 6.3

a fairly easy time identifying dominant appeals in advertisements, especially if the ad takes a simplistic approach to persuasion. For instance, the toothpaste ads shown in Figures 6.1, 6.2, and 6.3 were easy for my students to label as using ethical, logical, or emotional appeals.

Students had no trouble seeing how Figure 6.1 uses a celebrity spokesperson (ethos), how Figure 6.2 uses fear (pathos), and how Figure 6.3 uses claims about "scientific" proof and measurability (logos) to promote their products.

But academic arguments are far more complex than advertisements. Reading and writing academic arguments demands a sophisticated understanding of shared identification, human emotion, and logic. In teaching ethos, pathos, and logos, moving students past the threshold means moving them from a passive recognition of basic persuasive strategies to an expressive application of complex concepts.

Learning at the Threshold

Teaching in California, where a rhetorical approach to texts has been widely used over the last ten years, thanks to the CSU Expository Reading and Writing Course, I find that most of the recent high school graduates I encounter have at least heard of ethos, pathos, and logos. I suspect that with the Common Core's focus on argumentation this will increasingly be the case nationally, too. But having heard of the three rhetorical appeals and knowing how to use them with complex texts are two different things. Learning to analyze, integrate, evaluate, and apply the threshold concepts of ethos, pathos, and logos takes intellectual maturity.

What does an understanding of these three rhetorical appeals look like before students have crossed this developmental threshold? A beginner's use of these terms tends to be pretty simplistic. A student may even confuse the definitions like I did. This is a normal stage of intellectual growth. The point is never to deride beginners for being beginners but rather to help students recognize when they're progressing from emergent to advanced levels of proficiency.

How do we know when students haven't crossed the rhetorical appeals threshold yet? Essays that read like a Mad Lib of argumentation are a clue. You can almost see the embedded directions in the students' writing:

1. Name a rhetorical appeal
2. Name a logical fallacy
3. List a type of evidence
4. Make a counterargument or concession
5. List an emotion

This superficial use of rhetorical concepts exemplifies the "suspended state [of pretransformational learning] in which understanding approximates to a kind of mimicry or lack of authenticity" (Meyer and Land 2003, 10).

Another pitfall beginners tend to fall into is the thesis statement based on rhetorical appeals: "In [insert title of text], the writer uses ethos, pathos, and logos to [identify purpose]." The student who wants to mix things up a bit might swap out an appeal for "diction" or "syntax," but the resulting claim is just as vague and formulaic. Perhaps one of the greatest drawbacks to Aristotelian rhetoric is that its easy numerical divisions fit all too well into the five-paragraph essay structure—not that's there's any real sense to that move, as one of my students learned to her chagrin. When Anyssa proposed writing an argument essay with one paragraph on ethos, one on logos, and one on pathos, I asked her what that would look like in terms of content: "How will that organizational structure help you answer your question at issue?" She quickly stalled. Ethos, pathos, and logos are more about what a text does than says; they're the means a writer uses to achieve his or her end, not the end itself.

Author and teacher Carol Jago says we have to take the first-person *I* away from middle school writers so we can give it back to them in the twelfth grade. In the same way, it might not be a bad idea to take the terms *ethos, pathos,* and *logos* away from students for a while as they learn to write about the writer's image, the audience's frame of mind, and the text's content and structure.

Looking at the Three Appeals in Action: "Is Algebra Necessary?" by Andrew Hacker

The best way to help students integrate and apply the three appeals is to have them work with whole, authentic texts. Using the following article from the *New York Times,* my students and I analyze how political scientist Andrew Hacker uses ethos, pathos, and logos to argue against making algebra a high school graduation requirement. We typically do this kind of rhetorical analysis as part of the doubting game (see Chapter 2)—after we've faithfully worked to understand the writer's main idea in our first reading of the Hacker article. (You can find Hacker's full article at http://www.nytimes.com/2012/07/29/opinion/sunday/is-algebra-necessary.html?pagewanted=all&_r=0.)

As students reread the opening paragraphs of "Is Algebra Necessary?" I ask them to consider the following questions about ethos, pathos, and logos:

Questions About Ethos

1. What kind of persona does Hacker create for himself? Does he seem concerned? Compassionate? Reasonable? Informed? Reflective?

2. What role is Hacker taking in relation to his audience?

3. How does Hacker use his personal qualifications and experience to support his argument?

4. Why does Hacker use the words *I* and *we*?

5. What does it say about Hacker that his article is published in the *New York Times*? Hacker is also a frequent contributor to the *New York Review of Books*. How does that fact impact his ethos?

Questions About Pathos

1. Does Hacker use any emotionally charged, or "loaded," language? What words, if any, seem intended to draw out an emotional response from the audience? What are the connotations of these words?

2. What emotions (e.g., desire, fear, outrage, pity, compassion, frustration, etc.), if any, does Hacker appeal to?

3. What strategy does Hacker use to make the audience feel like it has a personal stake in this issue?

Questions About Logos

1. Does Hacker anticipate any counterarguments to his position? If so, how?

2. Does Hacker qualify any of his claims? If so, how?

3. Does Hacker make any concessions to the other side? If so, how?

4. What kind of evidence does Hacker use?

5. What assumptions does Hacker make, either explicitly or implicitly?

"Is Algebra Necessary?"
by Andrew Hacker

A typical American school day finds some six million high school students and two million college freshmen struggling with algebra. In both high school and college, all too many students are expected to fail. Why do we subject American students to this ordeal? I've found myself moving toward the strong view that we shouldn't.

My question extends beyond algebra and applies more broadly to the usual mathematics sequence, from geometry through calculus. State regents and legislators—and much of the public—take it as self-evident that every young person should be made to master polynomial functions and parametric equations.

There are many defenses of algebra and the virtue of learning it. Most of them sound reasonable on first hearing; many of them I once accepted. But the more I examine them, the clearer it seems that they are largely or wholly wrong—unsupported by research or evidence, or based on wishful logic. (I'm not talking about quantitative skills, critical for informed citizenship and personal finance, but a very different ballgame.)

This debate matters. Making mathematics mandatory prevents us from discovering and developing young talent. In the interest of maintaining rigor, we're actually depleting our pool of brainpower. I say this as a writer

FIGURE 6.4

Our PAPA Square for Andrew Hacker's article "Is Algebra Necessary?"

PAPA Square

Through a PAPA Square, students analyze the **P**urpose, **A**rgument, **P**ersona, and **A**udience of a text. Around the perimeter of the box, students answer the following questions in response to their own writing: Who is my audience? What is the persona, or public image, that I create for myself through my language choices and tone? What is my thesis or argument? What is my purpose or desired outcome of my argument (i.e., What would I like my reader to do if he or she is persuaded by me?)? In the center of the PAPA Square, students identify the stylistic devices and emotional, logical, and ethical appeals they use to persuade their audience. These may include types of evidence, figurative language, text structures (e.g., cause and effect), and tone. (Adapted from the CSU Expository Reading and Writing Course.)

PURPOSE

To bring attention to the problems caused by requiring algebra for high school graduation and college admission; to change educational policy

RHETORICAL DEVICES AND STRATEGIES

Pathos—loaded language: "toll," "precious," "onerous stumbling block," "shame," "exclude," "prohibitive mathematics," "struggled," "regiment," and "depressing"; uses dramatic numbers ("six million high school students") and frightening statistics ("one in four ninth graders fail to finish high school")

Figurative language—block, wall, huge boulder, hoop, badge, totem

Logos—makes frequent counterarguments and concessions; anticipates possible objections; uses numerical data and expert testimony

Ethos—establishes credibility through firsthand experience and academic qualifications ("I say this as a writer and social scientist . . ."); shares personal observations; relates stories from colleagues

Attention to audience—appeals to his audience members' dual interests in social justice and our national economy; suggests removing the algebra obstacle is good for students, businesses, and government because America will stop wasting resources and increase its talent pool

parenthetical asides to the audience—sounds like Hacker is speaking directly to his readers

multiple examples to show wide-reaching impact—suggests mandating algebra hurts students across class, social, regional, and institutional boundaries

AUDIENCE

Relatively affluent, well-educated readers of the *New York Times*; Hacker's audience is probably made up of mature professionals ranging in age from late 20s to 60s or 70s; these are people who care about education, social justice, and the economy and who are interested in politics, business, and culture; NYT readers can be fairly liberal but they might be fiscal conservatives.

ARGUMENT

"Making mathematics mandatory prevents us from discovering and developing young talent. In the interest of maintaining rigor, we're actually depleting our pool of brainpower" (Hacker).

Hacker argues that mandating successful completion of algebra hurts our country by wasting resources and excluding large numbers of students with the potential to excel in higher education.

PERSONA

Knowledgeable, concerned, experienced, and frustrated educator and scholar who values mathematics and uses it in his field but who is dismayed by American students' high failure rates in algebra

and social scientist whose work relies heavily on the use of numbers. My
aim is not to spare students from a difficult subject, but to call attention to
the real problems we are causing by misdirecting precious resources.

We discuss the preceding critical thinking questions, then complete a rhetorical analysis
through a PAPA Square (Figure 6.4). Students can work individually, in pairs, or as a whole
class to complete the PAPA Square (see Chapter 2 for tips on this strategy and Appendix 6
for a reproducible version).

From the PAPA Square analysis, we see how Hacker's ethos draws strength from both his
sense and sensibility. He's careful to present himself as someone who not only cares about a
serious problem but who also has the academic qualifications and intellectual discipline to
make a reasonable argument on the issue. Aristotle tells us there are three things that inspire
confidence in a speaker's character: good sense, good moral character, and goodwill (1984;
Book II, Chapter 1). Thus within the creation of a credible ethos, we see elements of reason,
character, and feeling all working together.

Going Deeper into Ethos

In its simplest, most spokesperson-y form, ethos is the appeal that doesn't require proof to
convince an audience. We believe simply because we trust the person talking to us. The writer
or speaker is such a role model, such a paragon of virtue, such a worthy leader or authority
that we're prepared to accept his or her words on faith. In Shakespeare's *Henry V*, for instance,
the king's battle cry of "Once more into the breach, dear friends!" (act 3, scene 1, line 1) relies
heavily on his ethos as their comrade "Harry" to move his soldiers to action (2008, 1503).

When it comes to academic arguments, however, ethos never does the heavy lifting all
by itself. Indeed, a critical part of an academic ethos is a writer's ability to attend to logos
(which means both "logic" and "word" in Greek). Students and scholars gain their readers'
trust by avoiding bias, making defensible claims, using appropriate disciplinary conventions,
and reasonably responding to counterarguments. Pathos can benefit an academic ethos, too,
particularly in arguments on issues of social justice. Sometimes a writer needs to demonstrate
her compassion in order to establish her credibility. The ideal academic image—the scholar
who is both ethical and effective, responsible and responsive—includes elements of all three
rhetorical appeals.

In addition to being integrative, the concept of ethos can also be transformative. A colleague
of mine at San Francisco State University, Nelson Graff, shared a classroom example that I
think brilliantly illustrates how a deep understanding of ethos can change the way students
think about writing. Nelson uses the idea of ethos to talk with students about how they choose
to start their essays. He points out that when students open their essays with sentences that
directly reference the assignment (e.g., "When I had to do this assignment, I decided to write
about . . ." or "I picked this chapter because we talked about . . ."), these writers are adopting

the persona of a student completing an assignment rather than a scholar addressing a shared problem. Sentences like these indicate that our students haven't yet developed that writerly voice in their head that asks, "How can I make a good first impression?" and "What do my readers need to know about me?" A surface-level understanding of ethos isn't enough to help students think like writers.

Classroom Activity: Pairs Conversation on Ethos

Edward P. J. Corbett and Rosa A. Eberly explain that, for Aristotle, ethos is "a constructed self, a mindful self, a public self" (2000, 10). The following pairs conversation can help students explore the persuasive power of a mindfully constructed public image.

> **Directions to Students:** In the following lines from rapper Macklemore's 2012 song "Wings," we can see how the ethos of someone like Michael Jordan can exert a powerful influence over young fans. Summarize and respond to the lyrics with a partner, then talk about the following questions: Have you ever been influenced by someone you wanted to be like? What are the benefits and dangers of this kind of influence? What qualities do you most admire in a person?

"WINGS" BY MACKLEMORE AND RYAN LEWIS

I was trying to fly without leaving the ground
Cause I wanted to be like Mike, right
Wanted to be him
I wanted to be that guy
I wanted to touch the rim
I wanted to be cool
And I wanted to fit in
I wanted what he had, America, it begins

After this warm-up, we brainstorm a list of other famous people who similarly inspire emulation. Now I can shift the discussion from the ways that celebrities influence us to the strategies and actions that contribute to a celebrity's image. Using our list of celebrities, we identify the choices they've repeatedly made about their careers, politics, lifestyle, language, fashions, and behavior to create a "public self." In the Greek lexicon, the word ethos [ἔθος] appears as "custom, habit" (Liddell and Scott 1968, 226). For the Greeks, character is based on repeated actions. Understanding how ethos relates to long-practiced habits helps students to see the personal history behind a compelling public image.

In a reflection she wrote for our class, one of my students, Stephanie, showed that these kinds of activities were helping her internalize the practice of considering how all three rhetorical appeals impact someone's image and credibility. "From time to time," Stephanie wrote,

"I find myself examining people's ethos and *the way what they do affects the way I see them.* Before this course I had never even heard of ethos, pathos, or logos and now I use them to examine my peers" (emphasis added).

Ethos and Tone

Aristotle says that not only should a speaker's own character look right but also "that he should be thought to entertain the right feelings towards his hearers" (1984; Book II, Chapter 1). I, for one, would certainly appreciate it if more of the writers whose work I read—student and otherwise—entertained the right feelings toward me. Unfortunately, many writers I read come across as irritated or resistant, if not downright hostile.

This seems to happen most often with student writers when they don't know their audience personally, as is the case with SAT essays or college placement tests. When I read these kinds of essays, I brace myself whenever I come across sentences that begin, "Anyone who believes this is . . ." fearing that I may be among the believers soon to be denounced. I similarly cringe whenever I encounter phrases like the following:

"To disagree is absurd!"

"Without a doubt, this is the stupidest . . ."

"Everyone knows . . ."

"Anybody who thinks . . ."

"The completely ignorant view that . . ."

Phrases like these signal to me that students haven't yet grasped the "goodwill" component of a credible ethos. These students aren't yet making the connections between how their word choice affects their tone and how their tone expresses their attitude not only toward their subject but also toward their readers.

Classroom Activity: Choosing an Academic Tone

The following activity helps students think more critically about how different tones impact a writer's ethos or image.

Directions to Students: Creating an effective "voice," or persona, can be the key to success in academic writing. If our readers like our tone and the image we present of ourselves, they are more willing to believe our arguments.

Consider the following tones and the effects they may have on a writer's image. List positive or negative connotations for each tone word. A few examples are given as a starter for you. How could each tone influence how we see the writer?

TONE	POSITIVE/NEGATIVE CONNOTATION	WRITER'S IMAGE
Inclusive	Positive—cooperative, invitational, pluralistic	Sees and accepts multiple points of view
Informed	Positive—educated, well read, knowledgeable	Responsible and careful researcher
Hostile	Negative—aggressive, unfriendly, intimidating	Suspicious of others; looking for a fight
Detached		
Compassionate		
Cynical		
Balanced		
Sarcastic		
Flippant		
Enraged		
Concerned		
Respectful		
Righteous		
Arrogant		
Reflective		

Ethos and Brand Image

Another way to extend students' thinking about character appeals is to have them analyze a company's brand image or logo. Companies that hire employees who serve as "brand representatives" (think Abercrombie and Fitch) are particularly good candidates for this kind of analysis. I show my students several well-known brands or logos (that's the plural of logo here, not the rhetorical appeal) and ask them what image or identity the brand or logo represents. I ask these questions: What kind of person would buy this product or be associated with this company or institution? What happens when people create knockoffs of the brand or parodies of the logo? What happens when a logo changes? Can a brand or logo become tainted by forgery? By scandal? What, if anything, can the company or institution do to save its image once this happens? Is image different from reputation? Why are logos important?

The University of California (UC) might have answers to some of these questions. In an attempt to update its classic, scholarly logo—complete with Latin motto—the UC launched a sleek new branding campaign for the university system in 2012 only to encounter a wave of controversy. It seems that the new logo regrettably looked more like the icon for a smartphone app than the hallmark of a world-class institution of higher learning. My students and I read a story from the *Los Angeles Times* on the UC logo redesign controversy and then compare images of the old and new logos (see Figures 6.5 and 6.6). We discuss what we notice. The opening lines from Larry Gordon's article in the *Los Angeles Times* capture the kerfuffle:

The new University of California logo is a no-go.

Responding to a wave of revulsion in the last week over the symbol's modern design, officials announced Friday that they would suspend further use of the logo and remove it where possible. (2012)

FIGURE 6.5
Old UC logo

FIGURE 6.6
New UC logo

As we analyze the two contrasting logos, we discuss the following questions:

What image does the century-old seal for the University of California convey? What details do you notice in the seal? Why are these important?

Why might the university system think it's time for a change?

How do you think students and alumni reacted to the new logo? Why?

How does a university's image impact its graduates' image?

The takeaway of our discussion is the power of shared identification. One UC student said that a positive outcome of the logo debate was that it showed how students and alumni "identify very closely with the UC system and what it represents for their lives" (Gordon 2012).

Credibility and the Question at Issue

Aristotle says that an admirable ethos is important because "we believe good men more fully and more readily than others" (1984; Book I, Chapter 2). How important is a credible ethos? Let's ask Lance Armstrong.

In California, several hundred high schools had been using an excerpt from *It's Not About the Bike,* Armstrong's 2001 autobiography with Sally Jenkins, as part of the twelfth-grade Expository Reading and Writing Course. The piece on Armstrong's battle with cancer was one of several texts in a unit that examined the question of how we should value human life. Students and teachers found the piece engaging and inspiring. After the stories broke on the champion cyclist's use of banned substances, however, Armstrong's ethos cratered, throwing his autobiography out of stasis (see Chapter 1) with the other texts in this unit.

It wasn't just not about the bike anymore; it wasn't even about the original issue. Achieving stasis in an academic argument depends on the participants all agreeing on the question at issue. Yet students were so distracted by Armstrong's fall from grace that the conversation over how life should be valued was completely derailed. Sure, Armstrong's many public denials of guilt and later admission of doping and lying provided a fascinating subject for an ethos analysis. Students were utterly engrossed in exploring the extent to which Armstrong's image and personal narrative had been constructed and maintained through a vigilant regimen of deceit.

But as a text participating in a conversation around how we should value human life, Armstrong's autobiography simply no longer worked. Students couldn't read his argument supportively because they were suspicious of everything he said. They couldn't even evaluate his claims and evidence critically because the problem with his ethos completely overshadowed the other appeals and strategies in the text. Indeed, the retrospective, postscandal readings of *It's Not About the Bike* revealed how fully the text relies on ethos—on Armstrong's early inspirational image as a sports hero and cancer survivor. Once his status as a role model had been obliterated, there was little logical reasoning holding the text together, and since nearly all the pathos in the text depends on our ability to feel sympathy and admiration for Armstrong, that fell apart, too.

The lesson learned is that sometimes a problem with a speaker's or writer's ethos is so significant that it not only undermines an argument but actually alters the conversation.

Creating an Academic Ethos

Students increase the likelihood that their readers will more fully and readily believe them when they are careful to create an academic ethos for themselves. One of the ways we do this in my classes is by using academic English in formal argument essays—and by avoiding language that is too casual or vague to be rhetorically effective.

Nearly twenty years ago, one of my master teachers taught me the trick of killing off "dead words" in my classroom that I didn't want my students using in their academic assignments. These included words like *get, go, very, really, thing, good, bad,* or *big* that were too informal or general to be of much help in academic writing. Later, I added my own words to the list—words that I thought were too difficult to defend logically in most cases: *always, never, everyone, no one,* and so on.

I start a dead word memorial service by bringing out my cardboard tombstone and calling for a moment of silence. Then, with as somber a face as I can manage, I inform students that I have, in fact, dispatched a particular word myself because it was too lazy and imprecise. It simply didn't do enough work for writers. I then go on to reassure students that we will cope just fine without the dead word, and to prove it, we're going to find at least thirty-six better words to use in its place. See Appendixes 15a and 15b for reproducible versions of this activity.

Directions to Students: **In each of the following sentences, replace the word *get* with a more precise word or phrase. Try not to use the same word more than once!**

1. What did you get on your test?

2. I don't get the joke.

3. We get to go camping often.

4. Get some milk on your way home from work.

5. Get the cat off the table.

6. Would you please get me a piece of pizza?

7. Did you get the assignment from Kristen?

8. Get out your pens and paper.

9. Get to the point.

10. Your train may get in late.

11. Get out of my house.

12. Did your parents get you to do your homework?

13. I can't get enough of this chocolate.

14. Get in your chair immediately.

15. Get away from the stove.

16. What are you getting your boyfriend for his birthday?

17. I'm not sure which shirt to get.

18. I got an A- on my math test.

19. Do you and your sisters always get in a fight?

20. I get the news on the radio when I'm driving home.

21. Did you get first or second place in the marathon?

22. I get a sick feeling whenever I have a geometry quiz.

23. Our carpet always gets so dirty.

24. Pedro gets up at 5:30 every morning.

25. Can I get you something to drink?

26. David doesn't get out much anymore.

27. Our camping group got to the summit just before sunset.

28. It seems like our parents are getting so much older.

29. Get all your assignments in on time.

30. Can you get your brother's car for the weekend?

31. Get your friend on the phone and ask her over for dinner.

32. How many tourists' stops did you get to?

33. This work gets so confusing!

34. I get all my books from the catalogues.

35. Do you get who the murderer was in that film?

36. Get everything you'll need for our skiing trip.

Students are impressed when they see that there really are at least thirty-six different words to use instead of "get." The elevated diction of the revised sentences seems to give students a nice confidence boost, too. They sit up straighter when saying, "May I offer you a drink?" or "Did you deduce who the murderer was in that film?"

The Language of Ethos

Teaching students how to recognize and apply the language used to signal an appeal to character helps them to be more effective readers and writers. As we read texts, we write down all of these phrases that we find. Here are some of our finds:

> From my vantage point
>
> In my view
>
> Because of my experience with/in . . .
>
> In my perspective
>
> As someone with expertise/experience in . . .

Just as there are rhetorically effective uses of sentence fragments and run-ons, there are also rhetorically effective uses of dead words, even in academic writing. After students understand the effects these kinds of words can have in different rhetorical contexts, we talk about why there might be strategic moments in their writing when they want to downshift to simpler diction. We also discuss situations where using overly formal language is rhetorically ineffective. An awareness of *kairos* (see Chapter 3) helps students make stylistic choices based on what is most appropriate for a given rhetorical situation.

I bring out this list again when it's time for students to write their own arguments.

Deepening Practice

The PAPA Square works well as a holistic rhetorical analysis, but there are times when I want my students to distinguish among nuances in appeal, so that they are ultimately able to see arguments in greater detail and complexity. For this purpose, I like to have them analyze individual rhetorical appeals. Breaking an appeal like ethos down into its working parts helps students see the strategic choices writers make. See Appendix 16a for a blank Ethos Analysis and 16b for a teacher-made example.

Take a look again at the PAPA Square on Andrew Hacker's article "Is Algebra Necessary?" on page 144. Now compare that to a student's Ethos Analysis of Hacker's article (Figure 6.7).

FIGURE 6.7

Sample student Ethos Analysis for "Is Algebra Necessary?"

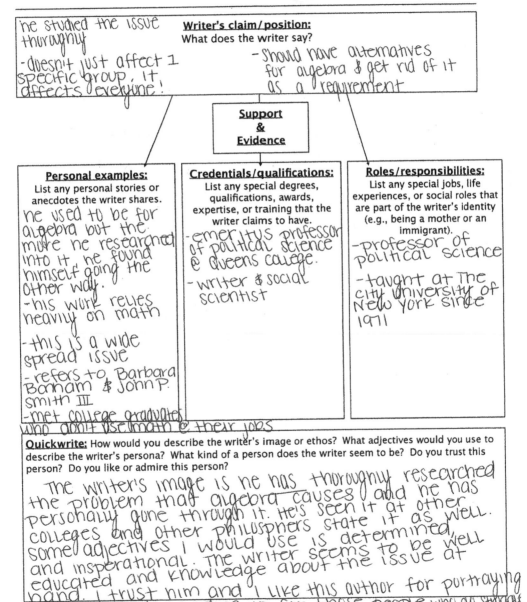

Ethos Analysis

he studied the issue thoroughly

-doesn't just affect 1 specific group, it affects everyone!

Writer's claim/position:
What does the writer say?

- Should have alternatives for algebra & get rid of it as a requirement

Support & Evidence

Personal examples:
List any personal stories or anecdotes the writer shares.

he used to be for algebra but the more he researched into it, he found himself going the other way.

-his work relies heavily on math

-this is a wide spread issue

-refers to Barbara Bonham & John P. Smith III

-met college graduates who don't use math @ their jobs

Credentials/qualifications:
List any special degrees, qualifications, awards, expertise, or training that the writer claims to have.

-emeritus professor of political science @ Queens College.

-writer & social scientist

Roles/responsibilities:
List any special jobs, life experiences, or social roles that are part of the writer's identity (e.g., being a mother or an immigrant).

-professor of political science

-taught at The city university of New York since 1971

Quickwrite: How would you describe the writer's image or ethos? What adjectives would you use to describe the writer's persona? What kind of a person does the writer seem to be? Do you trust this person? Do you like or admire this person?

The writer's image is he has thoroughly researched the problem that algebra causes and he has personally gone through it. He's seen it at other colleges and other philosphers state it as well. Some adjectives I would use is determined, and insperational. The writer seems to be well educated and knowledgeable about the issue at hand. I trust him and I like this author for portraying his voice and standing up for those people who no struggle

The Ethos Analysis in Figure 6.7 gets at the *how* behind Hacker's creation of his persona. While the PAPA Square lets students describe the writer's persona and see how ethos works in relation to the other components of an argument, the Ethos Analysis gives students a how-to guide for their own writing.

Going Deeper into Pathos

As the preceding examples and activities show, going deeper into ethos inevitably means going deeper into our understanding of human emotions, too—the realm of pathos. Still, pathos has several particularities of its own worth noting. For Aristotle, understanding how pathos functions in arguments involves understanding how our changing emotional states impact decision making. Emotions, he notes, affect our judgments (1984; Book II, Chapter 1). For instance, Aristotle observes that "when people are feeling friendly and placable, they think one sort of thing; when they are feeling angry or hostile, they think either something totally different or the same thing with a different intensity" (1984; Book II, Chapter 1). With pathos, the focus is on the audience's state of mind.

A good step toward helping students conduct a finer-grained analyses of pathos is to brainstorm a list of emotions as a class. This activity can also help build academic vocabulary while alerting students to the subtle connotation differences between related words. We start with the simple—*happy, sad, scared, angry*—and work toward nuance. After generating our list, students classify the emotions through a List, Group, Label activity.

Classroom Activity: Pathos List, Group, Label

If you've used List, Group, Label before (Taba 1967), you know it's a great way to help students make connections among ideas or terms. I like to use this sorting exercise as a prereading activity or to help students organize review material for tests. Here are my directions for a Pathos List, Group, Label.

> **Directions to Students:** Below is a list of human emotions writers may appeal to when using pathos to persuade their audience. You may work on your own or with others to organize related emotions into categories that make sense to you. Then give each category a label that describes its contents. Avoid overly general labels (e.g., "positive emotions" or "negative emotions").

outrage	pity	amusement	dejection
rage	envy	confidence	despair
guilt	shame	resolution	pain
wrath	joy	satisfaction	irritation
indignation	excitement	hilarity	hostility
fury	bitterness	contentment	annoyance
desire	agony	bliss	resentment

discontent	alarm	fascination	distrust
depression	insecurity	anxiety	determination
distress	shock	doubt	perplexity
regret	terror	suspicion	tranquility
dismay	dread	curiosity	enthusiasm
cowardice	grief	bravery	serenity
apprehension	worry	confusion	oppression

Students already know from their work with literature how challenging it can be to identify and describe the emotional vibe of a text—what in literary analysis we often talk about as the tone or the mood. Completing the Pathos List, Group, Label helps students grow beyond a vague understanding of this appeal. When my students say that a writer is using pathos, I always ask, What *kind* of pathos? Emotions are complex, I remind them.

Applying Their Learning

Once they're primed for describing emotions, I ask my students to put their knowledge into practice by identifying specific pathetic appeals at work in sample texts. The point is for students not just to recognize pathos or name an emotion but also to understand the dynamics behind that particular feeling and how it impacts decision making. Consider this opening from an article by Jordan Weissmann published in the *Atlantic* on November 5, 2012:

Should Science Majors Pay Less for College Than Art Majors?
Philosophy lovers, prepare to be outraged.

Down in Florida, a task force commissioned by Governor Rick Scott is putting the finishing touches on a proposal that would allow the state's public universities to start charging undergraduates different tuition rates depending on their major. Students would get discounts for studying topics thought to be in high demand among Florida employers. Those would likely include science, technology, engineering, and math (aka, the STEM fields), among others.

But Art History? Gender Studies? Classics? Sorry, but the fates are cruel. Unless a university could show that local companies were clamoring to hire humanities students, those undergrads would have to pay more for their diploma.

The writer of this article, Jordan Weissmann, knows his topic is likely to spark an emotional reaction in his audience, particularly in readers who are fans of the humanities. Weissmann even tells this subset of his audience what emotion they're going to feel: outrage. The classical reference in the sentence "Sorry, but the fates are cruel" further emphasizes the sense of personal injury and injustice some readers may feel over the Florida proposal to give discounts to college students in high-demand STEM majors. The feeling Weissmann invokes in this opening paragraph certainly matches Aristotle's definition of anger: "an impulse, accompanied by pain, to a conspicuous slight directed without justification towards what concerns oneself or towards what concerns one's friends" (1984; Book II, Chapter 2). We feel outrage, in other words, when we think something's not fair. This feeling puts us on our guard, making us more defensive and less willing to entertain other viewpoints—which, in turn, impacts how we make decisions. Analyzing the causes and effects of emotions takes students into a deeper understanding of pathos.

Giving Feedback on Students' Use of Pathos

Much of the modeling and mentoring I do to help students develop a deeper understanding of pathos happens when I give my students feedback on their writing. Adrianna, for instance, had written a strong first draft of a research paper on childhood that began with a compelling narrative about her early life in Mexico. While her opening story of the struggles and joys she had experienced caring for her younger siblings provided an apt frame for her subsequent research on the definition and boundaries of childhood, she related two more personal stories before introducing her first scholarly source. My comments on her paper told her she was on the right track but needed to be a little more strategic about her use of rhetorical appeals:

> Excellent start! Your opening story is beautiful and gives your reader a
> strong sense of your topic's importance. I do, however, think you need
> to include more scholarly evidence before you share your next anecdote.
> Remember to balance your logos with your pathos so that you maintain an
> academic ethos.

For her revision, Adrianna chose to move one of her personal anecdotes to her conclusion, where it provided a fitting illustration of why her argument mattered.

Classroom Activity: Pathos Analysis

Like the Ethos Analysis, a Pathos Analysis gets at the nuts and bolts behind an appeal to emotion. Notice how the following Pathos Analysis for "Is Algebra Necessary?" not only asks students to identify the complex emotions Hacker invokes in this article but also the ways his choice of diction, examples, and tone contribute to his desired rhetorical effect. See Appendix 17a for a blank Pathos Analysis and 17b for a teacher-made sample.

FIGURE 6.8

A student's Pathos Analysis for "Is Algebra Necessary?"

emotion
loaded lang.
audience frame of mind

Pathos Analysis

Author's claim/position:

Students are failing and dropping out of school. They are being expected to fail. Why are they subjecting students to this ordeal if they're just expected to fail?
6 million high school students and 2 million college students are struggling with algebra.

causing anger and stress.
So many talented students but can't get passed this huge road block

Support
&
Evidence

Personal examples/
anecdotes:
List any human interest stories or personal experiences the writer shares.

Bohan says, "there are students taking these courses 3, 4, 5 times, and many drop out."

Loaded language:
List any words that have strong emotional connotations.

ordeal
failing
expected
subject
exclude
many

Humor, irony, and/or
sarcasm:
List any jokes or funny/ sarcastic remarks the writer makes.

"How many college graduates remember what Fermat's dilemma was all about?"

Quickwrite: Describe the overall emotional impact of this text. How did the writer make you feel? Happy? Sad? Afraid? Hurt? Enthusiastic? Suspicious? Excited? Irritated? Brave? Angry? Amused? Concerned? How strong were your feelings while reading this text?

Hacker included some facts and quotes that made me feel a bit concerned and afraid. I personally feel this way because I'm going to a university and algebra is considered general ed which is mandatory. Although I may feel this way on a scale of 1-10, I'm about a 5.

Going Deeper into Logos

How much logical nuance and complexity can we reasonably expect from teenagers? According to the CCSS, a good bit. In terms of proficiency in logic, I think the goal at the high school level is not for students to know everything but for them to know what they don't know. We want them to get that funny feeling when they make an unsupported claim or sweeping generalization and ask themselves, "Can I really say that?" I call this logic radar.

I still do funky things in my own writing. But when I do, my logic radar usually says, "That's a mixed metaphor" or "That doesn't make any sense." I remember one education professor I had said you're a bad speller only if you don't know when you don't know how to spell a word. As long as you get that mental tug that says, "Hey, that doesn't look right"—and you consult a dictionary—you're fine. I think the same is true with logic. You're a poor logician only if you don't know when something doesn't make sense. If our students stumble in trying to follow circular reasoning like this—"Doing something that benefits only yourself is selfish"—they've already developed some logical skills.

When students ask me to take a look at their writing because something seems wrong, I make sure to compliment them on their "good eye." I want them to trust their own instincts and know that seeking help is an important and admirable skill in itself. That's our starting point. I'm happy when their logic radar detects any of the following dodgy moves:

Inventing facts

Sliding down the slippery slope

Not accurately following the writer's line of argument

Being distracted by minor claims

Misreading the writer's claims

Making sweeping generalizations

Writing off topic

Using circular reasoning (e.g., "When you tell a lie, you're being dishonest.")

Flip-flopping or contradicting oneself without explanation

Expressing opinions not backed by evidence

Not aligning evidence to claims

When my students or I see these signs in their writing, I know we need to spend more focused time on logos.

Logos in the Rhetorical Tradition

Aristotle tells us that one of the three ways we can persuade audiences is by proving the truth (or the probable truth) of the statements we make (1984; Book III, Chapter 1). This proof might be "hard" or "soft," depending on the academic discipline and task, but chances are most of the arguments high school students make and read aim for reasonable conclusions rather than absolute certainties. In "Three Ways to Persuade," John Edlund describes how we both favor and fudge logic in most twenty-first-century arguments:

> In our society, logic and rationality are highly valued and this type of persuasive strategy is usually privileged over appeals to the character of the speaker or to the emotions of the audience. However, formal logic and scientific reasoning are usually not appropriate for general audiences, so we must rely on a more rhetorical type of reasoning. (2013, 56)

A rhetorical type of reasoning allows writers to apply principles of logic even when the truth can't be known. These principles include supporting claims with evidence, responding to counterarguments, qualifying assertions, examining assumptions, avoiding fallacies, connecting ideas, and in general making a good faith effort to be sensible. The goal is an argument that is reasonable and defensible, not an airtight case.

As Edlund (2013) notes, there's a tradition of privileging logos over the other rhetorical appeals dating back to Aristotle. Given his druthers, Aristotle prefers that all arguments rest on logical proofs, but he also recognizes that knowing something is not the same as caring about it—hence the need for pathos.

George Hillocks follows this tradition when he calls logical appeals "the essence of argument" (2011, xvii). The CCSS also shows a preference for logic and rationality. Notice how the following ELA writing standards for grades nine and ten are full of the language of logos:

> CCSS.ELA-Literacy.W.9-10.1a Introduce precise claim(s), distinguish the claim(s) from alternate or opposing claims, and create an organization that establishes clear relationships among claim(s), counterclaims, reasons, and evidence.
>
> CCSS.ELA-Literacy.W.9-10.1b Develop claim(s) and counterclaims fairly, supplying evidence for each while pointing out the strengths and limitations of both in a manner that anticipates the audience's knowledge level and concerns.
>
> CCSS.ELA-Literacy.W.9-10.1c Use words, phrases, and clauses to link the major sections of the text, create cohesion, and clarify the relationships between claim(s) and reasons, between reasons and evidence, and between claim(s) and counterclaims. (NGA/CCSSO 2010)

While Common Core standards are critical components of academic literacy, I remind my students not to lose sight of purpose, audience, and occasion in making use of any of the appeals. There are some rhetorical situations in which the heavy use of logical reasoning might actually irritate or alienate the audience: a marriage proposal, for instance.

Making Defensible Assertions

An indefensible assertion is a claim that doesn't know its own limits. For high school students, more sophisticated reasoning starts with knowing what they don't know. Do you see assertions like these in your students' writing?

"There is no easy way out in any situation."

"All parents want the very best for their children no matter what."

"Society will never allow women to achieve equality with men."

"Judging someone based on looks is completely and totally wrong."

This is entry-level argumentation, and we want high school students to feel that it's OK to try on some claims to see how they fit. But once students understand the basics, they need to practice making defensible assertions—in other words, claims that can withstand counterattacks and be defended with evidence. And that means cutting things like unqualified generalizations ("There is *no* easy way out in *any* situation") out of their playbook. It's this respect for the limits of knowledge and the value of evidence that ultimately helps students make defensible assertions in their own writing.

When I see indefensible assertions in my students' writing, I try to respond with questions that will help them think more carefully about their logic:

"Are you ready to draw this conclusion yet?"

"What do your other sources have to say about this point?"

"Do you have evidence for this claim?"

"Do you have an academic source for this idea?"

"You've used the word *always* (or *never*)—are you sure there are no exceptions to the claim you're making?"

"What's the historical or cultural context for this claim?"

"How has this idea changed over time?"

Each of these questions is designed to activate students' logic radar. While high school students don't need a formal understanding of what makes an argument valid, they do need a practical understanding of what makes it sensible.

Supporting Claims with Evidence

One of the best ways to make a claim more defensible, of course, is to support it with carefully chosen evidence. This is why the believing game matters so much. Just as academic writing starts with academic reading, so too does logos begin with listening.

Students tend to forget the listening step. Providing support for claims sometimes seems like something students do for teachers because they know we like it. I think many developing writers see gathering evidence as just one more hoop English teachers make their students jump through.

When I ask students to describe how they pull quotations or paraphrases to use in their arguments, they often say they just start writing, and then when they remember something they read, they use it. Scholars and professional writers do this too, of course, but they tend to do something first that my students typically skip (unless I make them do it): Scholars usually summarize their sources through a literature review before they start using them. They know you have "to collect the dots before you can connect the dots," as a popular tweet puts it.

Students don't always know this. Even when I work with college seniors, I still encounter students who tell me, "I've pretty much finished my essay. Now I just have to go back and add my sources." Yikes! These students see quotations, paraphrases, and summaries as ways to accessorize their writing after they've already put the basic ensemble together. When this happens, I have to take the blame for these students seeing the form, but not the process, of academic writing. The lesson learned is that I need to show the behind-the-scenes brain work of composition explicitly.

To help make the invisible visible to more students, I share pages of my own prewriting notes for articles and essays I've written. We talk about how, in order to give ourselves loads of options so that we can choose the best support, we need to capture a whole lot more evidence than we plan to use. Going overboard on evidence gathering is also the best way to be sure we're being fair, informed, responsible, and responsive in our own stance—and not retrofitting evidence to support predetermined claims. We can't see the big picture if we're only looking for the quotations that support our own views.

I know my students are starting to get it when I write comments like these on their papers:

"Good improvement! I appreciate your more thorough response to the views of other writers."

"Better use of evidence—good!"

"More skillful integration of quotations—nice!"

Responding to Counterarguments

Playing the believing game can help students make defensible assertions because it enables them to respond to the views of those who might disagree with them. Understanding counterarguments through supportive, noncritical reading prepares writers to make concessions. Consider these statements:

> "I think that's a fair point."
>
> "This makes sense."
>
> "I can see your point of view."
>
> "I understand your perspective."
>
> "That's reasonable under the circumstances."

These are the kinds of responses to a text we coach our students to have when they're playing the believing game (see Chapter 1). Turns out, they're also the basic ingredients for making a concession—an important logical skill in argumentation. The ability to concede the value of a perspective that differs from our own is essential to establishing our own rationality. As a bumper sticker I saw in Santa Cruz, California, put it, "If you can't change your mind, how do you know you have one?" Being a reasonable—or logical—person includes this capacity to give way under compelling evidence, even if it contradicts or undermines our own position.

Playing the believing game also teaches us to take the views of others seriously. Instead of dismissing counterarguments to our claims as absurd or outrageous, we learn from reading with the grain how to postpone judgment, so that when it comes time to answer the questions or challenges of other writers, we're not tempted to say "That's just silly" or to ignore altogether those viewpoints that raise our hackles. Playing the believing game increases our tolerance for discomfort.

> Sometimes responding to counterarguments requires a bit of skillful redirection. What if—after listening to the views of others—we find that writers engaged in the conversation we're trying to enter are not yet addressing the points we think are most important? When this happens, I offer my students some language for responding to other viewpoints while steering the conversation in a new direction:
>
> X's point of view omits/ neglects/disregards/ overlooks/underestimates/ misrepresents/ misunderstands/ exaggerates the importance of/inflates/is preoccupied with/assumes that/shows an outdated concern with . . .

Classroom Activity: Qualifying Claims

Playing both the doubting and believing game can also help students understand what claims of their own they might need to qualify. This practice of methodological doubt and belief teaches students to acknowledge disagreement and ambiguity. If they're aware that there's no scholarly consensus on an issue, they can avoid going out on a limb. I tell students, if you don't know it, qualify it. Be honest about when you have to rely on speculation. And if speculation doesn't help your argument, leave it out.

Although there are tactical moments when we may want to make a bold assertion, I ask students to practice qualifying extreme claims from their own writing so they can at least see the differences between qualified and unqualified assertions. Using a projector or document camera, I share samples of extreme claims from my students' essays that could be made more defensible by adding more moderate qualifiers (e.g., *sometimes* rather than *always*, or simply the addition of *sometimes* before a verb). The following student sentences come from our unit on gender and math:

Directions to Students: Make each of the following claims more defensible by adding moderate qualifiers as appropriate.

1. Gender has been defining people for years; it decides for people what they should do, how they should do it, and what they can and can't say.

   Student Sentence: *Gender has been defining people for years; it <u>often</u> decides for people what they should do, how they should do it, and what they can and can't say.*

2. Society pushes men to do certain jobs like being a scientist, a doctor, or a construction worker and women to be models, secretaries, and executive assistants.

   Student Sentence: *<u>Contemporary American</u> society <u>frequently</u> pushes men to do certain jobs like being a scientist, a doctor, or a construction worker and women to be models, secretaries, and executive assistants.*

3. At a young age, kids are taught that looks are more important than being smart since they see models and actresses on TV who are thin and "perfect."

   Student Sentence: *At a young age, <u>many</u> kids are taught that looks are more important than being smart since they <u>often</u> see models and actresses on TV who are thin and "perfect."*

4. Many teenagers have already figured out that society only cares about how a person looks because that might be the only way society will accept them.

   Student Sentence: *Many teenagers have already figured out that our society <u>primarily</u> cares about how a person looks because that might be the main way society will accept them.*

Classroom Activity: Qualifiers and Persona

In this next activity, students consider the interaction between logos and ethos as they examine how the use of qualifiers impacts a writer's persona. (See Appendix 18 for a reproducible version.)

> **Directions to Students:** A qualifier is a descriptive word (either an adjective or adverb) that adds more information to a sentence. First, underline the qualifiers in each statement below (e.g., *all, always, never, some, few, often, no*, etc.). Then describe the kind of person who might make each statement. What is the image you get of this person? Opinionated? Unbiased? Moderate? Skeptical? Careful? Impulsive? Reasonable? Extreme? Observant? Open-minded? Determined? Absolute? Resolved? List adjectives describing the writer's persona under each statement.
>
> All children should always wash their own clothes.
>
> Most teachers usually just want what is best for their students.
>
> Many families often struggle to make ends meet.
>
> Some students occasionally cheat on tests.
>
> No cause is worth dying for.
>
> True friends will never let you down.
>
> *Quick-Write:* How does the use of qualifiers affect tone? How do qualifiers affect a writer's persona or ethos?

The point students should understand is that the use of a qualifier is a rhetorical choice and that the effectiveness of this choice depends on the text's audience, purpose, and occasion. Qualifiers do not automatically improve writing. There are some situations in which bold and assertive language might be the most rhetorically effective choice.

Examining Assumptions

An even more advanced rhetorical skill is the ability to examine assumptions. Being able not only to make a defensible claim but also to articulate what principles and ways of knowing are behind that claim is a truly sophisticated competency. This is deep logic. If claims and evidence are the visible tip of the iceberg, then assumptions and backing are the below-the-surface bulk that give weight to the whole argument.

In *The Uses of Argument,* philosopher and physicist Stephen Toulmin (1958/2008) takes a close look at the logical components that determine the validity of an argument. These include the data, the claim, the warrant, and the backing, as well as qualifiers (words like *necessarily* or *probably*). While the ideas of data (or evidence) and claims are pretty familiar to most high school students, the concepts of warrant and backing are not. A warrant is an underlying principle or assumption that authorizes the connection between the data and the claim (Toulmin 1958/2008). Students who drop random quotations into their essays regardless of their relevance ("There! I've included evidence!") could benefit from learning to identify warrants. As the implicit justification for an argument, a warrant can be a difficult, yet important, concept for students to grasp. Toulmin says that, unlike specific claims and evidence, warrants are "general, certifying the soundness of all arguments of the appropriate type" (1958/2008, 92). In other words, the warrant is what makes a claim "legit." (Think about how a judge issues a search warrant to authorize police officers to enter someone's home.)

The idea of a warrant (an authorization for a claim) is easier to understand through an example. Here's a simple illustration I share with my students:

Data:	My dog barks every time the doorbell rings.
Claim:	When my friend rings the doorbell tonight, my dog will bark.
Warrant:	Dogs have highly predictable behavior patterns.
Backing:	I know this because of my personal experience as a dog owner.

To agree with the claim, we have to accept the assumption that doggy behavior can be predicted based on established patterns. In this case, the warrant is founded on common sense and personal experience. While a zoologist might bring far more sophisticated and extensive backing to this claim (more on backing later), the basic warrant would probably be the same. Hillocks says warrants "may be simply common sense rules that people accept as generally true, laws, scientific principles or studies, and thoughtfully argued definitions" (2011, xxiii). We find the more formal kind of warrant, for example, in something like parliamentary procedure, where a key principle is that the majority rules.

In *Introduction to Rhetorical Theory,* Gerard A. Hauser offers a student-friendly explanation of Toulmin's model:

> *Data answers the question, "What have you got to go on?*
> *Claim is the inference drawn as a conclusion from the data.*
> *Warrant answers the question, "How did you get there?"*
> *Backing contains evidence and argument to support a warrant.* (2002, 266)
> (original emphasis)

I often like to use the word *assumption* instead of Toulmin's *warrant* or Aristotle's *premise* because high school students already understand that to assume something means to take it for granted. What we assume to be true usually goes without saying.

In a rhetorical analysis of academic texts, the ability to uncover and critique assumptions is an important part of reading against the grain. To experience this in action, let's take a second look at the

> Literacy scholars Michael D. Smith and Jeffrey D. Wilhelm offer another student-friendly alternative to Toulmin's terms, calling a warrant and its backing "connections" (2006, 133).

central claim in Andrew Hacker's "Is Algebra Necessary?" Hacker says that he wants to "call attention to the real problems we are causing by misdirecting precious resources" (2012). The big problem, according to Hacker, is this: "Making mathematics mandatory prevents us from discovering and developing young talent. In the interest of maintaining rigor, we're actually depleting our pool of brainpower" (2012). To support this claim, Hacker provides data on high school and college completion rates as well as anecdotal evidence from educators who cite algebra as the reason for students' academic problems.

But what's behind this way of thinking? If we agree with Hacker, what principles or definitions do we have to accept? When we read against the grain, we're testing, in Toulmin's phrase, the "soundness" of the argument—including the legitimacy of its warrants (1958/2008, 92). Can we accept all of the following underlying assumptions behind Hacker's central argument?

1. Educational resources should be used efficiently and productively.

2. A broad and diverse talent pool is beneficial to our society.

3. Unnecessary obstacles to education should be removed.

4. Mathematics isn't necessary to the development of young talent.

5. "Mandatory" means required for high school graduation and college admission.

Nowhere does Hacker directly say any of these things, yet these are the principles authorizing the logical connections between his evidence and his claims. By uncovering these warrants—and playing the doubting game with them—students can develop a far more nuanced response to Hacker's argument. They might find, for example, that they agree with warrants 1–3, but that they don't agree with warrants 4 and 5. Maybe they see the idea of development as including being a well-rounded person academically or maybe they see meeting graduation requirements as within a student's choice and control—and therefore not "mandatory."

If we want to stretch students' thinking even further, we can ask about the backing that supports these warrants. How, for instance, does Hacker's personal experience as an educator, disciplinary training as a political scientist, or use of quantitative research boost his confidence in the legitimacy of his argument?

Classroom Activity: Identifying Warrants

The following activity helps students articulate possible principles or rules behind arguments, using the topic of the gender gap in the STEM fields. As part of this unit of inquiry, my students read texts on issues such as the "pinkification" of math, the power of stereotypes, and the lack of female computer software engineers. All of the questions in the activity are loaded with hidden assumptions; that's why answering them helps students to uncover the warrants—or underlying principles—behind the implicit claims about the benefits or drawbacks of different efforts to close the gender gap in science, technology, engineering, and mathematics.

When we make arguments, we can't avoid also making assumptions. We just hope that our audience shares our assumptions.

Direction to Students: We need to be responsible about how we allow warrants to work in our arguments. And that means that we need to know our warrants and guard against unexamined assumptions. To practice these skills, identify the hidden assumption(s) behind each of the following "leading" questions and then share your answers with a partner. (Sample answers are provided in italics for teachers; these samples should not be shown to students.)

How can we encourage math teachers to include more word problems on topics that are interesting to girls, such as fashion, cosmetics, body image, shopping, and dating?

Assumption: *Girls' interests are different from boys' interests.*

Assumption: *Girls are interested in fashion, cosmetics, and body image, etc.*

Assumption: *Word problems on body image and dating will help girls perform better in math.*

Assumption:_____

How does playing with Barbies hurt girls?

Assumption: *Playing with Barbies hurts girls.*

Assumption: *Girls play with Barbies.*

Assumption: _____

How can we encourage more young women to choose math as their college major?

Assumption: *Not enough women are choosing math as their college major.*

Assumption: *More women should be choosing math as their major.*

Assumption: *We can do something to encourage more women to be math majors.*

Assumption: _____

How can we improve the image of female software engineers?

Assumption: *Female software engineers have a negative image.*

Assumption: *We should do something to improve the image of female software engineers.*

Assumption: _____

Why haven't women achieved equality with men?

Assumption: *Women haven't achieved equality with men.*

Assumption: _____

What teaching strategies would better meet the needs of girls in math classes?

Assumption: *Current teaching strategies are not adequately meeting the needs of girls in math classes.*

Assumption: *Girls have distinct educational needs.*

Assumption: _____

Pairs Conversation: What rules, principles, and/or definitions can you identify in your answers to these questions?

Understanding Backing

Backing is a way of knowing. It's also a doorway into rhetorical context. To understand the backing for a warrant, we have to know the values, methods, interests, beliefs, and even the worldview of that way of knowing. Backing that emerges from a religious or ethical framework, for instance, will be substantially different from backing based on scientific method or legal precedent. Toulmin talks about backing as "the credentials" of a warrant (1958/2008, 98). Examples of backing could be anything from academic subjects, such as medical science or postmodern literary theory, to cultural ideologies, such as fatalism, manifest destiny, faith in human progress, or the doctrine of self-reliance.

Here's where stasis theory and disciplinary contexts come back into play. If participants in a conversation don't share the same backing or credentials, they have a hard time achieving stasis. They may not be able to agree on the question at issue if they have radically different value systems, disciplinary methods, or definitions of key terms. Hauser explains that, for Toulmin, "arguments are field-dependent" (1958/2008, 266). Not only do different fields or disciplines ask different kinds of questions, but they also have different ways of drawing conclusions from evidence based on field-specific backing. Hauser gives an example: "What counts as a valid inference in theology, say, might be completely unacceptable in chemistry, and vice versa" (2002, 266). Being able to see the ways that backing makes an argument reasonable or logical *in its own context* can help students develop greater respect for intellectual and cultural differences.

When I want students to get at the backing behind a claim, I ask, "What way of knowing authorizes the assumptions underwriting the argument?"

Types of backing common to high school texts include the following:

Historical knowledge

Personal experience

Scientific method

Quantitative reasoning

Modern psychology

Religious faith

Philosophical beliefs

Constitutional law

Laissez-faire economics

Evolutionary biology

Authoritative or compelling backing can tip the scales in an argument's favor when the evidence, claims, and warrants aren't quite enough to get the job done on their own. Toulmin stresses the importance of "backing our warrants": "In defending a claim, that is, we may produce our data, our warrant, and the relevant qualifications and conditions, and yet find that we have still not satisfied our challenger"—especially if our challenger objects to our whole way of thinking (1958/2008, 95). In these cases, we need to provide assurances that the foundation of our reasoning is legitimate.

I think of the high school senior I observed who was making an argument about animals' capacity for pain and emotion in a class debate. When he claimed that animals don't suffer the same way humans do, he was challenged by his peers to demonstrate the source of his knowledge. "I don't know," the young man said defensively. "I'm not a scientist." This is why Toulmin says we need to know *how* we know what we know. If we can't back our warrants with authority, we might look like we're just making stuff up.

The field dependence of backing (i.e., the idea that backing comes from specific fields, such as physics, social science, or religious studies) connects us again to the importance of audience. Knowing what *kind* of backing is valued by a particular audience is key to effective argumentation. A speaker addressing a group of biologists will likely need to rely on different backing than the speaker addressing a group of lawyers. And, of course, anytime a writer or speaker can draw on specialized knowledge, that's going to be an ethos booster, too.

Backing and Students' Prior Knowledge

When we write argument prompts for our students, it's important to consider whether or not our students already have the backing to answer the question responsibly. If they don't—and we don't give it to them—we'll be grading a stack of essays full of factual errors and unfounded assumptions.

A colleague of mine made this point when she shared an aphorism reminiscent of one of my favorite lines from the 1987 film *The Princess Bride:* "Never go against a Sicilian when death is on the line!" My colleague's similarly sweeping and apt truism is "Never write a censorship question for an on-demand essay!" I look forward to the day when I'll be proved wrong on this account, but my experience thus far suggests that most students don't have the literary, legal, and ethical backing to answer a banned books question without substantial preparation. Think about it—how can students argue whether or not it's right or wrong to censor books if they don't know anything about constitutional law or the history of intellectual freedom? This doesn't mean they can't write superb essays as part of a full instructional unit. It just means that censorship tends not to bring out their best logical thinking when they're writing cold, because they usually can't ground their claims and evidence in an established body of knowledge.

Renewable energy questions related to our country's reliance on foreign oil also call for credentials most teenagers don't have. While sustainability is a timely and important topic, students need sufficient political, economic, and scientific knowledge to engage it responsibly. A question on the ethics of police collecting DNA samples during arrests presents a similar backing problem for most teens. Without legal knowledge of suspects' rights and how such evidence is used in court, it would be hard for kids to do more than speculate.

What's worse, questions like these can sometimes invite students to invent facts. Most of us have seen startling interpretations of the U.S. Constitution in our students' writing at one time or another. To hear my students paraphrase it, there are more freedoms in the Bill of Rights than were dreamt of in the founders' philosophy. What we don't want to do is hinder the development of students' logic radar by putting them in situations where they have to ignore what they don't know just to complete an assignment.

> Seeing backing as essential prior knowledge has important implications for lesson planning. If we want students to make informed and logically defensible arguments, we need to ask them questions that they can answer with the backing they have, or we must frontload them with the backing they need.

Avoiding Fallacies

Like invented facts, logical fallacies are signs of malfunctioning logic radar. Undetected sweeping generalizations are particular problems. At the risk of making a sweeping generalization of my own, I'd venture to say that any sentence that starts with "Society" could land the writer in logical trouble. Without Jane Austen's wry understanding of truths universally acknowledged, a broad, unqualified claim about what society thinks or does invites contradiction—and can make a writer seem naive and uninformed. In fact, logical fallacies of all sorts are ethos eroders. I make this point through the following activity.

Classroom Activity: Zombie Fallacies

The purpose of writing zombie fallacies is to create non-examples of defensible assertions. By using words that we've identified and prohibited as "dead words" because of their vagueness or extremity (e.g., *always, never, everyone, nobody,* etc.), students generate thesis statements that would be difficult to support logically. Zombie fallacies, in other words, are an exercise in how *not* to write a logical argument, the idea being that many students need to see a problem in order to avoid it. Resurrecting dead words also helps students see the connections among language choices, ethos, and logos.

Directions to Students: Write a thesis statement in which you "resurrect" as many dead words as possible, using a minimum of four from the list below. A dead word is a word that should generally be avoided or qualified in academic arguments because it is too vague, casual, or extreme, but for this exercise in how *not* to write a thesis, you get to bring dead words back to life! Try modifying a thesis you're currently working on or one that you've already written. After writing your "zombie" thesis, use the list below to identify the logical fallacies you've created. Remember: Zombies are the enemies of brains!

> Example: Because algebra has *always* caused graduation problems for *everyone*, it should *never* be an admission requirement for *any* college.

> Logical fallacies: Sweeping generalization and false causality

Dead Words
always, never, everyone, everybody, everywhere, all, none, good, bad, no one, everything, anything, perfect, nobody, obviously, totally, completely, no matter what, absolutely, any

Logical Fallacies (this is just a partial list)
Bandwagon: Appeal to the popular (e.g., "Everyone is doing it.")

False Causality: Claiming that something has caused something else when there is no logical connection or proof (e.g., "My boyfriend broke up with me because it was raining.")

Sweeping Generalization: Making a broad claim that doesn't account for variations and exceptions (e.g., "All women make good mothers.")

Hasty Generalization: Drawing a conclusion without sufficient evidence and analysis (e.g., "I'm a boy who likes to play video games. My brother likes to play video games. Therefore, all boys like to play video games.")

Appeal to Tradition: Basing an argument solely on long-standing practice (e.g., "We've always done things this way.")

False Analogy: Claiming that something is like something else without sufficient grounds for the comparison (e.g., "Eating a french fry is just like smoking a cigarette.")

Poisoning the Well: Unfairly prejudicing an audience against an alternative view (e.g., "Don't believe him—he's a liar and a cheat!")

Alexis's zombie rewrite of one of her thesis statements captures the spirit of this exercise beautifully; even the undead would be leery of defending the following argument. The italics show the dead words she added: "Media *obviously* distorts *all* views on gender by giving the idea that *everyone* should fit their gender's stereotype *no matter what*." Alexis correctly identified "sweeping generalization" as the fallacy created by this act of revivification.

Connecting Ideas

Much of the logical reasoning we want students to apply happens at the sentence and paragraph level in their own writing. This is logic as it relates to cohesive writing. As writers, we know we have a logical knot to untangle when we find ourselves stuck at a tricky transition. That feeling of "How am I going to get out of this one?" or "What have I gotten myself into now?" is an indication that our logic radar is working during the composing process.

Writers work to create logical cohesion when they do the following:

Make decisions about sentence or paragraph transitions

Cue the reader about an upcoming move

Prepare a reader for a controversial claim or unexpected conclusion

Tighten the link between a claim and its support

Classroom Activity: List, Group, Label Revisited

List, Group, Label (LGL) can give students practice creating logical coherence. Creating order from chaos was a favorite pastime of the ancient Greeks. Little surprise they were such huge fans of systems of classification. LGL, of course, is an exercise in taxonomy that requires students to think about both the associative (the groups) and the hierarchical (the labels) relationships within a disorderly assortment of stuff (the list).

To get my students thinking about the order-making, logic-focused aspect of LGL, I add the following directions:

Pretend you're an archaeologist who's just landed on an alien planet, and you've found a lot of alien-made stuff. You don't know what it is, and you don't have any preconceptions about what it might be. So you just start sorting and looking for patterns. What things seem to go together? What items belong in different categories? Are there any things that can't easily be classified? Any anomalies or outliers? How are the groups similar to each other? How are they different?

(For a sample list, see the inventory of emotions for the pathos LGL activity on pages 154–155 of this chapter.)

Following the activity, we have a discussion on these questions, noting the way their sorting choices create logical coherence.

LGL works particularly well as a prewriting activity to sort the evidence students have gathered for an essay. The resulting groups then become the "chunks" of the essay while the labels become part of the topic sentences. Having students write quotations, paraphrases, and summaries on individual index cards allows them to physically sort their evidence into the piles that will ultimately give them the structure of their essay. Using LGL to create an essay outline in this open-ended way is a particularly good idea for students who have a hard time breaking away from the five-paragraph essay.

Logos Analysis

Lastly, a detailed Logos Analysis (Figure 6.9 and Appendix 19) can help students move beyond a simple definition of logos as "a logical appeal" to a more complex understanding of how a writer's use of evidence, qualifiers, and counterarguments contribute to both the effectiveness of the argument and the credibility of the writer's ethos. (See Appendix 19a for a blank Logos Analysis and 19b for a teacher-made sample.) Compare the Logos Analysis for "Is Algebra Necessary?" shown in Figure 6.9 to the Ethos and Pathos Analyses on this same article (see Figure 6.7 and Figure 6.8 in this chapter) for a better understanding of the way these appeals interact in Andrew Hacker's argument.

FIGURE 6.9

Logos Analysis for "Is Algebra Necessary?">

Logos Analysis

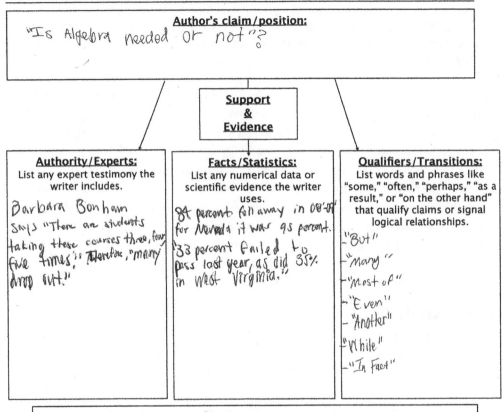

Author's claim/position:

"Is Algebra needed or not"?

Support & Evidence

Authority/Experts:
List any expert testimony the writer includes.

Barbara Bonham says "There are students taking these courses three, four, five times." Therefore, "many drop out."

Facts/Statistics:
List any numerical data or scientific evidence the writer uses.

84 percent fell away in 08-09 for Nevada it was 95 percent. "33 percent failed to pass last year, as did 35% in West Virginia."

Qualifiers/Transitions:
List words and phrases like "some," "often," "perhaps," "as a result," or "on the other hand" that qualify claims or signal logical relationships.

"But"
"Many"
"Most of"
"Even"
"Another"
"While"
"In Fact"

Counterarguments:
List any opposing views the writer mentions.

"Why do we subject American students to this ordeal? I've found myself moving toward the strong view that we shouldn't."

Quickwrite: How reasonable does this writer seem to you? Is the writer careful to make claims that can be supported by evidence? Does the writer seem fair and unbiased? Does the writer consider different viewpoints? Make concessions?

In my opinion, the writer seems reasonable because he states many facts and statistics that Algebra is a huge factor to why many students fail. Also, he seems fair because he does use numbers as he stated. In addition, he uses a couple view points as math is necessary in our society. He's credible to what others have to say.

Putting It All Together: The Rhetorical Analysis of an Argument Project

The final activity in this chapter is an extended exercise in integrating and applying the three appeals through a full rhetorical analysis of an argument. This assignment was created by Ernest Stromberg, my colleague at CSU Monterey Bay, and was adapted for high school students. I'm grateful to Loretta Bernasconi at Salinas High School (alma mater of John Steinbeck!) in Salinas, California, for her help reimagining the original college assignment for an audience of teenagers.

Because of the complexity of the tasks, this assignment is best suited to seniors (or nearly college-ready juniors) who have been working on rhetorical skills throughout the year. Even then, students will likely need a good bit of modeling, coaching, and reassurance. Breaking the process of rhetorical analysis down into manageable steps helps. Students will also need some time to work on the assignment in class.

RHETORICAL ANALYSIS OF AN ARGUMENT PROJECT (USED WITH PERMISSION FROM ERNEST STROMBERG)

> Analysis: "The separation of a whole into constituents with a view to its examination and interpretation" (*The American Heritage Dictionary*).

> Rhetoric: "The art of effective expression and the persuasive use of language" (*The American Heritage Dictionary*).

Directions to Students: **For this project, you will be creating two products: a group presentation and an individual essay. We'll complete the rhetorical reading process together in small groups, but you'll work through the rhetorical writing process on your own.**

Step 1: **In your assigned groups, choose an article from a newspaper, journal, or magazine (print or online) that makes an argument. Try looking at the op-ed pages of a newspaper for possible arguments to analyze. Many major newspapers are available online. You might also look at the opinion sections of magazines such as *Time* or *Newsweek* or at music or film reviews. After you've found your article, work together in your group to complete a rhetorical analysis of the writer's argument. To analyze an argument means to take it apart in order to understand how its various parts work together to achieve persuasion (or not). This kind of analysis helps us to evaluate the effectiveness of an argument. Use everything you know about playing the believing game, playing the doubting game, understanding the rhetorical situation, and analyzing ethos, pathos, and logos.**

Step 2: **As a team, you will now develop evaluation criteria for judging the effectiveness of an argument. If possible, review rubrics that have been used in the past to grade your essays. Create a bulleted list of criteria, or standards, for evaluating the argument you analyzed (see the sample provided).**

Step 3: Prepare a PowerPoint or Prezi group presentation showcasing the results of your rhetorical analysis. Create six to eight slides representing the main findings of your analysis. Identify the text's author, title, and source. Slides should include direct quotations from the text, as well as your analysis of the effects of the writer's choices. In other words, your slides should explain what the writer is saying and doing. Include your evaluation criteria and a visual that best represents the main argument your article makes. Present your analysis to the class as a group.

Step 4: Say "thank you" and "goodbye" to your group members. You will now individually write a three- to four-page essay analyzing and evaluating your selected argument. For this assignment, please use specific concepts and terms from our study of rhetorical reading and writing. This may include terms and ideas from Aristotle or Stephen Toulmin, along with other rhetoricians whose works you've read. For instance, maybe you see the writer as creating an especially effective ethos or using especially strong backing in support of his or her claims.

Prewriting Activities
Before you begin drafting your essay, please do the following:

- After rereading the argument your group analyzed, look closely at the text structure. First summarize each paragraph. Then find the argument's main claim (thesis) and underline it. Identify the main reasons offered in support of the main claim and circle them. If the argument engages any alternative perspectives, identify those perspectives and circle them in a different color.

- Try using the annotation and descriptive outlining strategies you've learned. Notice not only what the text says but also how it says it.

- Analyze the language and style of the argument. Does the argument use any metaphors or other types of figurative language? Is there any emotionally charged language in the text?

- Analyze the writer's ethos. Does the writer use *I* or *we*? Why or why not? How would you characterize the writer's tone—Angry? Funny? Serious? Sarcastic? Bitter? Joyful? Amused? Outraged? How does the writer come off as a person? What adjectives would you use to describe the writer's image? Does the writer have the authority to speak on the topic? Do you trust this writer? Why or why not?

- Analyze the logos. What kinds of data as support does the writer offer? Firsthand experience? Statistics? Interviews? Statements from authorities? Citations from research? Anecdotes? Does the data seem to support (warrant) the claims? Do you see any problems in the logic of the argument?

- Analyze the pathos and audience appeals. For whom do you think this argument was written? Do you see any evidence that it targets specific populations in terms of values, beliefs, education, economic class, race/ethnicity, or gender? Does the argument seem to try to stir up any specific emotions—anger, sympathy, disgust, joy, etc.? To what extent do you feel that you share the underlying values and assumptions of this piece?

- Make conclusions about the overall effectiveness. How successful is this argument, overall? What are the most important factors contributing to either its success or its failure? Explain what criteria you are using to evaluate this argument.

Write a First Draft

Introduction. Use the introduction to introduce your readers to the argument you are analyzing. Describe the question at issue and the argument's main claim. Let the readers know where it was published and who the author is.

The Body. Share your criteria for analyzing and evaluating the argument. Show your readers how the argument is effective or ineffective using the evidence you generated in your prewriting. Don't simply present your analysis as a list. Rather, decide which of the writer's choices contribute the most to the argument's success or lack of success, and make those rhetorical choices your focus.

Conclusion. Here is a place to make an overall evaluation of the argument. Based on all the evidence you have presented in the body of your essay, explain why you conclude that, overall, the argument is effective or not effective. Remember, you do not have to end by agreeing or disagreeing with the argument. Your task is to analyze and evaluate the rhetorical strategies the writer uses.

Criteria for Assessment

- The analysis demonstrates critical, analytical, and supportive rhetorical reading and writing skills (i.e., the analysis shows the student's ability to read with and against the grain).
- The analysis demonstrates a clear sense of purpose and provides good reasons and specific evidence to support its conclusion.
- The essay demonstrates the ability to ask relevant questions and critically identify and explore significant information.
- The essay respectfully addresses diverse points of view.
- The essay demonstrates the ability to make appropriate use of writing conventions, including grammar, spelling, punctuation, and organization.

This project takes a lot of time and effort both in and out of class, but when your students are finished, you'll have a summative assessment of their rhetorical literacy skills.

Conclusion

On the first day of class this year, one of my new students looked concerned after hearing that we would be using a rhetorical approach to argumentation. "Are we going to have to use ethos, pathos, and logos in all our essays?" she asked. "I find that really hard to do." Her question suggested that she saw the appeals as radically different and that swinging from intense emotion to cool logic would make her writing seem fickle and confused. Then I explained that using all three appeals just meant paying careful attention to your voice, your audience, and your language. As P. J. Corbett and Rosa A. Eberly explain, the key elements of reasoning are "language and human beings in relation with each other" (2000, 8)—components that involve ethos, pathos, and logos.

I know my students are starting to cross the threshold into a more sophisticated understanding of rhetorical appeals when they say things like this:

> "So I can write the principle first and then give an example *or* I can write the example first and then give the principle, right?"

> "I think I need a little more evidence for this claim before I move on."

> "I'm going to move my anecdote to my introduction so my reader knows why I care about this topic."

I love these moments. Ben, one of my summer bridge students at CSU Monterey Bay, made the genius discovery that he could distinguish between his ethos and the ethos of the writers he was citing in his paper by shifting to a slightly more casual and personal style when expressing his own ideas.

"Can I do that?" he asked in surprise.

"Well, does that move work for an academic audience?" I asked back.

"Yeah, maybe if I go right back to using an academic voice and evidence afterward."

Ben was learning what all mature writers learn at some point in their growth—that the effectiveness of our rhetorical choices depends on how we finesse the relationships among the writer (through ethos), the reader (through pathos), and the text (through logos). If we think we have enough reader trust and support for our claims, we can "bend the rules" a bit, provided we reassure our audience that we know our stuff and still have their needs and interests in mind. It's a matter of achieving the right balance.

Our ultimate goal is for students to make nimble use of the three rhetorical appeals as the rhetorical situation demands.

Points to Remember

As you plan your lessons and teach the concepts described in this chapter, you might want to refer to the following list of points to remember:

1.   Ethos, pathos, and logos are threshold concepts that require students to see texts differently.

2. Threshold concepts can be troublesome because they represent disciplinary ways of thinking that may be alien to many students (Meyer and Land 2003).

3. A deep understanding of the three rhetorical appeals includes the ability to analyze, evaluate, integrate, and apply them.

4. A writer's ethos is enhanced by his or her use of logical and emotional appeals.

5. Praising students' "instincts" for identifying faulty logic or syntax in their own writing helps to build their confidence and sense of self-efficacy.

6. Students need to read a wide variety of texts before they can understand that effective writing is based on choices, not rules.

7. Ethos, pathos, and logos have the same kind of provisional nature as occasion, audience, and purpose; what choices are effective depends upon a particular set of conditions.

Prompts for Quick-Writes or Pairs Conversations

The following prompts can be used before, during, or after a lesson to help students make personal connections, deepen their understanding, and reflect on their learning:

1. Describe a person you admire. What does this person represent to you?

2. Are you more motivated by love or fear? Why? What about anger?

3. Do commercials and advertisements that use statistics and scientific evidence persuade you to buy their products? If so, why? Describe an example.

4. Describe a time when you felt you had a chance to change your identity. What gave you the opportunity to be a "different" person? What happened?

5. How do you know when you've gone too far "out on a limb" in making an argument? What warning signs alert you to the danger of making claims that are too extreme or difficult to support?

6. Describe your process for gathering and organizing your evidence for an argument essay. How do you choose what evidence to include? How does your evidence influence the structure of your essay?

CHAPTER 7

Aristotle's Guide to Becoming a "Good" Student

It is not unimportant, then, to acquire one sort of habit or another, right from our youth. On the contrary, it is very important, indeed all-important.

— Aristotle

[Students who are college and career ready] habitually perform the critical reading necessary to pick carefully through the staggering amount of information available today in print and digitally.

—COMMON CORE STATE STANDARDS

This is not a chapter that you'll find in other books on rhetoric. Those books are for college students—or for high school students who are already so well prepared for college that it probably doesn't much matter what their teachers do. Those books launch straight into the nuts and bolts of argumentation as if students can't wait to party with logical fallacies, underlying assumptions, and discourse communities. But what about the students who have checked out before the fun even starts? *Preparing* students to be academically prepared sometimes means backing up a few steps and dealing with the reasons why some kids don't see themselves as "college material."

Consider the following scenario: It's sixth period in my sophomore English class. I assigned act 2 from *Julius Caesar* for the previous night's homework, and now I'm ready to discuss how Shakespeare's use of foreshadowing contributes to the play's rising action. "What signs do you see of trouble brewing?" I ask, my marker poised to record a flurry of responses on the whiteboard. Nothing. Not a single student read the assignment. Something has obviously gone wrong.

This scene will sound familiar to most teachers. Many of us, in fact, have given up assigning difficult texts for independent reading because we know our students simply won't do their homework, and we don't want the next day's lesson derailed by incomplete assignments. Yet we also know that our students need more than basic literacy skills to succeed in life beyond high school—and that advanced proficiency in rhetorical reading and writing requires hours of routine practice. So how can classroom teachers influence what happens outside of the classroom? How do we prepare students for academic work if they don't see themselves as students?

Why Should We Focus More on Habit and Identity?

Nurturing students' academic habits and identities can be an important place to start. Aristotle says that "we are completed through habit" (1999; Book II, Chapter 1, line 26); in other words, we are what we practice. He gives several examples: "We become just by doing just actions, temperate by doing temperate actions, brave by doing brave actions" (1999; Book II, Chapter 1, lines 2–3). If we accept this idea, then we have to believe that teenagers become independent and critical thinkers by repeatedly doing independent and critical brain work. Aristotle also wisely (and reassuringly) points out that teachers are needed to help habituate citizens into positive social roles because we are not born a "good" or "bad" anything (NE 1999; Book II, Chapter 2).

While the rest of this book targets those intellectual habits that characterize rhetorical literacy, this final chapter addresses some of the metacognitive and physical habits that are not commonly included in discussions of academic preparation. It's worth noting that classical rhetoric doesn't distinguish between "work habits" and proficiency in argument and reasoning. From Aristotle's perspective, how we think and how we live are two sides of the same coin.

Throughout this chapter, teachers will find strategies for promoting students' academic identities and habits. We might think of this as Aristotle's guide to becoming a good student—or as the prep work necessary for the rigorous, principled argumentation we want students to enjoy in our classrooms.

Why Logos Isn't Enough

The trouble with a strictly logical approach to academic preparation is that many of the teenagers we're trying to reach don't use deductive reasoning to make decisions about their schoolwork. Figures on the earning potential of college graduates, accountability measures like exit exams, expectations of college faculty and employers, reports of declining literacy skills, international comparisons of educational achievement—this kind of empirical evidence might convince teachers or administrators that academic preparation is important, but it rarely moves reluctant students to action. The time horizon is often too distant, the rewards and consequences too delayed or indirect.

That's why when it comes to increasing students' motivation, engagement, and self-efficacy, pathos and ethos can be more persuasive than logos, especially for our most vulnerable students. Many kids won't try the harder stuff in school unless they first see the fun and relevance of it. Before they tackle something like forensic rhetoric, students often need reassurance that they won't look fake or stupid doing this kind of brain work.

Ethos Revisited

Global economic competition may not matter much to teenagers, but social identity sure does. High school students know firsthand the problem of ethos that James Paul Gee describes in *Social Linguistics and Literacies:*

> Children are "hailed" ("summoned") to be different sorts of students in different classrooms, even in different domains like literature or science. In one and the same classroom, different children may be "hailed" to be different types of students. One, for example, may be "hailed" to be a "gifted student" and the other a "problem student." (2012, 2)

Gee's point about context shaping identity is an everyday experience for teenagers. Those students who have been "hailed" or identified as "problem students" because they struggle academically may find it particularly hard to create a credible ethos for themselves when it comes time to write or speak in a classroom.

The Academic Identity Confidence Survey

I invite students to explore the idea of situated academic identity early in the fall semester by having them complete an Academic Identity Confidence Survey. The statements in this survey ask students to assess how confident they feel in different scenarios or performing different academic tasks. What I'm after is an inventory of the school situations students already feel comfortable in, as well as those that tend to raise their anxieties. Because students respond to the survey using a scale from 1 to 5, I'm also trying to help students see that academic confidence can be mapped on a developmental trajectory. We all feel insecure when learning something new, and we become increasingly confident as we make progress toward mastery.

The directions and the first few statements for this activity follow. You'll find the full survey in Appendix 20.

Directions to Students: **Decide the extent to which you agree or disagree with each statement below. If you feel highly confident that the statement is true for you, write a number 5. If you feel the statement is not at all true for you, write a number 1.**

5 = strongly agree
4 = agree
3 = unsure
2 = disagree
1 = strongly disagree

____ I will be well prepared for the reading and writing demands of college and the workplace when I graduate from high school.

____ Twenty years from now I will be making important contributions to our society.

____ I can see myself as a successful student at a four-year university.

____ I have valuable ideas to contribute to our society.

____ Teachers are interested in my opinions.

____ Politicians are interested in my opinions.

____ Employers are interested in my opinions.

____ I can see myself giving a speech before an audience.

____ I can see myself publishing an article, poem, song, or book.

____ I have an important influence on my friends and family.

____ I know how to write an essay for an academic audience.

____ I know how to write a business letter.

____ I feel confident in my English class.

____ I feel confident in my math class.

This exercise can later be used as prewriting for either an essay defining college success or a literacy autobiography (see "College Success Letter" on page 189 in this chapter).

How Does Self-Perception Affect Performance?

Kids who see themselves as "good" students tend to trust their efforts. Because they believe in their ability to adapt and learn, these students have a high sense of "self-efficacy" (Ruddell and Unrau 2004). We can think of self-efficacy as a kind of faith in future results; it's a student's belief that, through personal effort, he or she can master new knowledge and skills. The idea of self-efficacy also reflects an understanding that academic competency is an acquired—not a natural—ability. Everyone can relate to the feeling of being a novice. We expect to make mistakes when learning to ride a bike, play soccer, or drive a car. However, some students don't see the same learning curve when it comes to their academic work. They see themselves as "bad" students who have "always" struggled in school. Revealing the process of apprenticeship that all learning requires can reassure many frustrated students—and help them understand that the first step toward better performance is to see themselves as capable of achievement. Students who develop this strong sense of self-efficacy are, not surprisingly, more motivated to improve their reading and writing skills.

Self-efficacy can be especially important for low-income and minority students.

Research suggests that sustained effort over time, as reflected by high school GPA, is a more accurate predictor of college success than high-stakes assessments like the SAT—a test on which students with high socioeconomic status typically outperform students with low socioeconomic status (Geiser and Santelices 2007). Personal attributes such as motivation, discipline, and perseverance—in other words, a high sense of self-efficacy—can be even more important indicators of academic preparation than traditional aptitude tests. This means that students who consistently trust their efforts have a better chance of completing a college education.

Expanding our sense of academic preparation to include the development of students' academic habits of mind and identities has significant implications for teachers. From this perspective, learning involves more than mastering new competencies; it requires new ways of being in the world. Elizabeth Birr Moje and Cynthia Lewis explain this broader view:

> Learning is thus not only participation in discourse communities, but it is also the process by which people become members of discourse communities, resist membership in such communities, are marginalized from discourse communities (or marginalize others), reshape discourse communities, or make new ones. (2007, 20)

Being college ready and career ready means being able to engage, resist, and reshape academic communities and conversations—and not be marginalized by them.

Insider Knowledge

Another activity that can support students' sense of a developing academic ethos is one I call Insider Knowledge. Like the Translating for Outsiders activity in Chapter 4, this learning experience draws on the confidence and expertise students may already enjoy in other areas of their lives to help them reflect on their in-school identity. It also serves as a good reminder that specialized knowledge requires specialized language. (See Appendix 21 for a reproducible version of this activity.)

Directions to Students:

Step 1: Generate a list of words from a subject you know well but that your teacher and classmates may know little about. For example, this could be your favorite style of music, computer game, sport, comic book series, after-school job, or any other subject you are an expert on. What specialized words do you use when you talk about this subject? Include slang and jargon if appropriate.

Step 2: Using words from your list, write a paragraph describing your subject. Try to make this paragraph challenging for an "outsider" to read. Feel free to use slang and jargon; your paragraph does *not* have to follow the rules of standard English.

Quick-Write: How does your insider knowledge of this subject affect your identity? In what ways does being an "expert" in this field impact how you see yourself?

Oscar chose to write his paragraph (Step 2) on the sport of track and field in the form of a conversation between two athletes:

A1:	Hey man, you ready to do work today?
A2:	You know it, bro, it's time to tear it up! Not only am I going for a P.R., but I'm going home with some hardware today.
A1:	That right? You know there's elite racing in your heat, right?
A2:	Yeah, it's all good, I brought that fuel that's gonna set me on fire, no worries.
A1:	Alright man, good luck out there. I'm going go get some strides in and get ready for showtime!
A2:	Just don't be the bandit that gets caught.

Oscar's quick-write on how his insider knowledge of running affects his self-perception shows a sophisticated understanding of the relationship between language and identity. This is the level of insight that will help Oscar transfer his insider experience to new tasks and contexts:

Being a runner for the past several years and knowing the insider
knowledge allows me to make immediate friends with others who are also
in the sport. When I talk this way with others I feel a sense of identity that
I belong there. It reassures my place in the sport and it is something that
no one can take away. Being an "expert" has impacted me in many ways.
I can communicate easily with others who are knowledgeable. I feel like I
can be a good coach to others. Thanks to this knowledge, my teammates,
and coaching staff, I feel proud of myself when I win races.

It's exciting to see the glimpse into students' lives this activity offers. Students who may have
shown only lukewarm reactions to the academic texts we read suddenly come to life when
writing about their insider knowledge. Describing her insider knowledge of music, Jenn
wrote that "it allows me to be who I am and to show what I like and what my passion is."
We conclude this activity by talking about the areas of their school lives where they enjoy, or
could enjoy, this same sense of member privilege.

Pathos and Passion

I rely on pathos early and often to engage reluctant learners in my classes. Remember that
list of human emotions from Chapter 6? *Anger, desire, joy, hilarity, amusement, enthusiasm,
excitement,* and even *shock:* These are powerful allies in our work to prepare more kids for
college and career. Pathos is about discovering what moves us; it's the catalyst that transforms
"I know it's good for me, but I still don't care" into "I'm doing this today."

When I asked recent high school graduates in our summer bridge program to write a letter
to themselves describing what it means to be successful in college, passion dominated over
pragmatics. Anyssa, for instance, wrote that to be successful in college "you must know the
difference between thriving and surviving. Students can muddle through college and pass their
classes with flying colors. However, they have only survived college. Who wants to survive
when you can thrive and take so much more away from the experience?" Alondra defined
college success as being "completely engaged academically, socially, and emotionally with a
foundation that includes a positive perspective in life." Most of the students in this program
were native Spanish speakers from the agricultural communities of the Salinas Valley. Attending college required significant financial sacrifices from these students and their families, but
most were still more motivated by the intrinsic rewards of the college experience than by the
material rewards of a college degree.

Connecting the Personal to the Academic

I love Alondra's definition of college success as being "engaged academically, emotionally, and
socially," and I look for learning experiences that create this holistic, integrative experience.
One I found is the Personal Argument Case Analysis Assignment, created by my colleagues

in the Division of Humanities and Communication at California State University, Monterey Bay. This writing assignment thoughtfully connects students' personal experiences and emotions to the study of argumentation.

Personal Argument Case Analysis Assignment

Directions to Students: Write a three- to four-page essay in which you identify, explore, and analyze your participation in an argument. By argument is meant a verbal or written exchange with one or more other person(s) in which you disagreed about something. This should be a situation in which you and the other participant(s) considered the outcome important (not an argument where you had little at stake, such as an argument about ice cream flavors), and you were both emotionally engaged.

In your analysis, please include the following:

- A detailed description of the situation: What was the argument about (the question at issue)? Who was involved? Why was the issue important? What were the positions?

- What was your position, and why did you take this position (your reasons)?

- What emotions did you and the other participant(s) feel?

- What reasons did the other participant(s) offer for their position(s)? Were you able to sympathize with the other participant(s)' reasons and understand their perspective? In other words, could you play the believing game?

- How did the argument conclude? Was it a satisfactory conclusion from your perspective? Why or why not? Was/were the other participant(s) satisfied with the outcome?

- What impact did this argument have on your relationship with the other person or people involved?

- In retrospect, would you have changed anything that you did? Why or why not?

Criteria for Assessment

- Demonstrates the ability to reflect, understand, and synthesize different points of view— your view, view of person(s) you argued with, and views of other involved parties.

- Demonstrates the ability to take apart a complex communication situation and analyze how its different elements contribute to the whole experience and message.

- Demonstrates the ability to communicate about a personal experience with insight and empathy.

- Demonstrates the ability to apply appropriate writing conventions, including grammar, spelling, punctuation, and organization.

This assignment offers a good opportunity for students to bridge their in-school and out-of-school experiences while exploring key components of arguments.

Developing Academic Skills and Identities

One of my favorite new ways to link rhetorical literacies to academic identity development is through an analytical reading of Joe Rodriguez's "10 Rules for Going to College When Nobody Really Expected You To" (2012). I learned about this text from Rick Hansen at Cal State Fresno, who included Rodriguez's article in a module he wrote for Cal State's twelfth-grade Expository Reading and Writing Course.

Rodriguez's newspaper column—adapted from a graduation speech he gave at Menlo-Atherton Computer Academy—also serves as a terrific text for reviewing *kairos*, ethos, and pathos with your students. Notice how Rodriguez's opening lines signal a unique historical moment in American education:

> A vital revolution in American education has launched a slew of academic programs and charter schools that pluck bright minority, poor and blue-collar students from the educational abyss and turn them into college-bound scholars. Teachers are inspiring them to dream while showing them how to study, do research, write term papers, think critically and effectively cram for finals.
>
> In many ways, the kids have learned the hard parts of surviving college. But when the mere act of attending college is totally unexpected, there are unforeseen obstacles—including family and friends—that tend to blow nontraditional students off their paths like land mines.

Rodriguez goes on to offer first-generation college students pointed advice, including some my own students find controversial. There's this, for instance: He tells minority and blue-collar students not to let their studies be derailed by serious issues at home, even if it seems like their families really need them. Some of my students have to work hard at postponing their judgment to understand Rodriguez's point about long-range goals taking priority over short-term emergencies.

But it's Rodriguez's top five rules that get at the heart of how affect and identity impact the first-year college experience:

> No. 5: You will become lonely or homesick and it will upset you very much . . . Don't question whether you belong there—you do.
>
> No. 4: Get to know students of different racial, ethnic or social backgrounds.
>
> No. 3: Ignore career confusion. Stay in school even if your dream job seems to become a delusion.
>
> No. 2: You are much more than a future employee, so don't think like one.
>
> No. 1: Remember where you came from and who helped you get this far.

After reading the text together to get the gist of Rodriguez's argument, I then ask my students to annotate the text as part of their second reading. I like to make my own notes on the article first and then use my annotations to alert students to interesting rhetorical choices Rodriguez has made. Depending on how much and what kind of modeling a class needs, I may also choose to share my annotations using a document camera or overhead transparency. While my annotations reflect the understanding of an "expert" adult reader rather than a typical adolescent reader, they still can show kids the extent and depth of analysis we're after when we ask students to annotate texts. In *Write Like This,* Kelly Gallagher offers a nice justification for why this kind of teacher modeling is important. "You are the best writer in your classroom," Gallagher tells us (2011, 8). Showing students our own prewriting notes lets students in on our trade secrets.

You may alternatively find it helpful to have your students conduct a whole-class analysis of Rodriguez's article by using the Annotation Cue Cards in Appendix 22. (See page 29 in Chapter 2 for teaching tips for this activity.)

Eventually, Rodriguez's article becomes one of the sources my students use to write a letter to themselves defining college success.

College Success Letter

Directions to Students: Write a 3–4-page, double-spaced letter to yourself answering this question: What does it mean to me to be successful in college? Draw on your reading as evidence to support your points illustrating the habits of mind and rhetorical literacies you will need to cultivate (or keep) to be successful in college.

Possible readings to use as research sources for this letter:

CWP, NCTE, and WPA (Council of Writing Program Administrators, National Council of Teachers of English, and National Writing Project). *Framework for Success in Postsecondary Writing.* Berkeley, CA: National Writing Project, 2011. Print.

Garcia, Diana. "A Lifetime of Learning." AVID Writers Conference. California State University, Monterey Bay, Seaside, CA. 22 Mar. 2011.

Graff, Gerald. "Hidden Intellectualism." In *"They Say/I Say": The Moves That Matter in Academic Writing,* ed. Gerald Graff and Cathy Birkenstein. 3rd high school ed. New York: W. W. Norton, 2014. 244–251. Print.

Rodriguez, Joe. "10 Rules for Going to College When Nobody Really Expected You To." Student Sites. SunShine Web Enterprise, 4 June 2012. Web. Mar. 2013. http://www.mercurynews.com/ci_20778835/10-rules-college-nobody-expected-blue-collar.

Schreiner, Laurie A. "The 'Thriving Quotient': A New Vision for Student Success." *About Campus,* 15(2), 2010.

Finding the Teachable Moments: *Kairos* Meets Ethos and Pathos

Rodriguez's article teaches the lesson that personal situations matter. The educational context of each student is unique. Where and with whom they live, whether or not they work, past school experiences, health, friends, safety, culture, gender, and language are among the many factors that shape the *kairotic* moments in our students' school lives. Add to this mix our institutional context—big or small school; urban, suburban, or rural; multicultural or mono-cultural; languages spoken on campus; resources; faculty; administration, and so on—and we start to see the full complexity of our learning environments. When we teach rhetorically, we enhance our ability to respond to the situated learning of the students in our classes.

Kairos, ethos, and pathos work together in shaping the academic lives and identities of our students. This lesson was brought home to me on one of those quiet fall Southern California afternoons when the sound of a passing airplane feels like a page turning in our lives. I'd lingered a bit after the lunch bell, straightening a stack of essays that never seemed to grow any smaller. Three students wandered in, all seniors. They said that they didn't really need anything but saw that my door was open and wanted to see what I was doing. So we made small talk for a bit before the truth started to spill out. They'd completed their college applications and were terrified at the prospect of what the future held for them. Afraid of the unknown, afraid of their inexperience, afraid of their impending separations from family and friends, afraid of making mistakes—they poured out their vulnerabilities to me. So I let the walls come down, too. I told them my story about grad school, how hard it was learning to be a teacher, how clueless I felt as a new mother, and they listened, wide-eyed and reassured. When I'd finished, they said, "I didn't know we could talk to teachers like this." And I thought, *I didn't know I could talk to students like this.* It was a magical moment of mutual recognition and empathy. I learned that we do our students no favors by obscuring personal experiences and self-perceptions that are central to learning.

The Importance of Modeling and Mentoring

In *Write Like This,* Kelly Gallagher reminds teachers that "students must see the process to understand the process. They must 'stand' next to you to see how you do it" (2011, 16). For me, this now includes the process of intellectual growth. Revealing what we've experienced over the course of our academic development is particularly important for the many multilingual and first-generation college-bound students we serve in our schools. When our students feel like academic life just isn't for them, we can be the ones to say, "It's OK—I felt like that, too."

One of my first moves is to self-disclose the times I've felt like a fraud or amateur in my academic life. When I was a new teacher, I was afraid if I showed anything less than perfect composure and expertise my students would eat me alive. However, I've learned that being candid about my own struggles has paradoxically enhanced my ethos with students, especially when I can stand in solidarity with them and say, "Look, you can expect to feel discouraged during some of the tougher transitions. That's why flexibility and resilience matter so much."

FLOURISHING IN AN ACADEMIC LIFE

Much of this sharing occurs when I write what I ask my students to write. For instance, the following is a list of quick-write prompts that I ask my students to respond to during the beginning, middle, and end of a semester. The prompts ask students to reflect on the ups and downs of a typical learning cycle and how their habits of mind can help them flourish in an academic life. You'll find my own response to the first prompt after the list.

- What assets (e.g., personal strengths, experiences, abilities, prior knowledge, etc.) have been important to your learning during the early weeks of the semester? What habits of mind best support your intellectual growth at this stage? Describe a specific example of your experience.

- In what ways are you connecting to your school community? What steps have you taken to be an engaged learner? Give a specific example of your experience.

- What obstacles to learning are you encountering during the middle of the semester? What habits of mind help you to meet these challenges? Describe a specific example of your experience.

- How do you see yourself using what you've learned in this course in other classes or disciplines? What steps will you take to continue developing your skills and knowledge after the class is over? Describe a specific example.

Teacher Model

What assets (e.g., personal strengths, experiences, abilities, prior knowledge, etc.) have been important to your learning during the early weeks of the semester? What habits of mind best support your intellectual growth at this stage? Describe a specific example of your experience.

As someone who has spent her life in education, I have a lot of new semesters to look back on for my own reflection. The one that stands out the most is my first term at Queen Mary College in London, where I was writing my doctoral dissertation. I think this was the first real moment in my intellectual growth when I became aware that I would need more than just academic knowledge and skills to succeed on the path I'd chosen. I'd also need a tremendous amount of resilience and flexibility—and I'd need to trust that my prior experiences and abilities were more valuable than they at first seemed.

This story begins in Mrs. Peet's boardinghouse. Resting at the suburban edge of London, Mrs. Peet's Victorian duplex provides quiet lodging for medical students from the East End hospitals. I found Mrs. Peet when I was searching for graduate housing through a website called "Doctor in the House." Since I was writing my doctoral dissertation on British literature, I thought Mrs. Peet and I could do business. Imagine my embarrassment when I learned my new landlady only rented me a room because she thought I was a budding neurosurgeon—not the California schoolteacher turned amateur scholar that I was.

My first night at Mrs. Peet's I faced some difficult questions: What was I doing here? What did I know about working as a full-time researcher? As it turned out, very little. Graduate study was as obscure a labyrinth to me as the tunnels of the London Underground. Without experience, I had no confidence, and without confidence, I had no identity. I was just an unemployed tourist in the wrong boardinghouse. It didn't help that, upon hearing that I'd sold my house and taken a year's leave of absence from my job as a high school teacher to come to London, Mrs. Peet said, "Wasn't that a bit drastic?"

Having to consciously struggle with how I saw myself in unfamiliar terrain made me mindful of the role identity and belonging play in new learning. I came to see that some of my best assets—like my willingness to take risks and my experience as a classroom teacher—would continue to serve me well even if I at first felt woefully in over my head and out of my element.

In Hindsight

Having been through this kind of experience several times, I now understand that this is just what it feels like to be new. Experience has taught me that what I used to take as signs that I was trying to be something I'm not are just the inevitable side effects of growth. Feelings of being an impostor still plague me at times. I'm not quick on my feet. I get nervous when I have to speak publicly. I feel overwhelmed when I start a new project. But I've learned that these feelings aren't indications that I'm overstepping my abilities—they're just predictable working conditions. In my maturity, I understand that feeling scared or underprepared is no reason to stop what I'm doing.

What Does Aristotle Say?

Year after year, I received the same suggestion from my high school students on my course evaluations: "Give less homework." While I had great compassion for the challenges my students faced out of school, I also believed that getting them to see homework as a habit and not a crisis would make their lives happier. Becoming a literate individual involves learning how to acquire habituated "virtues" in the midst of all the stresses high school students experience every day. For Aristotle, virtue of character—or ethos (see Chapter 6)—results from habit, not nature. Indeed, the Greek word for ethical character [ēthos] is a slight variation from the Greek word for habit [ethos] (NE 1999; Book II, Chapter 1). This kind of virtue is acquired or learned through repetition. As a philosopher in my department explains it, "We do the right thing because we've been doing the right thing." My students who consistently complete their homework after babysitting their younger siblings or working at their family's business have outstanding virtue of character.

Aristotle also discusses intellectual virtue, which requires experience, time, and teaching (NE 1999; Book II, Chapter 1). Like ethos, the Aristotelian virtues of thought (such as scientific knowledge, wisdom, deliberation, and comprehension) are likewise not "natural" but must be nurtured through instruction and choice. In the *Nicomachean Ethics,* Aristotle reminds his students that "excellence is an art won by training and habituation" (1999; Book II, Chapter 4; Book I, Chapter 7); it is daily living, in other words—and not a single, spectacular event—that most often determines success.

How Can We Help Students Create Engaged, Literate Lifestyles?

Our habits hence determine our lifestyle. When I was a beginning teacher, I didn't tell my students what I did with my personal time. It didn't occur to me that sharing my own lifestyle—even my literacy habits—might be relevant to my teaching goals. For example, I didn't tell my kids that I always have to read before I can write or that reading, for me, involves a good book, my favorite chair, and a cup of Earl Grey. Throw in Aaron Copland on my iPod and an early morning view, and I'm in reader's heaven. Reading is my favorite way to start the day—a combination of yoga and Starbucks for my mind, as necessary to my sense of purpose in life as faith and love and useful work.

This is not reading as most high school students know it. Reading for them is often a borrowed book in a stuffy classroom, ten minutes of enforced silence. No cup of tea or comfy chair for them. Yet, my students and I weren't discussing the differences in our reading habits. I would assign books but not address the experiential components—like furniture, food, atmosphere, and light—that could determine whether or not my students understood or enjoyed (or even read) the assigned text. In contrast, when teachers explicitly address how factors like time, space, and materials create academic "flow," we help our students understand that becoming an effective reader and writer largely depends on routinized literacy practices.

In *Flow: The Psychology of Optimal Experience*, psychologist Mihaly Csikszentmihalyi describes the energized focus that results from being totally immersed in doing something we love. Flow is the feeling of being "in the zone," "on point," or "on a roll"; it's a runner's high or musician's jam session. According to Csikszentmihalyi, an activity that creates flow is "so gratifying that people are willing to do it for its own sake" (1990, 71) or is, as Aristotle puts it, "choiceworthy in its own right" (NE 1999; Book X, Chapter 6). Positive psychologist Martin Seligman describes a life rich with flow as the "engaged life" (2011, 11).

In educational contexts, we can think of flow as the engine driving self-efficacy. Students who experience academic flow are so engrossed in their work that their efforts feel effortless. When we experience flow, we lose track of time, become completely preoccupied, and don't want to be interrupted or distracted. George Hillocks notes that under flow conditions students "want to learn more because it is fun and rewarding and makes them feel good about themselves" (2011, 1). Aristotle has his own version of this concept. He describes pleasure as uninterrupted activity and tells his students that "no activity is complete if it is impeded, and happiness is something complete" (NE 1999; Book VII, Chapter 12). How often do our students think of schoolwork as unimpeded happiness?

But many successful students know exactly what this feels like. They might remember spending an entire weekend building a model of King Arthur's Camelot or writing a song—or being so engrossed in a book that they missed their bus stop or forgot to eat dinner. We *know* millions of kids stayed up all night reading the final Harry Potter or Twilight book. Most teenagers, in fact, experience flow in some area of their life, just not in their academic work. In *Reading Don't Fix No Chevys* (2002) and *Going with the Flow* (2006), literacy researchers Michael W. Smith and Jeffrey D. Wilhelm offer numerous examples of teens' out-of-school flow experiences. The trick, as Smith and Wilhelm note, is helping more students apply the intrinsic motivation they feel when rebuilding an engine or playing a sport or computer game to independent reading and writing.

Identifying the characteristics and conditions of flow can enhance its portability; in other words, if students understand when, where, and why flow happens for them they can more easily create flow in new contexts. Smith and Wilhelm explain that the goal is "to make the literacy learning in school resemble the passionate engagements students seek outside the classroom" (2006, 3).

Consider Adrian. Fifteen-year-old Adrian had a gift for designing his own clothing. He would spend hours altering jackets and shirts, adding rivets, safety pins, zippers, and any other hardware he could find and then would laboriously hand-paint intricate images on the fabric. By consciously reflecting on how and why he did this intensive work (Where and when could he best concentrate? What materials did he need? How did he feel doing this work?) Adrian could identify the routines and environment that support his best efforts.

How Can We Help Our Kids Recognize Flow?

Csikszentmihalyi identifies key components of flow that apply to both academic and nonacademic activities. These include the following:

Clear expectations (it isn't fun if you don't know the rules)

Attainable goals (success is fun)

Appropriate level of difficulty (succeeding too easily isn't fun)

Immediate feedback (so you know what to do to succeed)

Loss of self-consciousness

Diminished awareness of time and place

Total absorption and concentration (Csikszentmihalyi 1990)

Well-prepared students (or what Joe Rodriguez might call "total" students) often enjoy their schoolwork precisely for these reasons; they are totally engrossed in challenging, attainable activities that offer them immediate feedback. When students make a habit out of academic flow, they develop a greater sense of self-efficacy because they feel their efforts are rewarded—both through the intrinsic pleasure of doing something they enjoy and through the long-term payoff of pursuing a goal they understand. Flow combined with self-efficacy is a potent package. As Ruddell and Unrau note, "A student with high self-efficacy will work harder, longer, and more willingly than one with low self-efficacy" (2004, 961)—and will likely have more fun doing it.

Reading and writing seem made for this kind of flow. Aristotle's teacher, Plato, understood this well. In *Phaedrus*, Plato describes the act of inspired composition as a type of divine madness in which the self is carried away by a higher power. In this famous dialogue, Plato's Socrates tells of a kind of "possession" by the Muses that "takes hold upon a gentle and pure soul [and] arouses it and inspires it to songs and other poetry" (1990, 123). In a twentieth-century context, writing scholar Peter Elbow similarly describes process writing as a transformative experience, fueled by almost magical forces. Elbow's *Writing Without Teachers* uses metaphors of cooking and fermentation to describe the organic interactions of high-energy writing (1998b). For Elbow, writing is a generative, surprising process full of "fecundity, novelty, richness" (52)—full, in Csikszentmihalyi's word, of flow.

Kids can recognize when they've achieved this kind of flow when they become "carried away" by a book or writing project. I remember how Chandra reacted when we were reading the final chapters of John Steinbeck's *Of Mice and Men* in class. She had become increasingly caught up in the story of George and Lennie's friendship and was deeply anxious about the plot's outcome. When she heard from older students that Lennie dies at the novel's end, she borrowed a book from our class set to read at home (ahead of schedule) so that she could confirm if her worst fears were true. She returned to school the next day looking angry and betrayed. "Why did you make us read this book?" she demanded. "It was horrible!" While I fully appreciated Chandra's sense of devastation, I also didn't believe she really thought the book was terrible. Her heartfelt reaction—and the superb essay she later wrote—instead testified to her profound engagement with this deeply moving text.

Tony was another student who got carried away with a text—in this case, his own. As a companion piece to a research project on the Salem witch trials, Tony decided to write a play about Puritan life. For weeks, he came into my classroom before school and during lunch to share his latest drafts, and I would often see him pacing the hallway, trying out lines of dialogue. Tony's finished project was brilliant.

In both of these examples, I had very little to do with the students' total immersion in their literacy experience. Indeed, a primary characteristic of both flow and self-efficacy is internal motivation. These kids had created for themselves what Judith Langer calls an "envisionment" (1995, 9), a dynamic and personal text-world. But what I could do was alert Chandra and Tony to the special thing that had happened to them. I could say, "Now, that's what it's supposed to feel like—go out and get some more of that!" Being aware of when reading or writing is more than just an assignment can motivate students to seek out other opportunities to develop healthy obsessions with academic work. We can do this by drawing students' attention to moments of inspiration in their own lives and helping them recognize and encourage those flashes of "divine madness" that threaten to carry them away in the best sense.

I also nudge students toward flow-consciousness by asking them to think about what habits they're developing as readers and writers. Not every rhetorical literacy strategy we teach is going to become a permanent part of our students' meaning-making repertoire. After our class has experimented with several strategies typically used by fluent readers and writers, my students complete a Reading Strategies Ranking (Appendix 23) and a Writing Strategies Ranking (Appendix 24) to identify their favorite ways of approaching texts. What I really want to know is which literacy practices are becoming internalized and automatic for my students (i.e., which strategies they're likely to deploy unconsciously under flow conditions). The ranking activities help students see their "go-to" literacy strategies, as well as letting them know it's OK if some strategies don't work as well for them. Our goal is for students to analyze and respond to complex texts independently, not to master Think-Pair-Share.

Reading Strategies Ranking

Directions to Students: Rank the following reading strategies according to your personal preferences. Write a number 1 next to the strategies you find very helpful, a 2 next to the strategies you find somewhat helpful, and a 3 next to any strategies that you do not find helpful.

___ Quick-writing to tap into prior knowledge

___ Reading the title, footnotes, subheadings, and discussion questions

___ Looking at pictures, graphs, and charts

___ Making predictions about the subject and confirming your predictions as you read

___ Asking questions about the text and finding answers as you read

___ Learning key vocabulary words

___ Asking questions about the author

___ Writing summaries of the main ideas

___ Completing graphic organizers of key concepts

___ Outlining or charting a text to see how it is organized

Quick-Write: Pick one of the strategies that you gave a 2 or 3 and explain why this strategy is less helpful to you than others. What are the steps of this strategy? How is this strategy supposed to help you read better? Why isn't this strategy as effective for you? Are you willing to give this strategy another chance?

Writing Strategies Ranking

Directions to Students: Rank the following writing strategies according to your personal preferences. Write a number 1 by the strategies you find very helpful, a 2 by the strategies you find somewhat helpful, and a number 3 by any strategies that you do not find helpful.

___ Quick-writing to brainstorm ideas

___ Completing a cluster or graphic organizer

___ Analyzing the writing prompt and understanding the directions

___ Looking at how the writing will be graded (e.g., rubric or evaluation criteria)

___ Discussing your thesis statement with a partner

___ Organizing the essay through an outline

___ Reading a rough draft aloud to a small group

___ Answering questions about plans for revision

___ Completing an editing checklist

___ Conducting peer evaluations using a scoring guide

Quick-Write: Pick one of the strategies that you gave a 2 or 3 and explain why this strategy is less helpful to you than others. What are the steps of this strategy? How is this strategy supposed to help you write better? Why isn't this strategy as effective for you? Are you willing to give this strategy another chance?

Note to Self: Go with the Flow

A strategy for encouraging inspiration-driven flow is to have students keep a Brainstorm Board. This could be a whiteboard, laminated sheet of paper, or even a page in a plastic sheet protector along with a dry erase marker or transparency pen that students keep someplace handy at home or wherever they do their best thinking. The idea is that students can use the Brainstorm Board to jot down ideas about a book or a writing project they're working on that occur to them as they go about their daily business. These could be questions, insights, memorable phrases, or anything else the student just happens to think of related to the text.

I keep a whiteboard in my bedroom closet just for this purpose because I always seem to think of titles for my writing projects when I'm drying my hair. The Brainstorm Board, in other words, is an inspiration-catcher. Adults who are deeply engaged in a project or issue know that our insights can appear at any time and place. We might be driving the car, putting away the groceries, or brushing our teeth, and—bam!—there's that idea we were looking for.

The digital voice recorder industry was built on this need to catch flashes of understanding as quickly as possible.

When students get to really live with and through a book or writing project, they also experience random jolts of insight, only they don't often write these ideas down or understand how capturing this heightened brain activity can help with their schoolwork. The goal is to feed the preoccupations that sustain flow.

Another fun and real-world approach to flow-friendly materials involves what we might call "unconventional school supplies." As students take increasing ownership for their out-of-school literacy experiences, they find that sometimes the best ideas occur to them when they're far from a computer or notebook. We can challenge students to catch these ideas on whatever materials they have at the moment—whether that's on a napkin, their cell phone, or a crumpled receipt. The professionals do no less; the ideas for the Pixar films *A Bug's Life, Monsters Inc., Finding Nemo,* and *Wall-E* were supposedly generated from some scribbled notes on napkins during a power lunch. I've had to use gum wrappers and lip liner a few times myself to record insights I wanted to remember.

Teachers can structure this experience by inviting students to Bring a Brainstorm to Class. In this activity, teachers might pose questions on the reading or writing assignments for students to think about as they go about their daily business (or might leave the brainstorming totally open) and then challenge students to capture a response with whatever they have handy *as the*

FIGURE 7.1

Bring a Brainstorm to Class: Paper bag notes on Shakespeare's comedies and tragedies
Photo by Jennifer Fletcher

idea spontaneously occurs to them. For example, students might consider the following kinds of muse-worthy questions: Why *is* Hamlet so indecisive? Does Emerson *really* mean imitation is suicide? What's a good hook for my essay? When a response occurs to them, students can then text themselves, record a voice message on their phone, write the answer on their arm or hand, scribble on a tardy slip, or use any other means to catch the brainstorm (see Figure 7.1 for an example). Students can then share their brainstorm experiences in class, reflecting on how this type of out-of-school thinking affects their lifestyle or self-perception.

Students brought the following brainstorms to class on yellow sticky notes. Their challenge was to find an engaging opening for their evaluative essay on zoos.

First Lines for My Essay:

"Zoos are not as entertaining and educational as you think they are." Daniel

"Zoos and aquariums are helpful to animals by lowering endangered species rank." Tania

"The love and care that zoos give is the example of life. Keep the zoos!" Hernan

"Keeping the animals in zoos is doing more harm than good. Take a stand." Lauren

"What do you think animals feel?" Abraham

"Do you like animals?" Cam

"It has been said that zoos are 'horror shows.'" Angelica

"Do you think zoos are good or bad for animals?" Ian

"Imagine being in their shoes with fear and distress in a cage." Destiny

"Let's go to the zoo!" Karla

"Zoos help save animals from extinction." Anna

General Ideas for My Hook:

"I'm going to start with sarcasm." Lydia

"Start with an interesting fact." Maria

"Start out with a fact." Anisa

"I am going to start with a real-life example of going to a zoo." Johnny

How Do We Help Students Make Time for Flow?

Making time for flow is the first, and probably most difficult, step toward creating a habit-centered literate lifestyle. High school students have to be about eight or nine different people in one day. They rush from one subject to the next in a frenetic schedule punctuated by interruptions. When I returned to the classroom after a year of graduate study in London, I remember thinking, *What are all these darn bells ringing for?* Just as we'd started a lively discussion, I'd have to dismiss the class for the passing period. It can be maddening to live in fifty-seven-minute increments (or fifty-one or forty-six). And that's just the in-school realities.

Outside of school, our kids deal with a whole other set of distractions. I think of Michelle, an honors student who worried about the assignments she missed during the two weeks she spent in a shelter for abused and neglected children. Or about Cristian, who had to convince her mom that studying for college didn't mean she was turning her back on her family. Or about Matt, whose family moved three times during his junior year. Then there were kids like Carlos, who loved everything about the college-going culture—the campus visits, information nights, football pennants—except the homework. How do we help these kids find protected time in their busy lives for the focused, energized brain work that develops advanced literacy skills?

Unfortunately, I don't have a perfect answer. But I do believe a rhetorical approach to college and career readiness includes developing students' conscious awareness of the relationships between time, effort, and achievement. Malcolm Gladwell's best seller *Outliers: The Story of Success* (2008) underscores the staggering time investment and discipline needed to achieve excellence. Hip-hop fans will appreciate Macklemore's 2012 take on the same subject in his song "10,000 Hours": "Put those hours in and look at what you get." Students who haven't yet experienced or witnessed this time commitment firsthand need our help seeing its importance.

By asking students to think rhetorically, and even *kairotically*, about time management, we're encouraging them to pay attention to where, when, how much, and why they study and how effectively they study under different circumstances. For example, are they most energetic in the morning or at night? Do they study at the same time each day? Do they "cram" at the last minute? Do they choose their own tasks? Have they carved out at least a solid hour for uninterrupted reading or writing each day? Sure, I'd love more kids to do the four hours of daily homework necessary for admission to selective colleges, but that protected first hour can go a long way if it's consistent.

The goal is to use time in a way that's habit forming since research suggests repetition is more important to academic preparation than bursts of quantity. Some of my students use a favorite music album as a timer, training themselves to read or write for the full length of the album—usually about an hour. We find both classical and dance music work pretty well for this purpose because they don't have distracting lyrics. I've also encouraged kids to establish and enforce their own "office hours" (e.g., M-W-F from 3:00 to 5:00) so that family and friends know when they're not available.

We can likewise help students learn to capitalize on moments of flow-induced productivity. Successful readers and writers know that some texts and tasks require more of a warm-up than others. Sometimes we have to prime our intellectual pump before we're ready to read Herman Melville or write a statement of purpose. This is where portable flow-creating skills come in handy. If students know that certain environments and activities get them into a heightened sense of energy and concentration, then they can use that knowledge to prepare for more demanding tasks. For example, planning to read for thirty minutes before writing a challenging essay can be one way to get the flow—well, flowing.

Style Imitation Two Ways

My students and I test this strategy for generating flow by trying two different approaches to the classic style imitation, a standard exercise in the rhetorical tradition. As Crowley and Hawhee note, the ancients believed that this kind of "patterned practice at composing can further enliven rhetorical habits of mind" (2009, xiv). First, I ask students to try a version of a style imitation that will look familiar to many AP English teachers. After completing a style analysis of a passage's sentence structure and word choices, students create their own paragraph using the grammatical and lexical choices of the original as their blueprint. The topic is different in the imitation, but the syntax and level of diction should be about the same. It looks like this:

Original passage from Mark Haddon's novel *The Curious Incident of the Dog in the Night-Time*

People think that alien spaceships should be solid and made of metal and have lights all over them and move slowly through the sky because that is how we would build a spaceship if we were able to build one that big. But aliens, if they exist, would probably be very different from us. They might look like big slugs, or be flat like reflections. Or they might be bigger than planets. Or they might not have bodies at all. They might just be information, like in a computer. And their spaceships might look like clouds, or be made up of unconnected objects like dust or leaves. (2004, 69)

Gloria's Imitation of Mark Haddon

Kids think that getting in gangs is so cool and killing each other and getting respect from other people and wearing their favorite color because they want to show off to their new cholo friends that they can wear blue or red. But kids, if they are cool, will probably try and avoid gangs. They could one day become teachers, or be the next president. Or maybe become an artist like Picasso. Or they might keep scribbling on better walls. They should keep going to school, like I am. And one day they can graduate, and be the good role model for the cholos and their friends.

My flow-enhanced modification to this exercise is to have students analyze the passage and then *read* that author's work for at least fifteen minutes. Instead of copying the structure of individual sentences, students try to write on their own in that style for another ten minutes or until they've written a full page. The idea is that we pick up moves from the writers we read, that what we read, in fact, gives a distinct flavor to our own work. For this activity, you will need to provide enough copies or excerpts of the model texts for each student to read silently for fifteen minutes or more (one half of a class set per text works if you plan to have students switch after the first reading). The excerpts included in the following activity description are not long enough to give your students the full flow-enhanced experience, but they do give you, the teacher, an idea of what kinds of selections you might be looking for.

Flow-Enhanced Style Imitation

Directions to Students: For this assignment, you will be writing two very different style imitations. For each imitation, begin by reading the model text for at least fifteen minutes. The more you read of the original, the easier it will be to imitate. As you read, try to identify the genre, audience, and purpose of each text. Follow the directions below to complete your flow-enhanced style imitation.

Write a one-page autobiographical incident describing something that happened to you in middle school in the style of Jeff Kinney's *Diary of a Wimpy Kid: Rodrick Rules* (2008). Try to recreate Kinney's tone, humor, syntax, and level of diction in recounting your own experience (see excerpt).

Write a one-page literary critique of a novel or short story you have read in the style of Toni Morrison's *Playing in the Dark* (1992). Your critique must analyze the significance of blackness or darkness in the work of literature you choose. Try to recreate Morrison's tone, syntax, imagery, and level of diction in writing your own analysis (see excerpt). Select from the following list or choose another relevant text:

> *The Crucible* by Arthur Miller
>
> *The Scarlet Letter* by Nathaniel Hawthorne
>
> "The Minister's Black Veil" by Nathaniel Hawthorne
>
> "The Black Cat" by Edgar Allen Poe
>
> *Beloved* by Toni Morrison
>
> *The Adventures of Huckleberry Finn* by Mark Twain
>
> *Billy Budd* by Herman Melville

Finally, compare the two style imitations you've written. What does it say about you that you can produce two such different texts? What have you learned about changing your style to meet the expectations of genre, audience, and purpose? What have you learned about how reading can help prepare you for different writing tasks?

Excerpt #1: from *Diary of a Wimpy Kid: Rodrick Rules* by Jeff Kinney (2008)
<u>Wednesday</u>

Rodrick has an English paper due tomorrow, and Mom's actually making him do it himself for once. Rodrick doesn't know how to type, so he usually writes his papers out on notebook paper and then hands them off to Dad. But when Dad reads over Rodrick's work, he finds all sorts of factual errors.

Rodrick doesn't really care about mistakes, so he tells Dad to just go ahead and type the paper like it is.

But Dad can't stand typing a paper with errors in it, so he just rewrites Rodrick's paper from scratch. And then a couple days later, Rodrick brings his graded paper home and acts like he did it himself.

This has been going on for a few years, and I guess Mom decided she's going to put an end to it. So tonight she told Dad that Rodrick was going to do his own work this time around, and that Dad wasn't allowed to help out.

Rodrick went in the computer room after dinner, and you could hear him typing about one letter a minute.

I could tell the sound of Rodrick typing was driving Dad totally bananas. On top of that, Rodrick would come out of the computer room every ten minutes and ask Dad some dumb question.

After a couple of hours, Dad finally cracked.

Dad waited for Mom to go to bed, and then he typed Rodrick's whole paper for him. So I guess this means Rodrick's system is safe, at least for now. (46–48)

Excerpt #2: from *Playing in the Dark* by Toni Morrison (1992)

National literatures, like writers, get along the best way they can, and with what they can. Yet they do seem to end up describing and inscribing what is really on the national mind. For the most part, the literature of the United States has taken as its concern the architecture of a *new white man*. If I am disenchanted by the indifference of literary criticism toward examining the range of that concern, I do have a lasting resort: the writers themselves.

Writers are among the most sensitive, the most intellectually anarchic, most representative, most probing of artists. The ability of writers to imagine what is not the self, to familiarize the strange and mystify the familiar, is the test of their power. The languages they use and the social and historical context in which these languages signify are indirect and direct revelations of that power and its limitations. So it is to them, the creators of American literature, that I look for clarification about the invention and effect of Africanism in the United States.

My early assumptions as a reader were that black people signified little or nothing in the imagination of white American writers. Other than as objects of an occasional bout of jungle fever, other than to provide local color or to lend some touch of verisimilitude or to supply a needed moral gesture, humor, or bit of pathos, blacks made no appearance at all. This was a reflection, I thought, of the marginal impact that blacks had on the lives of the characters in the work as well as the creative imagination of the author. To imagine or write otherwise, to situate black people throughout the pages and scenes of a book like some government quota, would be ludicrous and dishonest. (14–15) (*Teachers may want to use a longer excerpt than this one.*)

Student Samples

Giselle's flow-enhanced style imitations demonstrate her willingness to fully engage the spirit of each original text as well as her own versatility as a writer. Furthermore, her use of the first-person point of view in her imitation of Morrison's literary criticism shows that she's picked up a move from a real-world scholar that's not often modeled in school-based essays:

> #1: Last week I tried out for the cheerleading squad. What was I thinking, right? Anyways, my friend convinced me to try out and I know I shouldn't have been nervous but I totally was. What if I just full out sucked?! Yeah, yeah, I've done cheerleading since the third grade so I know that I shouldn't be letting it get to me. But the fact is, I didn't know any of these people that were supposed to be judges and I knew they were all teachers. What if I bombed my tryout and they remembered me for it and decided to fail me if I was ever in their class? That's a lot of pressure for a seventh grader!

> #2: The darkness in [*The Lord of the Flies*] compels the reader to delve into their fear of the unknown and the evil that lives within. The characters in the work are subject to the uncertainty that the darkness instills in them and are afraid of a "beast" that may be lurking on the island with them. I found that the convincing nature of the children's fear made for an interesting study of the darkness and all it encased in the work. One of the smaller children is unnervingly frightened by something "big and horrid moving in the trees" (85) during the night. I came across the idea that this fear of an unknown entity lurking in the shadow drew a line between the children's growing fear and the social unrest that continued to mount within the community of the shipwrecked boys. Upon noticing this link, I could immediately conclude that this "beast" was directly linked to the savagery that the boys were beginning to exhibit.

Well done, Giselle!

How Do We Help Students Find Space for Flow?

Creating or finding flow-friendly spaces is another key requirement for generating optimal academic experiences. Few of my students can retreat to a room of their own for their academic reading and writing. Fortunately, they've proven to me many times—contrary to Virginia Woolf's famous claims—that we don't have to have private space and money to do intellectual work. My students have found numerous creative ways to establish their own space-based academic routines that accommodate the different realities of their home lives while promoting the concentration and sense of control necessary for flow.

What these creative solutions have in common are effective boundaries for brain work. For my high school students, these boundaries were seldom four walls that they could call their own. Instead, they were often a symbolic means of saying, "Do not disturb; I'm doing something important here." These boundaries can be as simple as a regular spot at the kitchen table or a favorite corner of the school library—anything that gives a student a sense of proprietary control over his or her work space. In this case, imagination is nine-tenths of possession. If a student feels that she has claimed a study territory for herself, then she is likely to do good work there. And her confidence of ownership can send a message to others not to interrupt her. I always used to tell my Advanced Placement students to bring a pillow from home with them on the big test day. While I pretended that the pillow was for back support during the long exam, my real reason was for the students to feel "at home" in the test room. They always said it helped.

While it will be a stretch for most students, using Morrison's *Playing in the Dark* for a style imitation gets at a frequently lamented problem in high school English classes: We ask students to write literary criticism but rarely give them opportunities to read literary criticism, thus isolating them from the conversations we ask them to join. In this exercise, students learn to "put academic English in to get academic English out"—or, in this case, what we might call the discourse of literary criticism. Most of us find it easier to write criticism immediately after we've been reading criticism, especially if we've become absorbed in the reading.

Students who have little control over their home environments can often find a safe space to study at school. One of the delights of witnessing our new library open at Buena Park High School was watching how quickly students colonized this space. It was wonderful to see kids act as advocates for their own learning by staking their claims on their study territory, whether that territory was a corner table or a favorite computer terminal. If a school library is not a reliable option, teachers can help students brainstorm other places on campus (e.g., a classroom that's open during lunch, a computer lab, the quad, etc.) that could provide *regular* work space. Having our own space, poet and writing teacher Natalie Goldberg reminds us, means we take ourselves seriously (1986, 96). The following two activities ask students to reflect on how their work space can help them achieve flow.

The Writer's Work Space

Directions to Students:

Step 1: Respond to each of the questions below in a quick-write:

- Where do you write most often?

- Where do you like to write best?

- Describe your writing area (desk, computer, kitchen table, binder, school desk, library table, etc.).

- What resources do you like to have near you while you work?

- What books are close to your work space?

- Do you work best with or without music? If with, what do you like to listen to while you read and write?

- What snacks or drinks do you like to have when you read and write?

- What do you like to do when you need a break?

Step 2: Draw a quick sketch of your ideal work space. What kind of "office" space would you like to have for reading and writing?

Although Aristotle tells his students that material goods can be a hindrance to study, he admits that even a philosopher needs some stuff "for living a human life" (NE 1999; Book X, Chapter 8). One writer's work space is depicted in Figure 7.2.

FIGURE 7.2

"The Writer's Work Space" by Jenn Benge

Interruptibility Index

A blank version of the Interruptibility Index and a student's sample are provided in Appendix 25a and 25b.

Directions to Students: List and describe your options for places to read and write at school and at your home. Then rank your choices according to "interruptibility" on a scale of 1 to 6. Write a number 1 by the option that presents the fewest distractions; assign the highest number to the place where you are most likely to be interrupted. An example has been done for you.

Place (e.g., bedroom, kitchen, family room, office, garage, school library, computer lab, quad, etc.)	Resources (e.g., books, computer, paper, desk, etc.)	Distractions (e.g., TV, phone, younger siblings, noise, etc.)	Ranking (1 means LEAST "interruptible")
Example: *coffeehouse*	*table, chair, and snacks—must bring own school supplies*	*customers talking, noise of coffee machines, chance of seeing friends*	4

Quick-Write: Where do you see yourself as having the best chance of achieving flow? How can you minimize interruptions and distractions? Will you need to change your schedule in order to find *regular* work space?

Final Thoughts: Why Does This All Matter?

I once heard a Jesuit priest describe joy as knowing you are in the right place. This is how I want my students to feel in their academic lives. I want students to feel at home with rhetorical reading and writing, to feel that they're doing what they're supposed to be doing, becoming who they are supposed to be. The good news from both ancient and contemporary scholars is that we largely determine those feelings ourselves. Through our daily habits and pleasures, we claim our own territory, make our own moments, and choose our own identities. Becoming a "good" student or a "good" teacher just means showing up again and again for the things that matter. Will Durant provides an apt summary of this idea in his famous paraphrase of Aristotle: "We are what we repeatedly do" (1926/2005, 98). We want all our students to repeatedly do academic work that is personally relevant and intrinsically rewarding.

Points to Remember

As you plan your lessons and teach the concepts described in this chapter, you might want to refer to the following list of points to remember:

1. The *kairos* of a "teachable moment" is impacted by who we are as teachers (our ethos), how our students feel about new learning (pathos), and their own academic self-image (their ethos).

2. First-generation, multilingual, nontraditional, and low-income students benefit from explicit modeling and mentoring.

3. Threshold concepts mark a dividing line between insider and outsider knowledge.

4. Well-prepared students acquire habituated "virtues."

5. Well-prepared students often enjoy their schoolwork.

6. Well-prepared students have regular routines for academic work.

7. Well-prepared students have regular places for reading and writing.

8. Well-prepared students take responsibility for their own needs and growth.

Prompts for Quick-Writes or Pairs Conversations

The following prompts can be used before, during, or after a lesson to help students make personal connections, deepen their understanding, and reflect on their learning:

1. Describe a time when you were so engrossed in what you were doing that you lost all track of time (e.g., working on a car, writing music, reading a book, playing a sport or computer game, etc.). What was the activity? Why was it so engaging? How did you feel when you had to stop?

2. Describe your options for places to read and write at your home. Where are you most likely to be interrupted?

3. Where do you see yourself as having the best chance of achieving flow? How can you minimize interruptions and distractions? Will you need to change your schedule in order to find *regular* work space?

4. Describe the physical area around your most regular work space (e.g., kitchen, bedroom, library, etc.). What school supplies and resources do you have access to there? What would your "dream" office look like?

5. Describe your favorite place to study in the library: Where do you like to sit? What are the library's hours? Who helps you?

6. Describe a way that you've successfully established healthy boundaries for yourself. These could be boundaries that affect a relationship, your personal time, or space. What strategies did you use to give yourself some appropriate protection?

7. Why is it important for students to identify with writers and teachers? Why is it important that students identify with other students? Why is it important that teachers identify with students?

8. Describe a time when you were learning something new. This could be a sport, musical instrument, language, dance form, computer game, or anything else that took time and effort to learn. Who helped you? What skills did you learn most quickly? Most slowly? When did you stop feeling like a beginner?

9. When do you feel invited or encouraged to participate in classroom activities? When do you feel discouraged?

10. How would you describe your school identity?

11. Describe a time when you felt like you were being a "good student" in school. How did this identity affect your learning?

12. Describe a time when you did not want to participate in class. Why were you being resistant? What did you learn from this experience?

13. When have you experienced "flow"? Why did you experience "flow"? How can you experience "flow" again?

Appendix Contents

Appendix 1

Checklist for Listening to a Think-Aloud: Playing the Believing Game and the Doubting Game

Directions to Students: As your teacher models how to do a think-aloud, keep track of what he or she does while playing the believing game and the doubting game. You'll be using this same checklist for both games. First, place a plus sign (+) by everything you hear your teacher do during the believing game. Then, place a minus sign (–) by everything your teacher does when demonstrating the doubting game later on. Be sure to hang on to your checklist since you'll probably be playing the believing game and doubting game on different days. Some reading strategies may get a plus and a minus sign.

___ Identify the main idea

___ Postpone judgment

___ Identify underlying assumptions

___ Question the writer's authority

___ Identify the context

___ Notice text structure and organization

___ Evaluate the effectiveness of the writer's rhetorical

    choices

___ Identify important examples

___ Paraphrase key claims

___ Summarize the writer's argument

___ Question the relevance of the evidence

___ Challenge the writer's claims

___ Notice what paragraphs say and do

___ Identify the writer's purpose

___ Notice key transitions

___ Offer a personal response

___ See the issue from the writer's point of view

___ Suggest potential counterarguments

___ Question the writer's reasoning

___ Give the writer the benefit of the doubt

___ Clarify key terms

___ Disagree with the writer

Adapted from a unit designed by Mira-Lisa Katz and Meline Akashian for the CSU Expository Reading and Writing Course (2013, "Bring a Text You Like to Class," page 11).

Appendix 2

"The Olympic Contradiction"

By David Brooks

Abraham Lincoln said that a house divided against itself cannot stand. He was right about slavery, but the maxim doesn't apply to much else. In general, the best people are contradictory, and the most enduring institutions are, too.

The Olympics are a good example. The Olympics are a peaceful celebration of our warlike nature.

The opening ceremony represents one side of the Olympic movement. They are a lavish celebration of the cooperative virtues: unity, friendship, equality, compassion and care. In Friday's ceremony, there'll be musical tributes to the global community and the Olympic spirit. There will be Pepsi commercial-type images of the people from different backgrounds joyfully coming together. There will be pious speeches about our common humanity and universal ideals.

And there will be a lot of dancing. Because we're social, semi-herdlike creatures, we take a primordial pleasure in the sight of a large number of people moving in unison. Dance is physical, like sports, but, in many ways, it is the opposite of sports. In dance, the purpose is to blend with and mirror each other; in sport, the purpose is to come out ahead. Dancers perform for the audience and offer a gift of emotion; athletes respond to one another and the spectators are just there to witness and cheer.

Dancers, especially at the opening ceremony, smile in warmth and friendship. No true sport is ever done smiling (this is the problem with figure skating and competitive cheerleading).

After the opening ceremony is over, the Olympics turn into a celebration of the competitive virtues: tenacity, courage, excellence, supremacy, discipline and conflict.

The smiling goes away and the grim-faced games begin. The marathoner struggling against exhaustion, the boxer trying to pummel his foe, the diver resolutely focused on her task. The purpose is to be tougher and better than the people who are seeking the same pinnacle.

If the opening ceremony is win-win, most of the rest of the games are win-lose. If the opening ceremony mimics peace, the competitions mimic warfare. It's not about the brotherhood of humankind. It's about making sure our country beats the Chinese in the medal chart.

Through fierce competition, sport separates the elite from the mediocre. It identifies the heroes and standards of excellence that everybody else can emulate (a noble loser can serve as well as a talented winner). The idea is not to win friendship; it's to win glory. We get to see people experiencing the thrill of victory from the agony of defeat and judge how well they respond.

In sum, the Olympic Games appeal both to our desire for fellowship and our desire for status, to the dreams of community and also supremacy. And, of course, these desires are in tension. But the world is, too. The world isn't a jigsaw puzzle that fits neatly and logically together. It's a system of clashing waves that can never be fully reconciled.

The enduring popularity of the Olympics teach the lesson that if you find yourself caught between two competing impulses, you don't always need to choose between them. You can go for both simultaneously. A single institution can celebrate charitable compassion and military toughness. A three-week festival can be crassly commercial, but also strangely moving.

F. Scott Fitzgerald famously said that the mark of a first rate intelligence is the ability to hold two contradictory thoughts in your mind at the same time. But it's not really the mark of genius, just the mark of anybody who functions well in the world. It's the mark of any institution that lasts.

A few years ago, Roger Martin, the dean of the University of Toronto's management school, wrote a book called "The Opposable Mind," about business leaders who can embrace the tension between contradictory ideas. One of his examples was A. G. Lafley of Procter & Gamble.

Some Procter & Gamble executives thought the company needed to cut costs and lower prices to compete with the supermarket store brands. Another group thought the company should invest in innovation to keep their products clearly superior. Lafley embraced both visions, pushing hard in both directions.

The world, unfortunately, has too many monomaniacs—people who pick one side of any creative tension and wish the other would just go away. Some parents and teachers like the cooperative virtues and distrust the competitive ones, so, laughably, they tell their kids that they are going to play sports but nobody is going to keep score.

Politics has become a contest of monomaniacs. One faction champions austerity while another champions growth. One party becomes the party of economic security and the other becomes the party of creative destruction.

The right course is usually to push hard in both directions, to be a house creatively divided against itself, to thrive amid the contradictions. The Olympics are great, but they are not coherent.

Appendix 3

Annotation Cue Card Comments and Questions for "The Olympic Contradiction" by David Brooks

Comment: That's a pretty strong claim.

Question: What does Brooks mean by "best"? Most successful? Most admirable?

Question: Is this an oxymoron or paradox?

Question: Do they represent only one side?

Comment: This is a strong image—Brooks sounds pretty sarcastic.

Comment: I find this sentence annoying.

Question: Is Brooks a cynic?

Question: Why is Brooks so negative here?

Question: Does Brooks mean too much dancing?

Question: Aren't these performers usually volunteers rather than professionally trained dancers?

Comment: "Unison," "blend," and "mirror" all suggest cooperation and togetherness.

Question: Just "witness and cheer"? Sports fans don't experience an emotional gift?

Comment: Some performances during past Olympic opening ceremonies have been serious and historical.

Comment: He must know he's irritating some readers here, right?

Question: Is there really a total transformation or switch from cooperative to competitive virtues? Or is the same spirit present throughout the Olympics?

Question: If one is totally replaced by the other, doesn't that undermine Brooks's claim about the importance of simultaneously accepting contradictions?

Comment: It seems like Brooks is contradicting himself.

Comment: Brooks's verb phrases suggest intense physical activity.

Comment: The image of the pinnacle suggests there's room for only one at the top.

Comment: The repetition of the sentence structure emphasizes the balance of opposites.

Question: How does the idea of the noble loser work with Brooks's image of the pinnacle?

Comment: Brooks's pairings of "opposites" are not as neat here, which helps support his argument about allowing contradictions to coexist.

Comment: While "victory" and "defeat" are antonyms, "friendship" and "glory" are not. And "fellowship" and "status" are not mutually exclusive desires.

Question: But would the festival be even more moving if it weren't crassly commercial?

Comment: These examples show that contradictions can coexist but not that their coexistence makes people or institutions better or more enduring.

Comment: Brooks hasn't really proved his point yet about contradictions being good.

Comment: In his Olympics examples, Brooks doesn't really stress the importance of opposites being present at the same time.

Question: Does being "two-faced" enhance our chances for survival?

Comment: Brooks doesn't give a concrete example of someone who truly sees or accepts only one side. Maybe he knows human beings are more complex than that.

Comment: This example doesn't seem as strong or interesting as the business examples.

Comment: This sounds like an exaggeration.

Comment: Write your own comment on this card and say it aloud whenever it naturally fits into the group analysis of the text.

Comment: Write your own comment on this card and say it aloud whenever it naturally fits into the group analysis of the text.

Question: Write your own question on this card and ask it whenever it naturally fits into the group analysis of the text.

Question: Write your own question on this card and ask it whenever it naturally fits into the group analysis of the text.

Appendix 4a

Adapted from *Reading Rhetorically* by John C. Bean, Virgina A. Chappell, and Alice M. Gillam.

Descriptive Outlining

Paragraph[s]:

SAYS:

DOES:

Paragraph[s]:

SAYS:

DOES:

Paragraph[s]:

SAYS:

DOES:

Paragraph[s]:

SAYS:

DOES:

Paragraph[s]:

SAYS:

DOES:

Paragraph[s]:

SAYS:

DOES:

Paragraph[s]:

SAYS:

DOES:

Paragraph[s]:

SAYS:

DOES:

MAIN ARGUMENT:

Descriptive Outlining

Paragraph[s]: 1

Says: Picture sending a mean email out of anger

Does: Gives a scenario to make the point that anger can get the best of someone

Paragraph[s]: 2-4

Says: A teens brain is wired to act before thinking. The brain cant catch up until the 20's

Does: gives the general info and then in ¶ 3rd & 4 it gets more specific and scientific

Paragraph[s]: 5-6

Says: We used to think the brain was mature by 13 or 14, but the limbic system matures before the prefrontal cortex (which matures in your 20's)

Does: gives general info and then gives specific scientific details

Paragraph[s]: 7-8

Says: Teens make rushed, "bad" decisions because of the way their brain development is.

Does: Summarizes main idea and shows the result of ¶ 5-6 (gives ex)

Paragraph[s]: 9-11

Says: The brain needs to prune and go through myelination to be more efficient.

Does: ¶s are general & then specific. Scientific definitions are explained

Paragraph[s]: 12

Says: Teens control how their brain develops

Does: giving example of the scientific stuff from ¶ 9-11

Paragraph[s]: 13

Says: you can make smart choices

Does: Makes it personal by saying "you"

Paragraph[s]: 14

Says: Think before acting

Does: listing of tips

Main Argument:

What this article talks about is in how teens make bad decisions due to their surroundings. They get influenced by bad people and who they hangout with.

Descriptive Outlining

Paragraph[s]:

Says: Picture sending a mean email out of anger.

Does: Gives a secenario to make the point that anger can get the best of someone.

Paragraph[s]: 2-4

Says: A teens brain is wired to act before thinking. The brain can't catch up until 20s

Does: Gives the general info and then in ¶ 3 & 4 it gets more specific & scientific

Paragraph[s]: 5-6

Says: We used to think the brain was mature by 12 or 14, but the limbic system matures before the prefrontal cortex (which matures in your 20s)

Does: Gives general info and then gives specific scientific details.

Paragraph[s]: 7-8

Says: Teens make rushed "bad" decision because of the way their brain development is

Does: Summarizes main idea & shows the result of ¶ 5 & 6
                    ((Gives ex)

Paragraph[s]: 9-11

Says: The brain learns to speed up messages and get rid of connection not being used.

Does: Defined words and explained them

Paragraph[s]: 12

Says: The activities a teen does shape the way the teen's brain develops.

Does: Summarizes the idea of Myelination and pruning and offers positive steps

Paragraph[s]: 13

Says: Telling you to make smart choices now that you understand the brain.

Does: Making it personal by using the word "you".

Paragraph[s]: 14

Says: Think before you act so your brain can weigh the consequences

Does: list tips for good decision making skills.

Main Argument:

The main argument of the article is that teens can control the way their brain develops. Although the part of the brain that controls emotion is in control they can strengthen the part that controls logic.

Believing, Doubting, and Transforming

Directions: The following activity can help you determine your position on an issue. After reading about an issue, respond to the questions in each section of the three-column chart below.

BELIEVING Which claims, if any, do you believe?	DOUBTING Which claims, if any, do you doubt?	TRANSFORMING What claims could be changed or modified to better represent how you think?

QUICK-WRITE:
What is your position overall?

PAPA Square

Through a PAPA Square, students analyze the **P**urpose, **A**rgument, **P**ersona, and **A**udience of a text. Around the perimeter of the box, students answer the following questions in response to their own writing: Who is my audience? What is the persona, or public image, that I create for myself through my language choices and tone? What is my thesis or argument? What is my purpose or desired outcome of my argument (i.e., What would I like my reader to do if he or she is persuaded by me?)? In the center of the PAPA Square, students identify the stylistic devices and emotional, logical, and ethical appeals they use to persuade their audience. These may include types of evidence, figurative language, text structures (e.g., cause and effect), and tone. (Adapted from the CSU Reading and Writing Course.)

PURPOSE

AUDIENCE   **RHETORICAL DEVICES AND STRATEGIES**   **ARGUMENT**

PERSONA

Appendix 7

Kairos Analysis

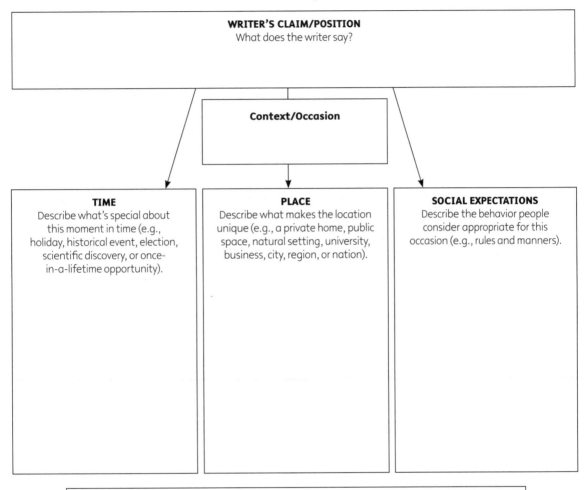

WRITER'S CLAIM/POSITION
What does the writer say?

Context/Occasion

TIME
Describe what's special about this moment in time (e.g., holiday, historical event, election, scientific discovery, or once-in-a-lifetime opportunity).

PLACE
Describe what makes the location unique (e.g., a private home, public space, natural setting, university, business, city, region, or nation).

SOCIAL EXPECTATIONS
Describe the behavior people consider appropriate for this occasion (e.g., rules and manners).

THE LANGUAGE OF *KAIROS*
List any words or phrases in the text that suggest the importance of time.

Quick-Write: How would you describe the *kairos* of this text? How do time, place, and social expectations impact the writer's argument? Do you think the writer has chosen the best opportunity to make his or her argument?

Audience Analysis

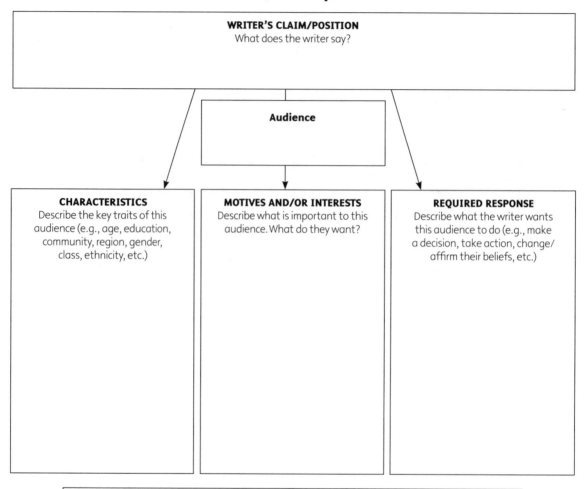

WRITER'S CLAIM/POSITION
What does the writer say?

Audience

CHARACTERISTICS
Describe the key traits of this audience (e.g., age, education, community, region, gender, class, ethnicity, etc.)

MOTIVES AND/OR INTERESTS
Describe what is important to this audience. What do they want?

REQUIRED RESPONSE
Describe what the writer wants this audience to do (e.g., make a decision, take action, change/affirm their beliefs, etc.)

WORLD VIEW
What values, beliefs, or assumptions might members of this audience share?

Quick-Write: How would you describe the audience of this text? How are the writer's rhetorical choices (e.g., language, style, structure, evidence, appeals, etc.) suited to the needs, interests, and expectations of this audience?

Translating for Outsiders

Directions to Students: Think of a subject that makes you feel like an expert, or insider. This might be your favorite sport, a style of music, a video game, anime, graphic novels, a hobby, a job, or "digitalk," like texting. Then use special "insider language" to express each of the ideas in the following chart. Feel free to use slang, dialect, emoticons, abbreviations, or jargon to express your ideas. Then translate exactly what your insider language means for an outside audience in the final column.

What subject are you an "expert" on? _____

How would say each of the following ideas if you were talking with other experts, or insiders, about your subject? (For example, how would a surfer describe the perfect wave to another surfer?)

IDEA	INSIDER LANGUAGE	OUTSIDER TRANSLATION
That's good.		
That's bad.		
That's frustrating.		
Hello		
Goodbye		
That's scary.		
That's funny.		

Appendix 9b

Answering Outsiders' Questions

Part I

Directions: Describe the importance of a subject you know well but that your teacher and classmates may know little about. For example, this could be your favorite style of music, computer game, sport, comic book series, after-school job, or any other subject you are an expert on. Why does this subject interest you? Use your "insider knowledge"—including specialized words, slang, and jargon—to describe the importance of your subject. Imagine you are writing this description for other insiders who will know exactly what you are talking about.

Part II

Directions: Now imagine an "outsider"—someone who isn't familiar with your subject—has read your description and asked you the following questions. Respond to each question using language and examples you think an outsider might understand.

"I don't get it. What's your point?"

"What do those words mean?"

"Why can't you say this in plain English?"

"Why should I care about this?"

"How is this relevant to me?"

Analyzing Target Audiences

Directions to Students: Use the concentric circles below to chart the levels of intimacy of participants in an ongoing conversation on an issue. Place those folks at the heart of the issue in the very center. Then identify other participants in this conversation according to their level of involvement. For instance, for a conversation that originates from a conference presentation, you might place the original panelists or speakers in the first circle, then the people in the room, then the readers of the journal that published the conference paper, then the scholars in the field, then the students of those scholars, and so on.

Hint: To find the names of other scholars in a field who are part of a text's audience, check the names in a writer's works cited list. If the writer is listening to those folks, chances are he or she is speaking to them, too. Endnotes are an additional clue to who's in the audience. In works that have endnotes, the scholars who are cited are typically the ones who agree or disagree with the author. Endnotes are thus a kind of transcript of a scholarly debate.

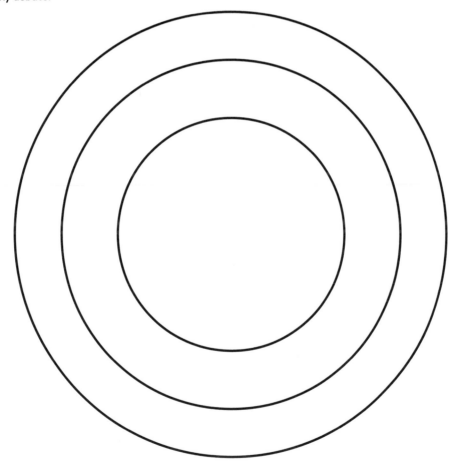

Forensic Rhetoric:
Accusation and Defense

Directions: Use the following graphic organizer for forensic analysis.

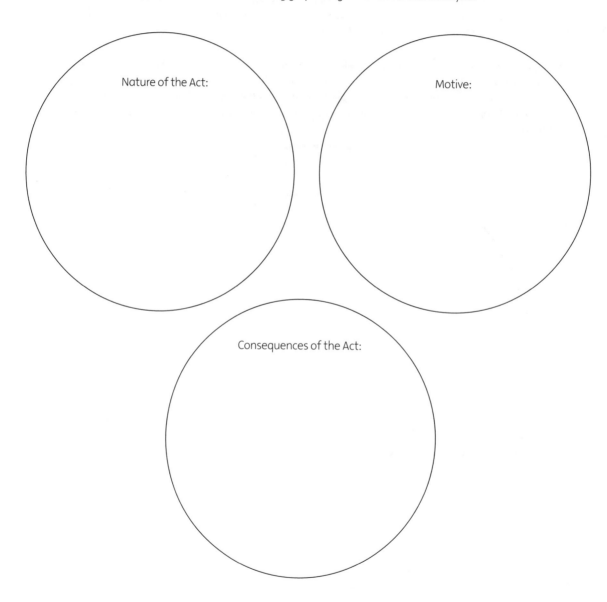

Nature of the Act:

Motive:

Consequences of the Act:

Epideictic Rhetoric:
Ways to Praise

According to Aristotle, praise can be deserved for being the first, the last, the only, the best, and the most consistent. He tells us we can praise something or someone by generating examples and by making positive and negative comparisons. The following prewriting exercise can help you think of support for an epideictic argument.

Subject for praise (X):_____.

EXAMPLES OF EXCEPTIONALITY

Directions: Complete all that apply.

1. X is/was the only _____to_____.

2. Every_____is/was _____by X.

3. X is/was the first to _____.

4. X is/was the last to _____.

5. X is/was/has the largest _____.

POSITIVE AND NEGATIVE COMPARISONS

Directions: Use Aristotle's model language to write your own comparisons.

1. X is/was better than Y.

_____.

2. X is/was the best _____.

3. Y is/was worse than X.

_____.

4. X was more consistent than Y.

_____.

Appendix 13

"A Lifetime of Learning"

By Diana Garcia

Keynote address given at the AVID (Advancement Via Individual Determination) Writers Conference on March 22, 2011, at California State University, Monterey Bay

Take risks. Stay curious. Be ambitious. Learn to recognize opportunities. Learn from your failures. Never give up. If I could sum up a lifetime of learning, my own successes and failures would fall into several of these categories.

Growing up in the 50s and 60s, taking risks for a Chicana in the San Joaquin Valley was not considered acceptable behavior. As a female child, I learned to keep my voice low, my head lower, and my hands folded in my lap. No shouting, no running, no getting dirty. One of my earliest memories was coming to Monterey with my parents, my maternal grandparents and my brother who was one year younger. I was probably five years old. When we got to the beach, my grandfather, father and brother got out of the car and climbed down the shore toward the rocky outcroppings.

Mesmerized by the ocean, the waves crashing onto the shore, the powerful thunder they made as they attacked, I tried to get out of the car. My father yelled something about it was too dangerous. I remember thinking, if my younger brother could climb down, why couldn't I? I watched my brother scramble from one rock to the next, bending, stooping, yelling, tossing shells, rocks, and sand into the air. He was having fun. I was trapped between my mother and grandmother in the back seat of the car, safe, and furious. My father called me ungrateful when I refused the handful of sea glass that my brother offered me when they returned. The gift paled in comparison to the adventure he'd had. Even then, I knew that's what I wanted. I wanted my life to be an adventure.

As toddlers, we stumble from our beds in the morning conscious of cool tile beneath our feet, the brush of air along our arms, the way the fine hairs on our cheeks respond to changes in temperature. We race outside and see the intimate immensity of sky and yard. Each moment, each discovery, is fresh and new and brilliant. We know nothing and want to understand everything. We hide in the hollow of a tree trunk and imagine a fantastic world where birds talk a language we understand. We live in an ever-changing present, overwhelmed with what is, aware of how much we need to understand, unafraid of a future because the now is what concerns us. Life is an adventure . . . and then we forget. Perhaps repetition and familiarity breed insensitivity. Perhaps red marks on math and English homework erode our willingness to take risks. Perhaps we learn that risk can result in failure, that adventure can lead to setback.

I moved to San Diego at age 23, a single mother on welfare. I knew no one, I had no place to live, but I had a job at SDSU. Over the next three years, I worked at Children's Hospital and then the San Diego County Department of Education, each time moving into positions that involved more responsibility, better pay, and better benefits. With several letters of recommendation, outstanding LSAT scores and a full scholarship, I also went to law school. Never mind that I didn't even have a BA at the time. I knew how to research and how to write: I could do anything.

Here's where the failures began to creep in. I was working full-time during the day at the Dept. of Education and going to law school at night. I saw my son before and after school and during dinner, then I'd drop him at a friend's house while I went to law school. I won the Am Jur award for legal writing and quit my job so that I could accept a position as a poorly paid law clerk for the most prestigious real estate law firm in the county. Within a week I knew I'd made a big mistake. These were wealthy, powerful people working with and for wealthy, powerful people. I was neither. I hated how they talked about Chicano Park and poor people and Mexicans as if I weren't even there. I was invisible. In retrospect, I should have applied to work with one of the immigration rights law firms or with the public defenders' office. I just didn't know. So, I quit. I quit the firm, quit law school, and let regret eat at me each time I saw the list of names of former classmates who had passed the bar exam. What I hadn't done was talked to any of my law professors or to the two attorneys who had written letters of recommendation for me. They could have offered me informed insight. They might have helped me avoid wasting those two years I'd already spent in law school. I gave up my dream of becoming an attorney, perhaps even a judge.

Soon after, my husband and I started a retail electronics store in San Diego's Old Town. We lost the store. I learned I wasn't meant to work in retail. During our going-out-of business sale, a couple from Washington DC came into our store and started talking about a sentencing project they worked for back east. They left town, and we started our own business writing sentencing recommendations in criminal defense cases. I finally got a chance to put law school and legal writing to work. For the next 15 years, I worked on the Spanish-speaking cases part-time and at night. I relished knowing that judges followed our recommendations almost 90% of the time. Even better, I loved when judges told defendants to call us.

During the day, for three years I worked as a personnel manager for an electronics research, development, and manufacturing firm. I knew nothing about the world of electronics research or personnel management, but I recognized an opportunity when I saw it. I was bilingual, I knew shorthand, and I was a strong researcher and convincing writer. I learned my way around the growing field of computer technology, patent applications, and business licensing. I learned how to put together an employees' handbook and a personnel manual. I learned how to conduct new employee orientations and seminars on patent law documentation procedures.

One day, the president of the electronics firm asked me when I planned to finish my degree. He told me I was ambitious. The first time he called me ambitious I wondered what I'd said or done to make him think so poorly of me. After all, in my culture, to be ambitious means you set yourself above the other members of your community. To be ambitious means that you want to leave that community behind, shake its dust from your heels, and pretend the past never existed.

When he called me ambitious a second time, I thought about how much I respected him. I considered his renown as a physicist and mathematician, the fact that he loved opera and was a wonderful writer. He seemed to think ambition was an admirable quality. I paid attention and went back to college part-time. When the electronics firm lost a major contract and had to lay off a quarter of our workforce, I laid myself off, too. What some people saw as a terrible decision, I recognized as an opportunity. I went back to college full-time.

Probably the biggest risk I took was switching from a major in business psychology to an English major with a creative writing emphasis. Yet, that decision changed my life. After 21 years of going to school part-time, applying for leaves of absence, and generally muddling through a degree program, I finally got a BA.

Growing up, I didn't know of any Chicana or Chicano writers. Sandra Cisneros and Gary Soto were born a few years after me. I read Shakespeare and Dostoevsky, Bocaccio and Beowulf. Once at age 19, I registered for an introduction to creative writing class at Fresno State. I walked in the door and turned around and walked out. There were no female students in the class. I was too insecure and unself-confident to imagine placing my own words next to those of all those guys. Years later I hosted the professor of that course, the remarkable poet Philip Levine, in a party at my home in San Diego. When I told him that story, he gave me a look that said I was crazy and said, "You should have taken the course."

Yes, I might have become a writer sooner rather than later. But I became a writer out of the fire and the intensity of my life. I became a writer because I love writing. I took a chance that I could make a life as a writer. I wrote dozens of poems and short stories each semester. I went to two different creative writing workshops during the summer, once as part of the CSU Summer Arts Program and once at the Squaw Valley Poetry Workshop. I was accepted as a writing fellow at Cottages at Hedgebrook on Whidbey Island. In my last year in the program, I submitted five of my best poems to *The Kenyon Review*, a major literary journal. The editor, poet Marilyn Hacker, accepted all five poems. When I went to campus and showed the letter to one of my mentors, he told me he'd never had a poem accepted for publication in that journal.

A year after earning my MFA, I took another huge risk and accepted a position as a visiting poet at Central Connecticut State University in New Britain, CT. When I told my husband I would have to leave the state to get my career started, he said, "We'll do whatever we have to do." I moved to Connecticut and climbed trap rock, stood beneath sycamore and hickories in jeweled colors, and shoveled my share of 100 inches of snow that winter. I also started the Central Connecticut Poets in the School Program. At the end of the first year, the dean offered me a tenured position. I declined. He suggested I call my husband before making a final decision. When I called my husband to tell him about the offer, he said, "What an adventure!" He knew me better than I knew myself.

If I hadn't taken a chance on becoming a writer, I might never had had a chance to teach at the University of Freiburg in Germany, take part in the El Otro Lado Conference at the University of Edinburgh in Scotland, or read at the Smithsonian's American Museum of History in honor of their exhibit on the Bracero Program.

Being a writer means I go into the world like a child. I love being around other writers for days at a time. We hear ourselves marveling at the smallest wonders, saying there's a poem in that and there's a story there. Being a writer means that I don't have to feel foolish for driving twelve hours to see nesting pairs of rose-breasted becards or blue-footed boobies. Being a writer means I am charmed by the world I enter each and every moment.

When I was a store owner, a personnel manager, and a sentencing consultant, I worked 60-hour weeks. I knew then what I know now: if you want to be successful at something, you have to work longer and harder than the person next to you. I learned that even working all those hours, you might fail. I learned that even my failures prepared me for the next stage of my life. I learned there are worse things than failure. I learned I might have become a lawyer and never have enjoyed the rich and varied life I enjoy as a writer and as a professor.

At each and every point of your life, you're going to be presented with opportunities. When I quit law school, I never imagined the opportunities that would develop. Opportunities might not be immediately recognizable. You have to learn to listen and analyze and interpret what's being presented. When my former boss told me I was ambitious, I thought he was insulting me. After much thought, I realized he was paying me the highest compliment. You have to learn to be ambitious for yourselves and have faith in yourselves. That is the hardest and the loneliest lesson you have to learn. No one else can learn it for you. Identify what drives you to succeed. Identify your passions. Then, learn from the experts in your chosen fields.

I flew to Rhode Island to interview the poet C. D. Wright and then to El Paso to interview the poet Pat Mora. I wanted to talk to women my age who had successfully navigated being writers, mothers, wives and academics. I needed to know that what I was imagining for myself was possible. Both women remain two of my heroes to this day. They were generous with their time, they encouraged me in my dream, and they inspired me to take risks that made me tremble.

Trust that the ones who love you will support you. They might not always understand, but if they truly love you, they will recognize the passion that drives you to succeed. My husband urged me to go to Connecticut and encouraged me to stay, even though we ended up having to live across the country from each other for three years. Those were some of the richest years I experienced as a writer because I was alone and had to learn how to be a writer and artist in a community of writers and artists.

Perhaps you remember someone telling you when you were five years old, "Stop asking so many questions!" That was a long time ago. Now is the time to be curious. There is so much to know. Often the simplest questions raise the most complicated answers. Learn to relish complexity. When you've exhausted your sources, go and experience for yourself. Be ready to leave familiar surroundings and explore new parts of the world. By the way, learn at least one other language. The world grows smaller each day.

There will always be a new app and new software and the latest and fastest technology to capture your attention. Just remember, don't let technology be a substitute for your life. Life is for living. Remember to be there for those who love you, for those who encourage you, for those who have faith in you.

Finally, remember to breathe. Take long walks through fields of native wildflowers. Turn your face towards a clear sky; pretend you're a suncup in April. Play. Pretend. Imagine.

Your life is an adventure. Don't settle for less.

Purpose Analysis

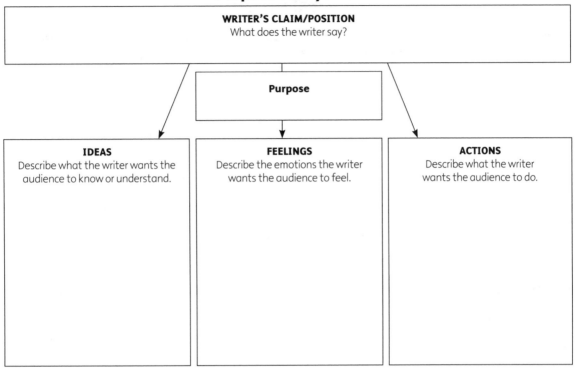

WRITER'S CLAIM/POSITION
What does the writer say?

Purpose

IDEAS
Describe what the writer wants the audience to know or understand.

FEELINGS
Describe the emotions the writer wants the audience to feel.

ACTIONS
Describe what the writer wants the audience to do.

PAST, PRESENT, OR FUTURE
Explain whether the writer wants the audience to make a judgment about the past, understand a statement about the present, or decide a course of action for the future.

Quick-Write: How would you describe the purpose of this text? What do you think the writer hopes to accomplish through his or her argument? Does the argument serve multiple purposes? If so, which one(s) is/are most important?

Appendix 15a

Replacing Dead Words
Get Rid of *Get*

Directions: In each of the following sentences, replace the word *get* with a more precise word choice or word phrase. Try not to use the same word more than once!

1. What did you get on your test?

2. I don't get the joke.

3. We get to go camping often.

4. Get some milk on your way home from work.

5. Get the cat off the table.

6. Would you please get me a piece of pizza?

7. Did you get the assignment from Kristen?

8. Get out your pens and paper.

9. Get to the point.

10. Your train may get in late.

11. Get out of my house.

12. Did your parents get you to do your homework?

13. I can't get enough of this chocolate.

14. Get in your chair immediately.

15. Get away from the stove.

16. What are you getting your boyfriend for Christmas?

17. I'm not sure which shirt to get.

18. I got an A- on my math test.

19. Do you and your sisters always get in a fight?

20. I get the news on the radio when I'm driving home.

21. Did you get first or second place in the marathon?

22. I get a sick feeling whenever I have a geometry quiz.

23. Our carpet always gets so dirty.

24. Pedro gets up at 5:30 every morning.

25. Can I get you something to drink?

26. David doesn't get out much anymore.

27. Our camping group got to the summit just before sunset.

28. It seems like our parents are getting so much older.

29. Get all your assignments in on time.

30. Can you get your brother's car for the weekend?

31. Get your friend on the phone and ask her over for dinner.

32. How many tourist stops did you get to?

33. This work gets so confusing!

34. I get all my books from the catalogues.

35. Do you get who the murderer was in that film?

36. Get everything you'll need for our skiing trip.

Appendix 15b

Go Away, *Go*

Directions: In each of the following sentences, replace the word *go* (and in some cases its preposition) with a more precise word.

1. Kimiko goes to the dance classes after work.

2. Please take my car and go to the market for me.

3. Then he goes, "There's no way I'll take that job!"

4. We'll be going to Europe this summer.

5. The Cuthbys go to their grandmother's house every July.

6. What's going on here?

7. I'm afraid your aunt is going insane.

8. Go over these accounts to see if I have made a mistake.

9. Did you go through what we can give away or keep yet?

10. I'll go with you to the park.

11. If this interview goes smoothly, I will have a new job.

12. Turn on your headlights when we go through the tunnel.

13. Is she planning to go for a triple jump?

14. They've been going around in circles in the desert for two days.

15. Why do you just go along with what your friends do?

16. My dog goes crazy every time I give her a biscuit.

17. The directions said to go left at the next stoplight.

18. My Uncle Samson can go on about his hip surgery for an hour.

19. Will you go with me to the prom?

20. Hester is terrified as she goes up the stairs to the scaffold.

21. What time will the actors go on?

22. Jan goes through the slalom faster than other downhill racers.

23. Teenage boys go through a tremendous amount of food.

24. It's a mystery why my grandfather just goes away sometimes.

25. This car goes too slow.

26. The military standoff has gone for six weeks now.

27. Does your teacher go over the answers with you?

28. My brother claims he can go for a month without television.

29. When we run out of food, we can still go on just the water for days.

30. How long will it take you to go through that book?

31. What time do you have to go catch your plane?

32. That is a great rule to go by!

33. That new sports car goes for a fairly steep price.

34. His property goes almost to the river.

35. Will these clothes go in your suitcase?

36. That old house is definitely starting to go.

Teaching Argument: Rhetorical Comprehension, Critique, and Response by Jennifer Fletcher. Copyright © 2015. Stenhouse Publishers.

Ethos Analysis

WRITER'S CLAIM/POSITION
What does the writer say?

**Support
&
Evidence**

PERSONAL EXAMPLES	**CREDENTIALS/QUALIFICATIONS**	**ROLES/RESPONSIBILITIES**
List any personal stories or anecdotes the writer shares.	List any special degrees, qualifications, awards, expertise, or training that the writer claims to have.	List any special jobs, life experiences, or social roles that are part of the writer's identity (e.g., being a mother or an immigrant).

Quick-Write: How would you describe the writer's image or ethos? What adjectives would you use to describe the writer's persona? What kind of a person does the writer seem to be? Do you trust this person? Do you like or admire this person?

Ethos Analysis

WRITER'S CLAIM/POSITION
What does the writer say?
Requiring algebra for high school graduation and college admission hurts a wide range of students, wastes precious resources, and reduces our nation's talent pool. Instead of the traditional math sequence, we should create exciting alternatives to develop students' quantitative reasoning skills.

**Support
&
Evidence**

PERSONAL EXAMPLES
List any personal stories or anecdotes the writer shares.

"I say this as a writer and social scientist whose work relies heavily on the use of numbers."

"... the more I examine them ..."—suggests ongoing study of the issue

"Most of the educators I've talked with ..."

"The City University of New York, where I have taught since 1971 ..."—establishes extensive experience in higher education

"I've observed a host of high school and college classes ..."

CREDENTIALS/QUALIFICATIONS
List any special degrees, qualifications, awards, expertise, or training that the writer claims to have.

writer and social scientist

professor at City University of New York since 1971

ROLES/RESPONSIBILITIES
List any special jobs, life experiences, or social roles that are part of the writer's identity (e.g., being a mother or an immigrant).

American

advocate of responsible citizenship

classroom observer

scholar who uses math

teacher at a university with high failure rates for math

Quick-Write: How would you describe the writer's image or ethos? What adjectives would you use to describe the writer's persona? What kind of a person does the writer seem to be? Do you trust this person? Do you like or admire this person?

(Student answers will vary.)

Article analyzed: Hacker, Andrew. 2012. "Is Algebra Necessary?" Op-Ed. *New York Times.* July 28.

Pathos Analysis

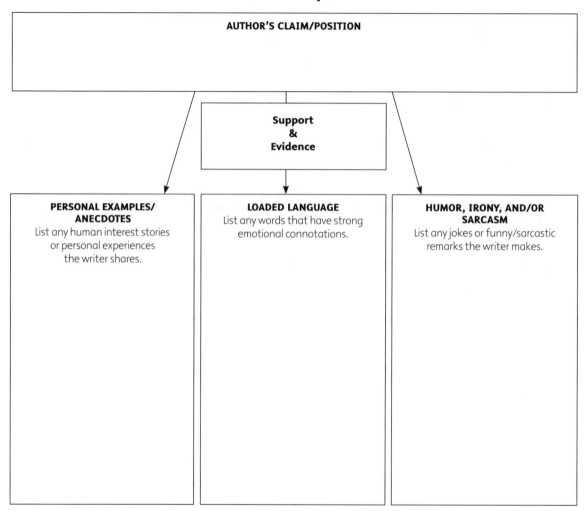

AUTHOR'S CLAIM/POSITION

Support
&
Evidence

PERSONAL EXAMPLES/ ANECDOTES
List any human interest stories or personal experiences the writer shares.

LOADED LANGUAGE
List any words that have strong emotional connotations.

HUMOR, IRONY, AND/OR SARCASM
List any jokes or funny/sarcastic remarks the writer makes.

Quick-Write: Describe the overall emotional impact of this text. How did the writer make you feel? Happy? Sad? Afraid? Hurt? Enthusiastic? Suspicious? Excited? Irritated? Brave? Angry? Amused? Concerned? How strong were your feelings while reading this text?

Pathos Analysis

AUTHOR'S CLAIM/POSITION

Requiring algebra for high school graduation and college admission hurts a wide range of students, wastes precious resources, and reduces our nation's talent pool. Instead of the traditional math sequence, we should create exciting alternatives to develop students' quantitative reasoning skills.

Support & Evidence

PERSONAL EXAMPLES/ ANECDOTES	**LOADED LANGUAGE**	**HUMOR, IRONY, AND/OR SARCASM**
List any human interest stories or personal experiences the writer shares.	List any words that have strong emotional connotations.	List any jokes or funny/sarcastic remarks the writer makes.
Shares perspective of Shirley Bagwell, a longtime Tennessee teacher	"ordeal"	"But there's no evidence that being able to prove $(x^2+y^2)^2 = (x^2-y^2)^2 + (2xy)^2$ leads to more credible political opinions or social analysis."
Uses examples of veterinary and medical students to show pointless suffering of students who struggle with math	"onerous"	
	"subject"	"(How many college graduates remember what Fermat's dilemma was all about?)"
Admits that he's changed his own view on the value of mandatory algebra	"warns"	
	"expected to fail"	
	"struggling"	
	"nation's shame"	
	"toll"	
	"exclude"	
	"depressing"	
	"chagrin"	
	uses numbers for emotional impact: "six million," "two million," "43 percent"	

Quick-Write: Describe the overall emotional impact of this text. How did the writer make you feel? Happy? Sad? Afraid? Hurt? Enthusiastic? Suspicious? Excited? Irritated? Brave? Angry? Amused? Concerned? How strong were your feelings while reading this text?

(Student answers will vary.)

Article analyzed: Hacker, Andrew. 2012. "Is Algebra Necessary?" Op-Ed. *New York Times*, July 28.

Qualifiers and Persona

Directions: A qualifier is a descriptive word (either an adjective or adverb) that adds more information to a sentence. First, underline the qualifiers in each statement below (e.g., *all, always, never, some, few, often, no,* etc.). Then describe the kind of person who might make each statement. What is the image you get of this person? Opinionated? Unbiased? Moderate? Skeptical? Careful? Impulsive? Reasonable? Extreme? Observant? Open-minded? Determined? Absolute? Resolved? List adjectives describing the writer's persona under each statement.

All children should always wash their own clothes.

Most teachers usually just want what is best for their students.

Many families often struggle to make ends meet.

Some students occasionally cheat on tests.

Few mothers would work if they could afford to stay home.

No cause is worth dying for.

True friends will never let you down.

Quick-Write: How does the use of qualifiers affect tone? How do qualifiers affect a writer's persona or ethos?

Appendix 19*a*

Logos Analysis

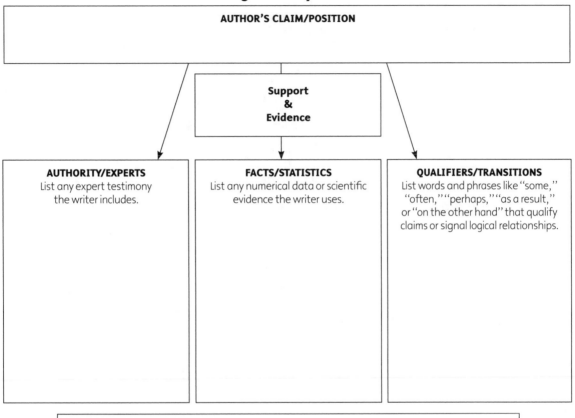

AUTHOR'S CLAIM/POSITION

Support & Evidence

AUTHORITY/EXPERTS
List any expert testimony the writer includes.

FACTS/STATISTICS
List any numerical data or scientific evidence the writer uses.

QUALIFIERS/TRANSITIONS
List words and phrases like "some," "often," "perhaps," "as a result," or "on the other hand" that qualify claims or signal logical relationships.

COUNTERARGUMENTS
List any opposing views the writer mentions.

Quick-Write: How reasonable does this writer seem to you? Is the writer careful to make claims that can be supported by evidence? Does the writer seem fair and unbiased? Does the writer consider different viewpoints? Make concessions?

Logos Analysis

AUTHOR'S CLAIM/POSITION

Requiring algebra for high school graduation and college admission hurts a wide range of students, wastes precious resources, and reduces our nation's talent pool. Instead of the traditional math sequence, we should create exciting alternatives to develop students' quantitative reasoning skills.

Support & Evidence

AUTHORITY/EXPERTS
List any expert testimony the writer includes.

List any expert testimony the writer includes.

City University of New York faculty report

Barbara Bonham, Appalachian State University

John P. Smith III, educational psychologist at Michigan State University

Peter Braunfeld, University of Illinois

FACTS/STATISTICS
List any numerical data or scientific evidence the writer uses.

Cites data on high school and college completion rates ("33 percent failed last year in Oklahoma") ("one in four ninth graders fail to finish high school")

"a definitive analysis by the Georgetown Center on Education and the Workforce"

QUALIFIERS/TRANSITIONS
List words and phrases like "some," "often," "perhaps," "as a result," or "on the other hand" that qualify claims or signal logical relationships.

"too"
"but"
"largely or wholly wrong"
"major"
"all kinds"
"for instance"
"hence"
"of course"
"for example"
"only"
"many"
"may"
"instead"

COUNTERARGUMENTS
List any opposing views the writer mentions.

List any opposing views the writer mentions.

"A skeptic might argue that, even if our current mathematics education discourages large numbers of students, math itself isn't to blame."

"What of the claim that mathematics sharpens our minds . . .?"

Quick-Write: How reasonable does this writer seem to you? Is the writer careful to make claims that can be supported by evidence? Does the writer seem fair and unbiased? Does the writer consider different viewpoints? Make concessions?

(Student answers will vary.)

Article analyzed: Hacker, Andrew. 2012. "Is Algebra Necessary?" Op-Ed. *New York Times*. July 28.

Appendix 20

Academic Identity
Confidence Survey

Directions: Decide the extent to which you agree or disagree with each statement below. If you feel highly confident that the statement is true for you, write a number 5. If you feel the statement is not at all true for you, write a number 1.

5 = strongly agree

4 = agree

3 = unsure

2 = disagree

1 = strongly disagree

___ I will be well prepared for the reading and writing demands of college and the workplace when I graduate from high school.

___ Twenty years from now I will be making important contributions to our society.

___ I can see myself as a successful student at a four-year university.

___ I have valuable ideas to contribute to our society.

___ Teachers are interested in my opinions.

___ Politicians are interested in my opinions.

___ Employers are interested in my opinions.

___ I can see myself giving a speech before an audience.

___ I can see myself publishing an article, poem, song, or book.

___ I have an important influence on my friends and family.

___ I know how to write an essay for an academic audience.

___ I know how to write a business letter.

___ I feel confident in my English class.

___ I feel confident in my math class.

___ I would like to help make decisions that will affect our country's future.

___ I believe that my potential income is related to my literacy skills.

___ I can see my friends graduating from college.

___ I would feel comfortable having a conversation with a doctor, lawyer, or college professor.

___ I believe that colleges care about the success of high school students.

___ I understand the college admissions process.

___ I know how to find grants, loans, and scholarships for college.

___ I feel confident that I will be able to understand a college lecture after I graduate from high school.

___ I know how to take notes during a college lecture.

___ I am willing to move away from home to attend a university.

___ I share common interests and/or hobbies with college professors and students.

___ I enjoy reading in my free time.

___ I keep a personal journal.

___ I enjoy talking about my studies with my friends.

___ I will be an independent reader after I graduate from high school.

___ I believe a college education leads to a more fulfilling personal life.

___ I believe a college education leads to a more fulfilling professional life.

___ I believe a college education enables people to make greater social contributions.

___ I could see myself becoming a scientist, doctor, researcher, teacher, professor, or other profession requiring higher education.

___ Today's jobs require higher levels of literacy than were needed twenty years ago.

___ I know how to write a persuasive essay.

___ I know how to write an expository essay.

___ I know how to avoid spelling and grammar mistakes.

___ I know several prewriting strategies that can help me generate ideas.

___ I know how to write an essay outline.

___ I know how to organize my ideas into paragraphs.

___ I know how to include direct quotations in my writing.

___ I know how to conduct research.

___ I know how to revise an essay draft.

___ I understand logic.

___ I am open to new ideas.

___ I enjoy class discussions.

___ I ask questions when I don't understand a lesson or reading assignment.

___ I seek help from a tutor or the Writing Center when I need it.

___ I take pride in my academic success.

___ I feel happy when a teacher praises my work.

___ I feel like a member of my school community.

___ I see my teachers as members of an educational community that includes colleges and universities.

___ I see myself as a future member of a college community.

___ When I'm working on an assignment I enjoy, I lose all track of time.

___ I feel a rush of energy when I'm being creative or intellectually challenged.

___ I believe that knowing the processes historians or scientists use (i.e., the how) is as important as knowing the content of history or science (i.e., the what).

___ I understand how to change my writing style and form for different audiences and purposes.

Appendix 21

Insider Knowledge

Directions:

Step 1: Generate a list of words from a subject you know well but that your teacher and classmates may know little about. For example, this could be your favorite style of music, computer game, sport, comic book series, after-school job, or any other subject you are an expert on. What specialized words do you use when you talk about this subject? Include slang and jargon if appropriate.

Step 2: Using words from your list, write a paragraph describing your subject. Try to make this paragraph challenging for an "outsider" to read. Feel free to use slang and jargon; your paragraph does not have to follow the rules of standard English.

Quick-Write: How does your insider knowledge of this subject affect your identity? In what ways does being an "expert" in this field impact how you see yourself?

Appendix 22

Annotation Cue Card Comments and Questions for "10 Rules for Going to College When Nobody Really Expected You To" by Joe Rodriguez

Note: For more information on using cue card comments and questions in a whole-class analysis of an article, see page 29 in Chapter 2.

Question: Is Rodriguez exaggerating or is he being sincere?

Comment: This phrase in the first sentence suggests a new wave of college access programs.

Comment: Rodriguez's verb tense shows ongoing action.

Comment: The word "but" marks a distinction between academic skills and college-ready attitudes and behaviors.

Comment: This sentence strikes a balance between dreams and effort.

Comment: This phrase suggests these students are overconfident.

Comment: This section talks about unexpected challenges.

Question: Why does Rodriguez talk about his personal experience here?

Comment: This language suggests Rodriguez is someone who has "been there."

Question: Who was the original audience for this speech?

Question: What kind of students graduate from Menlo?

Comment: This rule shows Rodriguez's familiarity with his audience's interests and values because he knows they like to buy nice stuff.

Comment: "Eight years" shows the cost of not being prepared to handle the personal obstacles Rodriguez describes.

Question: Does Rodriguez expect his audience to answer "no" to this question?

Comment: The balanced sentence shows the contrast between short-term goals and long-term goals.

Comment: These extreme and frightening examples show the extent of the commitment nontraditional students must be willing to make.

Comment: The word "almost" is a slight qualification.

Comment: This suggests students should be ready for resistance from their parents.

Question: Is Rodriguez warning students to guard against being persuaded by pathos?

Comment: Rodriguez here reassures students they're doing the right thing.

Comment: This rule emphasizes the contrasts between high school and college.

Comment: This rule suggests feelings of loneliness and isolation are not limited to certain kinds of college campuses.

Comment: This advice is about not giving in to feelings of being an outsider.

Comment: "Armageddon" is a scary word.

Comment: Rodriguez is using fear to persuade students to stay in college.

Comment: The extreme reference to the end of the world shows how high the stakes are.

Question: Isn't that kind of harsh?

Question: Are first-generation students really that different?

Comment: Here Rodriguez is using joy and passion to persuade his audience.

Comment: This conclusion is all about love of family and community.

Comment: The conclusion softens the earlier advice about not letting family get in the way of a college education.

Comment: Write your own comment on this card and say it aloud whenever it naturally fits into the group analysis of the text.

Comment: Write your own comment on this card and say it aloud whenever it naturally fits into the group analysis of the text.

Question: Write your own question on this card and ask it whenever it naturally fits into the group analysis of the text.

Question: Write your own question on this card and ask it whenever it naturally fits into the group analysis of the text.

Appendix 23

Reading Strategies Ranking

Directions: Rank the following reading strategies according to your personal preferences. Write a number 1 next to the strategies you find very helpful, a 2 next to the strategies you find somewhat helpful, and a 3 next to any strategies that you do not find helpful.

___ Quick-writing to tap into prior knowledge

___ Reading the title, footnotes, subheadings, and discussion questions

___ Looking at pictures, graphs, and charts

___ Making predictions about the subject and confirming your predictions as you read

___ Asking questions about the text and finding answers as you read

___ Learning key vocabulary words

___ Asking questions about the author

___ Writing summaries of the main ideas

___ Completing graphic organizers of key concepts

___ Outlining or charting a text to see how it is organized

Quick-Write: Pick one of the strategies that you gave a 2 or 3 and explain why this strategy is less helpful to you than others. What are the steps of this strategy? How is this strategy supposed to help you read better? Why isn't this strategy as effective for you? Are you willing to give this strategy another chance?

Writing Strategies Ranking

Directions: Rank the following writing strategies according to your personal preferences. Write a number 1 by the strategies you find very helpful, a 2 by the strategies you find somewhat helpful, and a 3 by any strategies that you do not find helpful.

___ Quick-writing to brainstorm ideas

___ Completing a cluster or graphic organizer

___ Analyzing the writing prompt and understanding the directions

___ Looking at how the writing will be graded (e.g., rubric or evaluation criteria)

___ Discussing your thesis statement with a partner

___ Organizing the essay through an outline

___ Reading a rough draft aloud to a small group

___ Answering questions about plans for revision

___ Completing an editing checklist

___ Conducting peer evaluations using a scoring guide

Quick-Write: Pick one of the strategies that you gave a 2 or 3 and explain why this strategy is less helpful to you than others. What are the steps of this strategy? How is this strategy supposed to help you write better? Why isn't this strategy as effective for you? Are you willing to give this strategy another chance?

Interruptibility Index

Directions to Students: List and describe your options for places to read and write at school and at your home. Then rank your choices according to "interruptibility" on a scale of 1 to 6. Write a number 1 by the option that presents the fewest distractions; assign the highest number to the place where you are most likely to be interrupted. An example has been done for you.

Place (e.g., bedroom, kitchen, family room, office, garage, school library, computer lab, quad, etc.)	Resources (e.g., books, computer, paper, desk, etc.)	Distractions (e.g., TV, phone, younger siblings, noise, etc.)	Ranking (1 means LEAST "interruptible")
Example: coffeehouse	table, chair, and snacks—must bring own school supplies	customers talking, noise of coffee machines, chance of seeing friends	4

Teaching Argument: Rhetorical Comprehension, Critique, and Response by Jennifer Fletcher. Copyright © 2015. Stenhouse Publishers.

Appendix 25b

INTERRUPTIBILITY INDEX

Directions: List and describe your options for places to read and write at school and at
your home. Then rank your choices according to "interruptibility" on a scale of 1 to 6.
Write a number "1" by the option that presents the fewest distractions; assign the highest
number to the place where you are most likely to be interrupted. An example has been
done for you.

Place (e.g., bedroom, kitchen, family room, office, garage, school library, computer lab, quad, etc.)	Resources (e.g., books, computer, paper, desk, etc.)	Distractions (e.g., TV, phone, younger siblings, noise, etc.)	Ranking ("1" means LEAST "interruptible")
Example: *coffee house*	*table, chair, and snacks--must bring own school supplies*	*customers talking, noise of coffee machines, chance of seeing friends*	4
kitchen	table, chair, laptop music	People walking in and out, food Phone	1 ✳
library	table, chair, snack, group of people to work with	Staff talking, noise, phone	2
Bedroom	table, chair, music computer, sofa	TV, people walking in, cousins, Phone	4
quad	snack, supplies from school, music	People, phone	3

References

ABC Publisher's Statement. September 2011. OCR Branded Editions. Quoted by the website for the *Orange County Register*. http://www2.ocregister.com/advertise/community.php.

Aristotle. 1984. *Rhetoric*. Translated by W. Rhys Roberts. New York: McGraw-Hill.

———. 1999. *Nicomachean Ethics*. Translated by Terence Irwin. Indianapolis, IN: Hackett.

Armstrong, Lance, and Sally Jenkins. 2001. *It's Not About the Bike: My Journey Back to Life*. New York: Berkley Books.

Armstrong, William H. 1995. *Study Is Hard Work*. 2nd ed. Boston: David R. Godine.

Bartholomae, David, and Tony Petrosky. 2002. *Ways of Reading: An Anthology for Writers*. Boston: Bedford/St. Martin's.

Bazerman, Charles. 1995. *The Informed Writer: Using Sources in the Disciplines*. 5th ed. Boston: Houghton Mifflin.

Beach, Richard, Amanda Haertling Thein, and Daryl Parks. 2008. *High School Students' Competing Social Worlds: Negotiating Identities and Allegiances in Response to Multicultural Literature*. New York: Lawrence Erlbaum.

Bean, John C., Virginia A. Chappell, and Alice M. Gillam. 2011. *Reading Rhetorically*. 3rd ed. New York: Pearson.

———. 2014. *Reading Rhetorically*. 4th ed. Upper Saddle River, NJ: Pearson.

Bitzer, Lloyd F. 1968/1999. "The Rhetorical Situation." In *Contemporary Rhetorical Theory: A Reader,* ed. John Louis Lucaites, Celeste Michelle Condit, and Sally Caudill, 217–225. New York: Guilford.

Booth, Wayne C. 1983. *The Rhetoric of Fiction*. 2nd ed. Chicago: University of Chicago Press.

Brooks, David. 2012. "The Olympic Contradiction." Op-Ed. *New York Times*. July 26.

Burke, Kenneth. 1941. *The Philosophy of Literary Form*. Baton Rouge: Louisiana State University Press.

———. 1969. *A Rhetoric of Motives*. Berkeley: University of California Press.

California Reading and Literature Project (CRLP). 2005. *Secondary Academic Language Tools for Teaching Content Area Literacy*. La Jolla, CA: CRLP, UCSD.

Card, Orson Scott. 1977. *Ender's Game*. New York: Tor Books.

Chang, Alicia. 2012. "How Old Is Grand Canyon? New Study Puts Age at 70 Million Years." Associated Press. November 29.

Cicada. 2013. "Cicada Magazine for Teens Ages Fourteen and Up." http://www.cricketmag.com/22-Submission-Guidelines-for-CICADA-magazine-for-teens-ages-14.

Collins, Billy. 1998. "Marginalia." In *Picnic, Lightning*. Pittsburgh, PA: University of Pittsburgh Press.

Corbett, Edward P. J., and Robert J. Connors. 1999. *Classical Rhetoric for the Modern Student*. 4th ed. New York: Oxford University Press.

Corbett, Edward P. J., and Rosa A. Eberly. 2000. *The Elements of Reasoning*. 2nd ed. Boston: Allyn and Bacon.

Crowley, Sharon, and Debra Hawhee. 2009. *Ancient Rhetorics for Contemporary Students*. 4th ed. New York: Pearson Longman.

Csikszentmihalyi, Mihaly. 1990. *Flow: The Psychology of Optimal Experience*. New York: HarperCollins.

CSU (The California State University). 2009. *Focus on English*. Long Beach: California State University Office of the Chancellor. http://www.calstate.edu/sas/ept.pdf.

CWPA, NCTE, and NWP (Council of Writing Program Administrators, National Council of Teachers of English, and National Writing Project). 2011. *Framework for Success in Postsecondary Writing*. Berkeley, CA: National Writing Project.

Deford, Frank. 2013. "Pete Rose Should Enter the Hall of Fame with Ichiro Suzuki." National Public Radio. August 14. http://www.npr.

org/2013/08/14/211657813/pete-rose-should-enter-the-hall-of-fame-with-ichiro-suzuki.

Dickens, Charles. 1846–1848/2008. *Dombey and Son.* Oxford, UK: Oxford University Press.

———. 1855–1857/1999. *Little Dorritt.* Oxford, UK: Oxford University Press.

Durant, Will. 1926/2005. *The Story of Philosophy.* Nook edition. New York: Simon and Schuster.

Edlund, John. 2006. "Rhetoric for Teachers." ERWC Leadership Conference. Los Angeles, CA. July 28.

———. 2013. "Three Ways to Persuade." Expository Reading and Writing Course, 2nd ed. Long Beach: California State University.

Eidenmuller, Michael. 2014. "Scholarly Definitions of Rhetoric." *American Rhetoric.* http://www.americanrhetoric.com/rhetoricdefinitions.htm.

Elbow, Peter. 1986. *Embracing Contraries: Explorations in Learning and Teaching.* New York: Oxford University Press.

———. 1998a. *Writing with Power: Techniques for Mastering the Writing Process.* New York: Oxford University Press.

———. 1998b. *Writing Without Teachers.* 2nd ed. New York: Oxford University Press.

Elbow, Peter, and Pat Belanoff. 2000. *A Community of Writers: A Workshop Course in Writing.* 3rd ed. Boston: McGraw-Hill.

Eminem. 2002. "Lose Yourself." Shady Interscope UMG Soundtracks.

ERWC Task Force (California State University, Task Force on Expository Reading and Writing). 2013. *Expository Reading and Writing Course.* 2nd ed. Long Beach: California State University.

Eskin, Catherine R. 2002. "Hippocrates, *Kairos,* and Writing in the Sciences." In *Rhetoric and* Kairos: *Essays in History, Theory, and Praxis,* ed. Phillip Sipiora and James S. Baumlin, 97–113. New York: State University of New York Press.

Fisher, Doug, and Nancy Frey. 2010. "Modeling Expert Thinking." *Principal Leadership.* November: 58–59.

http://www.nassp.org/Content.aspx?topic=Modeling_Expert_Thinking.

Gage, John T. 2000. *The Shape of Reason: Argumentative Writing in College.* New York: Pearson.

Gallagher, Kelly. 2004. *Deeper Reading: Comprehending Challenging Texts, 4–12.* Portland, ME: Stenhouse.

———.2009. *Readicide: How Schools Are Killing Reading and What You Can Do About It.* Portland, ME: Stenhouse.

———. 2011. *Write Like This: Teaching Real-World Writing Through Modeling and Mentor Texts.* Portland, ME: Stenhouse.

Garcia, Diana. 2000. *When Living Was a Labor Camp.* Tuscon: University of Arizona Press.

———. 2011. "A Lifetime of Learning." AVID Writers Conference. California State University, Monterey Bay, Seaside, CA. March 22.

Gaskell, Elizabeth. 1857/2005. *The Life of Charlotte Brontë.* 1857. New York: Barnes and Noble Classics,

Gee, James Paul. 2012. *Social Linguistics and Literacies: Ideology in Discourses.* London: Taylor and Francis.

Geiser, Saul, and Maria Veronica Santelices. 2007. "Validity of High School Grades in Predicting Student Success Beyond the Freshman Year: High-School Record vs. Standardized Tests as Indicators of Four-Year College Outcomes." Research & Occasional Paper Series. Berkeley: University of California.

Gladwell, Malcolm. 2008. *Outliers: The Story of Success.* New York: Little, Brown.

Goldberg, Natalie. 1986. *Writing Down the Bones: Freeing the Writer Within.* Boston: Shambhala.

Gordon, Larry. 2012. "UC Drops Controversial New Logo." *Los Angeles Times.* December 15. http://articles.latimes.com/2012/dec/15/local/la-me-uc-logo-20121215.

Graff, Gerald. 2003. *Clueless in Academe: How Schooling Obscures the Life of the Mind.* New Haven, CT: Yale University Press.

———. 2010. "Hidden Intellectualism." In *"They Say/I Say": The Moves That Matter in Academic Writing,* ed. Gerald Graff and Cathy Birkenstein, 198–205. 2nd ed. New York: W. W. Norton.

Graff, Gerald, and Cathy Birkenstein. 2006. *"They Say/I Say": The Moves That Matter in Academic Writing.* New York: W. W. Norton.

———. 2010. *"They Say/I Say": The Moves That Matter in Academic Writing.* 2nd ed. New York: W. W. Norton.

———. 2014. *"They Say/I Say": The Moves That Matter in Academic Writing.* 3rd high school edition. New York: W. W. Norton.

Green Fire Productions. 2012. *Ocean Frontiers: The Dawn of a New Era in Ocean Stewardship.* DVD and film website. La Grande, OR: Authors. http://ocean-frontiers.org/the-film/.

Hacker, Andrew. 2012. "Is Algebra Necessary?" Op-Ed. *New York Times.* July 28.

Haddon, Mark. 2004. *The Curious Incident of the Dog in the Night-Time.* New York: Vintage.

Hairston, Maxine. 1986. *Contemporary Composition.* Florence, KY: Cengage.

Hauser, Gerard A. 2002. *Introduction to Rhetorical Theory.* 2nd ed. Long Grove, IL: Waveland.

Hillocks, George, Jr. 2011. *Teaching Argument Writing, Grades 6–12: Supporting Claims with Relevant Evidence and Clear Reasoning.* Portsmouth, NH: Heinemann.

Huxley, Aldous. 1932/2006. *Brave New World.* New York: Harper Perennial.

ICAS (Intersegmental Committee of the Academic Senates of the California Community Colleges, the California State University, and the University of California). 2002. *Academic Literacy: A Statement of Competencies Expected of Students Entering California's Public Colleges and Universities.* Sacramento: Intersegmental Committee of the Academic Senates of the California Community Colleges.

Kennedy, George A. 1994. *A New History of Classical Rhetoric.* Princeton, NJ: Princeton University Press.

Kinney, Jeff. 2008. *Diary of a Wimpy Kid: Rodrick Rules.* New York: Amulet Books.

Kipling, Rudyard. 1902. *Just So Stories.* Toronto: George S. Morang.

Kolln, Martha, and Loretta Gray. 2013. *Rhetorical Grammar: Grammatical Choices, Rhetorical Effects.* 7th ed. Boston: Pearson.

Krakauer, Jon. 1996. *Into the Wild.* New York. Random House.

Langer, Judith. 1995. *Envisioning Literature: Literary Understanding and Literature Instruction.* New York: Teachers College Press and the International Reading Association.

Leonard, George. 1992. *Mastery: The Keys to Success and Long-Term Fulfillment.* New York: Plume.

Liddell, H. G., and Robert Scott. 1968. *An Intermediate Greek-English Lexicon: Founded upon the Seventh Edition of Liddell and Scott's Greek-English Lexicon, 1889.* Oxford, UK: Oxford University Press.

Lindemann, Erika. 2001. *A Rhetoric for Writing Teachers.* 4th ed. New York: Oxford University Press.

London, Jack. [1908] 2007. *To Build a Fire and Other Stories.* New York: Bantam Classics.

Lunsford, Andrea A. 1992. "Rhetoric and Composition." In *Introduction to Scholarship in Modern Languages and Literatures,* ed. Joseph Gibaldi. 2nd ed. New York: Modern Language Association.

Lunsford, Andrea A., and John J. Ruszkiewicz. 2010. *Everything's an Argument.* 5th ed. Boston: Bedford/St. Martin's.

Macklemore and Ryan Lewis. 2012 "10,000 Hours" and "Wings." *The Heist.* Seattle, WA: Macklemore LLC.

Meyer, Jan H. F., and Ray Land. 2003. "Threshold Concepts and Troublesome Knowledge: Linkages to Ways of Thinking and Practising Within the Disciplines." Occasional Report 4. ETL Project. Edinburgh, UK: University of Edinburgh School of Education. http://www.colorado.edu/ftep/documents/ETLreport4-1.pdf.

Meyer, Jan H. F., Ray Land, and Caroline Baillie. 2010. *Threshold Concepts and Transformational Learning.* Boston: Sense.

Miller, Carolyn R. 2002. "Foreword." In *Rhetoric and Kairos: Essays in History, Theory, and Praxis.* Ed.

Phillip Sipiora and James S. Baumlin New York: State University of New York Press.

Miller, Kathleen E. 2002. "Energy Drinks, Race, and Problem Behaviors Among College Students." In *Rhetoric and Kairos: Essays in History, Theory, and Praxis.* Ed. Phillip Sipiora and James Baumlin. New York: State University of New York Press.

Mintz, Howard. 2013. "Time Could Be Right for Gay Marriage." *Monterey County Herald.* March 24.

Moje, Elizabeth Birr, and Cynthia Lewis. 2007. "Examining Opportunities to Learn Literacy: The Role of Critical Sociocultural Literacy Research." In *Reframing Sociocultural Research on Literacy: Identity, Agency, and Power,* ed. Cynthia Lewis, Patricia Enciso, and Elizabeth Birr Moje, 15–48. Mahwah, NJ: Lawrence Erlbaum.

Moore, Alan. 2000. *League of Extraordinary Gentlemen. Vol. I.* La Jolla, CA: WildStorm Productions, an imprint of DC Comics.

Morrison, Toni. 1992. *Playing in the Dark: Whiteness and the Literary Imagination.* New York: Vintage.

National Assessment Governing Board. 2008. *Reading Framework for the 2009 National Assessment of Educational Progress.* Washington, DC: National Assessment Governing Board.

NGA/CCSSO (National Governors Association Center for Best Practices, Council of Chief State School Officers). 2010. *Common Core State Standards for English Language Arts & Literacy in History/Social Studies, Science, and Technological Subjects.* Washington, DC: Authors. www.corestandards.org/read-the-standards. (Note: Some citations in the chapters of this book are to the print version of the ELA Common Core standards, which are downloadable from this url. Other citations are to specific standard code numbers; you can navigate to those coded standards from this url as well.)

Orange County Register Media Kit. 2014. "A Well-Positioned Market." *Orange County Register.* http://www2.ocregister.com/advertise/market.php.

Oxford English Dictionary. 2013. s.v. "keynote." http://www.oed.com/.

Plato. 1990. "Phaedrus." In *The Rhetorical Tradition: Readings from Classical Times to the Present,* ed. Patricia Bizzell and Bruce Herzberg, 113–143. Boston: Bedford/St. Martin's.

Roberts, Jennifer L. 2013. "The Power of Patience: Teaching Students the Value of Deceleration and Immersive Attention." *Harvard Magazine.* Nov–Dec. http://harvardmagazine.com/2013/11/the-power-of-patience.

Rodriguez, Joe. 2012. "10 Rules for Going to College When Nobody Really Expected You To." *San Jose Mercury News.* June 3.

Ruddell, Robert B., and Norman J. Unrau. 2004. "The Role of Responsive Teaching in Focusing Reader Intention and Developing Reader Motivation." In *Theoretical Models and Processes of Reading,* ed. Robert B. Ruddell and Norman J. Unrau, 954–978. Newark, DE: International Reading Association.

Schreiner, Laurie A. 2010. "The 'Thriving Quotient': A New Vision for Student Success."*About Campus* 15(2): 2–10.

Seligman, Martin E. P. 2011. *Flourish: A Visionary New Understanding of Happiness and Well-being.* New York: Free Press.

Shakespeare, William. 2008. *The Life of Henry the Fifth* and *The Tragedy of Julius Caesar.* In *The Norton Shakespeare.* Ed. Stephen Greenblatt, Walter Cohen, Jean E. Howard, and Katherine Eisman Maus. 2nd ed. New York: Oxford University Press.

Slater, Wayne H. 2004. "Teaching English from a Literacy Perspective: The Goal of High Literacy for All Students." In *Adolescent Literacy Research and Practice.* Ed. Tamara L. Jetton and Janice A. Dole. New York: The Guilford Press.

Smith, Michael, and Jeffrey D. Wilhelm. 2002. *Reading Don't Fix No Chevys: Literacy in the Lives of Young Men.* Portsmouth, NH: Heinemann.

———. 2006. *Going with the Flow: How to Engage Boys (and Girls) in Their Literacy Learning.* Portsmouth, NH: Heinemann.

Sproat, Ethan, Dana Lynn Driscoll, and Allen Brizee. 2012a. "Elements of Rhetorical Situations." Purdue

University Online Writing Lab. http://owl.english.
purdue.edu/owl/resource/625/02/.

———. 2012b. "Aristotle's Rhetorical Situation." Purdue
University Online Writing Lab. https://owl.english.
purdue.edu/owl/resource/625/03/.

Taba, Hilda. 1967. *Teachers' Handbook for Elementary
Social Studies.* Reading, MA: Addison-Wesley.

Toulmin, Stephen E. 1958/2008. *The Uses of Argument.*
Updated ed. New York: Cambridge University
Press.

Vergano, Dan. 2013. "Human Embryos Cloned for Stem
Cells: Researchers See Key Step for Future Treat-
ments." *USA Today.* May 15.

Vygotsky, Lev. 1978. *Mind in Society: The Development
of Higher Psychological Processes.* Cambridge, MA:
Harvard University Press.

Watterson, Bill. 1989. "Mother's Day Poem." Calvin &
Hobbes. May 14.

Weingarten, Gene. 2007. "Pearls Before Breakfast: Can
One of the Nation's Great Musicians Cut Through
the Fog of a D.C. Rush Hour? Let's Find Out."
Washington Post. April 8.

Weissmann, Jordan. 2012. "Should Science Majors Pay
Less for College Than Art Majors?" *Atlantic.*
November 5. http://www.theatlantic.com/business/
archive/2012/11/should-science-majors-pay-less-for-
college-than-art-majors/264417/.

Whitney, Anne Elrod, Michael Ridgeman, and Gary
Masquelier. 2011. "Beyond 'Is This OK?': High
School Writers Building Understandings of Genre."
Journal of Adolescent and Adult Literacy 54(7):
525–533.

Index